SOLDIERS
ON THE
STEPPE

SOLDIERS
ON THE
STEPPE

ARMY REFORM
and
SOCIAL CHANGE
in
EARLY MODERN RUSSIA

Carol Belkin Stevens

Northern Illinois University Press   DeKalb   1995

© 1995 by Northern Illinois University Press
Published by the Northern Illinois University Press,
DeKalb, Illinois 60115
Manufactured in the United States using
acid-free paper
Design by Julia Fauci

Library of Congress Cataloging-in-Publication Data
Stevens, Carol Belkin.
Soldiers on the steppe: army reform and so-
cial change in early modern Russia / Carol Belkin
Stevens.
p.   cm.
Includes bibliographical references and index.
ISBN 0-87580-198-6 (alk. paper)
1. Russia—History—1613–1689.   I. Title.
DK114.S74   1995
947'.04—dc20   94-20855
                              CIP

For my father

CONTENTS

PREFACE

The long-term impact of Muscovy's military revolution on Russian provincial life is analyzed in this study. The Russian state essayed a massive transformation of its army beginning in the seventeenth century. Resulting military change was successful, in that it ably supported Russian expansion southward across the steppe, to the west, and into Siberia. It was the innovative use of existing political, social, and economic arrangements, I argue here, that, on the one hand, helped to accomplish this remarkable and rapid "military revolution." On the other hand, these same arrangements, often local or regional in nature, limited the exercise of state power. The Russian government of the seventeenth century cannot be simply viewed as authoritarian and centralized; it was also led by circumstance into compromise, contradiction, and regional adaptation. Those arrangements and compromises also helped to set Russia on its own distinctive path to military modernization, in which considerations of steppe defense, in-kind resource extraction, and the political impact of enserfment loomed large. As in other countries undergoing the early modern "military revolution," furthermore, the result of army reform was dramatic. In the Russian south, the interaction of military policy with regional political considerations, the needs of atypical populations, and the local economic conditions had a profound impact. The traditional underpinnings of Russia's social elite were eroded by military change; the result was to bring into being a new social order that would subsequently be enforced by Peter I.

This work has emerged from three historical issues that have interested me since before I began graduate school at the University of Michigan. I have long been curious about (1) the way in which Russia fits into European history more broadly cast, where the prevailing paradigms and availability of research materials have differed from those current among most Russian historians; (2) the ways in which early modern states and governments were influenced and transformed by noninstitutional figures, particularly given the institutional bias of surviving Russian documents; and (3) the way that, during the early modern period, the impact of the mundane on national politics becomes more visible. In this book, we shall see how the course of Russian military reform was heavily influenced by issues such as the availibility and supply of food, and the status and condition of the farmers.

This study, which focuses on the southern military-administrative regions of Belgorod and Sevsk, is based upon archival research accomplished during two visits to the then Soviet Union. The material comes primarily from what used to be called the Central State Archive of Ancient Acts, referred to throughout the notes by its current name, RGADA; *fond* 210 (f. 210) holds the records of the Military Chancellery, or Razriad, the institution with principal military and civilian jurisdiction in the southern provinces for much of the seventeenth century. The chancellery's raison d'être was the organization and administration of the military forces. I am grateful to the Russian archives, to numerous archivists, and most recently to Svetlana Romanovna Dovgalo for their patience, cooperation, and aid in pursuing my research.

Military Chancellery sources are useful in part because they provide a statistical snapshot of late seventeenth-century military life. Using the statistics, of course, raises questions about the reliability of Muscovite numerical documents. If one thing is clear, it is that the Muscovites themselves placed great value on accuracy in record keeping; they planned their armies, their supplies, and their future military behavior on the kinds of accounts used in this study. This, of course, does not suggest that those accounts are infallible or even very accurate; contemporary audits and the cross-checking of resources make it clear that the Muscovites themselves did not suffer from that delusion (see, for example, Richard Hellie, *Enserfment and Military Change*, p. 273). There may indeed be little point in pursuing complex "arithmetical exercises" with some of this material, but that is at least in part because of irregular rates of survival and widely varying methods of collecting and recording data (see John L. H. Keep, *Soldiers of the Tsar*, p. 89). Where such problems can be overcome, the numbers provide us with a glimpse (often in considerable detail) of how the Muscovites themselves understood their military forces to operate under the pressures of constant activity and ongoing reform in the late seventeenth century.

Quite apart from questions about the reliability of statistics, historians of the pre-Petrine period are faced with irresolvable questions about the translation of the intricate terminology of their period into intelligible English. A glossary supplies the Russian-to-English translations I have used in the text; however, one particular set of terms has been rendered in so many different ways as to require separate comment, namely, terms relating to the elite of Muscovite society. This group of families might broadly be described as the equivalent of a European nobility, but they were also servitors of the state, whose rank and prestige depended not only on lineage but also on the office they performed. They have been referred to as "noble servitors" (Keep, *Soldiers*, chap. 1). This general term conceals a number of subdivisions, including a group of military men who served "in the provinces," and were of lowlier social origins (*dvoriane, deti boiarskie*), and others, of higher rank, whose lives revolved around the court and capital. These two groups have respectively been rendered in English as "gentry" and "aristocracy," but only accompanied by explanations of the peculiarly Muscovite connotations (Robert O. Crummey, *Aristocrats and Servitors*; Thomas Esper, "The *Odnodvortsy* and the Russian Nobility," p. 124). Such translations have the advantages of being easily used in English sentences and of conveying meaning to an English-speaking audience. Richard Hellie refers to these two groups with great precision as the "middle" and "upper service classes" in his *Introduction to Muscovite Society*, his *Enserfment and Military Change*, and elsewhere. The material in this book deals almost exclusively with the provincial elite (*deti boiarskie, dvoriane*). For the purposes of euphony, I have usually referred to them as "hereditary servicemen." The term at once conveys the importance of their rank of military service, and offers an understanding of their lineage that is appropriately less exalted-sounding than "noble." Translating *deti boiarskie* and *dvoriane* as "gentry" seems to me somewhat misleading because to most English-speaking audiences it carries very British connotations inappropriate to Muscovy. I have also used "members of the middle service class" or "middle-level servicemen" where it was possible to do so without introducing unnecessary stylistic awkwardness.

Finally, throughout the text, weights and measures have been translated into their American equivalents. Many of these are necessarily approximate; weights and measures were not standardized throughout seventeenth-century Muscovy, and we do not currently calculate measurements using the same bases. Justifications for conversion are offered in the notes on the first occasion of use, raw measurements are given throughout, and the conversion rates are supplied again below. Conversion of the dry measure *chetvert'* posed a particular problem: it existed in two official versions, one for depositing grain in state coffers (*priemnaia chetvert'*) and another for withdrawing grain from state granaries (*otdatochnaia chetvert'*); the latter measured three-quarters of the former. In addition, the deposit *chetvert'* was raised from the weight of 6 *pudy* (216 lbs.) to 8–9 *pudy* (288–325 lbs.) in the 1670s, with the equivalent impact on the issuing *chetvert'*. More information on my translation of *chetvert'* and related terms can be found in note 17 of chapter 2. For further detail on this and other weights and measures, see E. I. Kamentseva and N. V. Ustiugov, *Russkaia metrologiia*. All transliterations from the Russian are according to the simplified Library of Congress system (without diacritics).

In undertaking the writing of a dissertation and its transformation into a book, authors incur intellectual debts, more perhaps than they remember, but certainly more than they have space to acknowledge. I should like generally to thank the many friends and colleagues who contributed directly and indirectly to this book in the course of its preparation. Particular mention should go to my mentors: the late Horace W. Dewey of the University of Michigan, who supervised my dissertation but did not live to see the appearance of this volume; J. D. Basil of the University of South Carolina, who interested me in food supply questions; Charles Tilly and Louise Tilly, who later encouraged and refined that interest; John V. A. Fine, Jr., whose meticulous reading of an early version is deeply appreciated; Ladislaw Matejka, Owen Connelly, Gerasimus Augustinos, and Peter Becker for intellectual encouragement at key moments. None is responsible for any of the book's errors, of course. Dan Field, Tim Mixter, Ann Lane, Walter Pintner, Richard Hellie, and Dan Little deserve thanks for their interest and illuminating comments (which they may not remember having made), and the patience and attention of the Press in preparing the manuscript merit special mention. Most particularly, I am deeply grateful to Brian Davies for sharing his opinions, notes, and erudition during the many years of our joint toil in the fields of southern Russia. Philippe Uninsky has provided years of loving support, incisive comment, and editing beyond the call of duty, and our daughter, Maya, has added a note of cheerful infant insouciance. Thanks are also due Bowdoin College, Colgate University, Harvard University (especially its Ukrainian Research Institute), the International Research and Exchanges Board, and the University of Michigan for their financial and institutional support.

SOLDIERS
ON THE
STEPPE

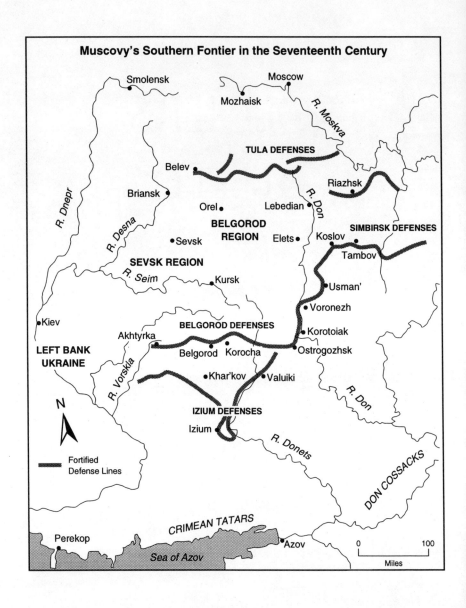

Muscovy's Southern Fontier in the Seventeenth Century

TOWN INDEX AND LOCATOR

Akhtyrka   W end of Belgorod defenses. On map.

Belev   Sevsk region, near Tula defenses. On map.

Belgorod   Toward W end of Belgorod defenses. On map.

Bogodukhov   Between Izium and Belgorod defenses.

Bolkhov   Sevsk region.

Briansk   Sevsk region, on Desna River. On map.

Chern'   Belgorod region, N of Belgorod defenses.

Chuguev   Between Izium and Belgorod defenses.

Dankov   Belgorod region, N of Belgorod defenses, on Don River.

Efremov   Belgorod region, N of Belgorod defenses.

Elets   Belgorod region, N of Belgorod defenses. On map.

Epifan'   Belgorod region, N of Belgorod defenses.

Iablonov   E of Belgorod on defensive line.

Izium   Near center of Izium defenses. On map.

Karachev   Sevsk region.

Karpov   W of Belgorod on defensive line.

Khar'kov   Between Izium and Belgorod defenses. On map.

Khotmyzhsk   Between Belgorod and Akhtyrka on defensive line.

Komaritskii district   Former court lands near Sevsk fortress.

Korocha   NE of Belgorod on defensive line. On map.

Korotoiak   At "elbow" of Belgorod defenses on Don River. On map.

Kozlov   Toward NE end of Belgorod defenses. On map.

Krasnyi Kut   SW of Akhtyrka.

Kursk   N of Belgorod on Seim River. On map.

Lebedian'   Belgorod region, N of Belgorod defenses on Don River. On map.

Livny   Belgorod region, N of Belgorod defenses.

Mtsensk   Belgorod region, N of Belgorod defenses.

Novobogoroditsa   Fortress built after 1687 near confluence of Samara and Dnepr Rivers, upstream of Dnepr River rapids.

Novyi Oskol   W of Belgorod on defensive line.

Oleshnia   N of Belgorod defenses near Akhtyrka.

Orel   Sevsk region. On map.

Ostrogozhsk   At E "elbow" of Belgorod defenses. On map.

Perekop   At Crimean isthmus. On map.

Poltava   S of Akhtyrka on Vorskla River.

Putivl'   Sevsk region, NNW of Akhtyrka.

Riazhsk   ESE of Tula, on a segment of sixteenth-century defensive line. On map.

Ryl'sk   Sevsk region, on Seim River.

Sevsk   Center of Sevsk region. On map.

(Staryi) Oskol   Belgorod region, just N of Belgorod defenses.

Sumy   N of Belgorod defenses at Akhtyrka.

Tambov   NE end of Belgorod defenses. On map.

Tula   Center of Tula defenses. On map.

Usman'   NE of Belgorod on defensive line, between Voronezh, Kozlov. On map.

Valuiki   Toward NE end of Izium defenses. On map.

Verkhososensk   E of Belgorod on defensive line.

Vol'nyi   Toward W end of Belgorod defenses.

Voronezh   NE of Belgorod on defensive line, on Don River. On map.

INTRODUCTION

This book is about the decisive and far-reaching consequences of military revolution on seventeenth-century Russian provincial life. As Muscovy restructured and expanded its army, the country as a whole was impelled to reconsider the world it had known. Each effort at military reform led to ever-widening and intersecting circles of change. Over the course of the seventeenth century, Muscovite power holders were forced to consider political alliances with new social groups, new forms of bureaucratic organization, and new perspectives on their economy. These broad reconsiderations were neither uniformly accepted nor uniformly implemented. Different parts of the empire defended their particular interests, and the central state enforced its will with varying enthusiasm, ability, and success.

The social and economic changes that resulted from the military revolution in one particular region, the Russian south, are examined in this book. Two of the requirements of military change experienced all over Russia acquired primacy in the south: first, the need to recruit more and more men to fill the new regiments, which meant that the old social system had to accommodate to a new and incompatible military structure, and second, the need to finance the new army, whose cost was levied from the southern population not primarily through cash taxation but by in-kind collection of grain used to feed the troops. Each of these demands was the subject of intense, if not explicit, negotiation and compromise between the central state and the southern population. I argue that regional imperatives interacted with the efforts at military reform, catalyzing the destruction of old social and political understandings, and that the resultant new social forces and new forms of social organization became important legacies to the centralized, reformist state of Peter I.

A few explanatory words are in order. The military revolution of early modern Europe broadly refers to the gradual shift from relatively disorganized, cavalry-dominated, feudal-style military forces to large, trained and salaried, infantry-based armies—a shift that took place in western and central Europe from the fifteenth through the seventeenth centuries. The process is acknowledged to have exerted intense pressure on almost all European societies. The need to recruit and train masses of infantry in the use of firearms violated an older social order that had associated nobility with the autonomous efforts of the cavalry knight. If such cavalry warriors, with their own training and resources, were not to dominate national armies, then states had to extract the resources needed to pay their soldiers, to train them, and eventually to equip and supply them. The collection of adequate financial resources required bureaucratic reorganization; the process as a whole demanded the consent of a redefined nobility and the cooperation of the taxable classes, some of whom by the seventeenth century were involved in new commercial activities.

Russia belatedly undertook the wholesale reforms that led the rest of Europe to create regular standing armies in the early modern period. Although it boasted siege artillery and a small number of infantry troops at the end of the sixteenth century, the Muscovite army remained fundamentally unchanged, with the focus and organization of a steppe cavalry force. Not until the middle of the seventeenth century did Muscovy commit itself to the development of a bureaucratic army.

The delays in adopting military reforms were not surprising. Although the military revolution was not confined to western and central Europe, it was military success that carried the impulse to such thoroughgoing reform beyond its original boundaries. Only in the face of such success did states with different social and political configurations and widely differing economic resources confront the problems of replicating military change. Until the seventeenth century Muscovy remained on the periphery of Europe. Its southern neighbors and frequent military foes—the Tatar khanate and the Ottoman Empire—were oriented to cavalry conflict on the open steppe. On its western borders, Sweden alone mustered a small, but regionally effective, modern army before 1600; in the wake of unhappy encounters with Gustavus Adolphus and an increasingly well-armed Swedish force in the 1620s, Poland overcame its resistance to military change and attempted to reorganize its army.[1] Muscovy's commitment to military reform could thus be said to flow in part from acknowledging the newly acquired military might of its northwestern neighbors. Russia's policies toward both its western and southern neighbors at this time became unabashedly expansionist: it attempted to regain territory lost to Poland early in the century, annex Ukraine, and extend its empire southward into the open steppe.

Once the decision to reform was taken, Muscovy moved swiftly from the introduction of modern troops (which it called the "new formation") to exceedingly rapid expansion of those forces in a process of growth at first more rapid than elsewhere in Europe. Large western European states fielded armies of 40,000 men in the mid-sixteenth century, gradually increasing these to 150,000 men by the 1630s. Muscovy, on the other hand, entered the Thirteen Years' War (1654–1667) with a force of 40,000 men but finished that conflict with 100,000 troops in the field;[2] it used this larger army intensively and persistently until the turn of the century.[3] This made Russia, with its relatively limited population, one of the more highly mobilized European states of the time.[4]

Muscovy's efforts to create, maintain, and eventually increase the number of its new formation troops confronted two structural obstacles. First, the fundamental social and political principles of the Russian state were antithetical to the rapid growth of a bureaucratic army. In this regard Russia was far from unique. Attitudes incongruent with the new standing armies also appeared in Poland and the Ottoman Empire; even in France, where the reforms had been underway for more than a century, remnants of the nobles' hostility to particular aspects of the new armies persisted.[5] But, hostility or no, Russian military reform could not succeed unless the Muscovite elite accepted positions in the new army, which violated their sense of hierarchy and of social place. Recruitment and conditions of military service thus became matters of social and political dispute. Muscovy compromised by mixing the new army with old values, a process fraught with complications for both military institutions and prevailing definitions of the social order. The new organization of the army, whose advantages were generally acknowledged by the second half of the seventeenth century, was enforced by a powerful central state apparatus. The price of military reform, however, was the realignment and rigidification of the social hierarchy, on the one hand, and limitations on the extent and character of reform, on the other.[6] This process had a particularly acute impact in Russia's southern provinces, where the social elite was atypically represented.

The second obstacle to Russian military reform was the unproductive Muscovite economy. The shift to a paid, trained army throughout Europe was perceived as an expensive necessity. Many governments, unable to accomplish the task entirely themselves, first embraced private resources, relying heavily on mercenaries to fight, private entrepreneurs to supply, and tax farmers to pay for the new armies. But European governments also paid for change by increasing taxation, searching for new ways of extracting cash and goods from their populations, and resorting to extraordinary exactions. On occasion they came perilously close to bankruptcy. These crises inspired a search for new financial resources outside as well as inside their borders.[7] The need for rising revenues partially inspired the institution of mercantilist policies to increase the volume of (taxable) trade. Governments with the ability to borrow plunged deeply into international markets. As the century wore on, some states, frequently the solvent ones, moved to limit the involvement of mercenaries and civilians in the administration of their military machinery and to replace them with their own nationals and state bureaucrats.[8] By then, Great Britain, the Dutch Republic, and France were at times investing upwards of 70 percent of their new and larger state budgets in military activity.[9]

Muscovy's economic problems were not replicas of those in Europe; distinctive issues of extraction and also of production and organization were involved. The Muscovite population was far-flung and its agriculture unproductive. At the beginning of the century service to the state was still largely remunerated by land distribution, for reasons relating to economic conditions and elite social preferences. Trade and urban activities, though growing by the end of the century, still occupied a modest share of the population, and the economy actually appears to have been short of specie.[10] Though Russia may have had its mercantilists, it could not seriously consider funding its army through commercial expansion and its taxation, and it could not easily rely on individuals outside its own structure to help in the organization of the military. Nor were efforts at finding foreign lenders particularly successful.[11] As a result, despite serious geographic and organizational limitations, Muscovite bureaucrats tried whatever new and old ways of extracting existing surpluses came to hand; they experimented with salt taxes, debasement of the currency, and other devices to little long-term benefit.

It is difficult to imagine how a cash-short economy might pay its expanding army in specie. Indeed, unwilling to relinquish military gain for financial reasons, Moscow relied heavily on noncash remuneration of its troops through continued distribution of land and continued extraction and redistribution in kind. Muscovy's use of land and in-kind payments, though unconventional and even self-defeating by western European standards, inventively responded to the highly complex problems of military support. It is a measure of their different economies and extractive devices, as well as different military organization, that Britain, at war in 1689, had to resort to deficit spending, exceeding its revenues by two million pounds to support a military force of 116,000, while Russia, at war in 1680, spent approximately one million rubles, about half its revenues, to support a field army of similar size mustered against the Ottomans.[12]

One particularly important result of Russia's collections and payments in kind for its armed forces was the growth of a military food supply system, which operated largely outside Muscovy's limited cash-market economy. As western Europe had already discovered, the armies of the early modern period required more than salaries; they had to be fed, moved, trained, equipped, and otherwise provided for. In some countries, cash was used to pay the networks of contractors and purchasers, the bureaucrats who arranged for the delivery of goods, and the hired specialists who snaked out across Europe, attempting to meet the needs of armies of

100,000 men and more. Of all supply requirements, the provision of food was essential and logistically most demanding. Soldiers traveled on their stomachs, and that required wagon loads of supplies, even if the wagons carried only *sukhari* (hardtack). For the most part, grain was the staple, and feeding a force of 100,000 with one and a half or two pounds of bread daily was no mean feat. Not only did grain have to be amassed, but it also had to be prepared, transported, and distributed. During the seventeenth century some European states perfected quite elaborate provisioning systems. The Spanish Road, in particular, was known for its chain of advance depots, which allowed troops to move along a predetermined route with speed and efficiency. By the end of the seventeenth century the Army of Flanders was supported by a well-organized commissariat, which relied on contractors to feed its men. But these were exceptional cases. Departure from established routes almost immediately caused problems for even the best-supplied forces. European armies in the field foraged and looted, leaving devastation in their wake; when matters deteriorated beyond the limit of their tolerance, hungry men abandoned armies, and wars were lost. It could even be argued that, in the seventeenth century, military supremacy depended as much on effective supply as on victory in the battlefield.[13]

The food requirements of the Russian army could not successfully be approached by using the same mechanisms that had been developed to draw upon more commercialized economies. In Russia neither commerce nor established contractors could be relied upon to help the state feed the military. Grain surpluses already on the market could not simply be redirected, away from local and regional consumers to the army, because these surpluses were inadequate to provision the forces.[14] Instead, Muscovy's extractions in kind drew grain and other foodstuffs for its army directly from the producers during the latter decades of the seventeenth century; such payments compensated for a cash-short economy, while also feeding the troops. The state used long-established mechanisms for collecting grain and then prepared, delivered, and distributed the food itself, thus in large part avoiding the cash nexus. These efforts made major organizational demands, and they were not uniformly successful.

The shortcomings of its system notwithstanding, Muscovite supply efforts were of enormous significance. First, the limitations of supply severely curtailed the range and effectiveness of armies. Because efforts to improve on this situation—to remodel the army into a more regular, standing force, paid and supplied in peace as in war—were outpaced by the rapid expansion of the army, Muscovy struggled with limited solutions to problems of military supply and finance through the end of the century. Such struggles had far-reaching social impact. Cash taxation levied funds from both the commercial and agricultural populations, albeit unequally. Grain payments, however, had economic impact specifically on landowners, who were also the military service elite. Because elite social standing and wealth were broadly related, grain extraction contributed to the social realignment already associated with the new armed forces. The impact of grain extraction on the ongoing social reordering was again particularly acute in Russia's southern provinces, where, because of the area's atypical character, fiscal contributions to military change were limited primarily to grain.

Although military transformations in seventeenth-century Russia did not follow precisely a western European pattern, there is every reason to suspect that similarly important social, political, and economic changes resulted from the military revolution there. And, despite a growing literature,[15] that relationship, which has been so fruitfully examined for other countries,[16] has been woefully neglected for Muscovy.[17] It is difficult to conceive how that relationship can be examined without broaching yet another theme: the articulation by local and regional elites of political and social differences within the structures of autocracy.

Seventeenth-century Muscovy is commonly and accurately perceived as a highly centralized tsardom, legitimated by religious and political ideologies, and reinforced by favors and patronage dispersed from the court at its center. This conception has encouraged the study of Muscovy as a unified whole, from the perspective of the central state and a Moscow-based elite. At the level of provincial landholders, peasants, towns, and churches, however, not only were government policies differentially applied from region to region, but they encountered differing local economies, social arrangements, and perhaps even cultures.

Many would argue that it is misleading to emphasize such local arrangements; seventeenth-century Muscovy remained institutionally and socially a highly centralized body, whose efforts were directed largely at incorporating regions into the center. But the absence of locally organized institutions does not imply the absence of regional identity, especially in the political and ideological context of Muscovy. Informal oligarchies appear to have run local affairs in a variety of cities. In periods when the central state was weakened (and in the seventeenth century one might point to 1600–1619, 1633–1653, 1676–1695) evidence of local identities and their linkages to the center became sharper.[18] One area, Siberia, was (and remained) so radically distinct economically and socially as even to retain separate institutional structures in Moscow, despite the centralizing trend of government.[19] The ways in which different regions retained, recognized, and articulated their differences have only recently begun to be examined anew.[20] Regional identity is a potentially important part of the interplay between state and society and cannot be disregarded in studying the impact of military change in Muscovy. This book therefore examines the consequences of the military revolution on the economic and social relations of one particular region, the Russian south, with a view to exploring the implied relationship between the central state and that region.

Encompassing an area somewhat larger than the United Kingdom or the former West Germany, the southern frontier was located directly south of the town of Tula, itself some 110 miles south of Moscow. In the seventeenth century the south was not only pronouncedly different from central Muscovy in important ways, it was uniquely positioned for the study of military change. Due in part to recent settlement, the south's population was socially quite uniform for most of the century, with an unusually large proportion of landholding servicemen (the provincial elite, in Muscovite terms). Its people shared a range of quite consistent social and economic concerns, which they did not hesitate to articulate. Because of the south's strategic location, it would experience exceptionally high military demands for much of the century; it faced frequent raids from the Tatar khanate of Crimea, and its western border was the launching site for Muscovite attempts to annex Polish Ukraine. Persistently, in the name of these efforts, Moscow called upon local landholders and others to make up the ranks of both new formation regiments and older units, with all the social disruption this implied. Finally, heavy participation in the military forces did not immunize the south against contributing to the support of the new army. Because the south was a relatively cash-poor territory, its wealth was not mobilized through taxation in cash; instead, its landholders (and their peasants) contributed grain and labor to a supply system that provided food to the new formation troops. Thus the landholders of this particularly coherent region experienced unusually severe economic and social demands through much of the seventeenth century. How did they respond? What was the impact of military change on the Russian south?

Part I argues that the Russian south possessed an institutional framework that recognized its concerns and peculiarities for most of the seventeenth century; during the period of military change, both the grain collection system supplying the army and the military recruitment process played this role. Chapter 1 lays the groundwork for the examination that follows by establishing the regional character of the south within the larger Muscovite context as it developed in the first half of the seventeenth century. Chapter 2 focuses on the first half century, concluding that a southern regional identity was both created and fostered by conditions of relative poverty and heavy military engagement. The regional anomalies acknowledged by 1650, however, were called into question by the military changes taking place between 1650 and 1663. Chapter 3 argues that between 1663 and 1683 this regional focus was nevertheless recognized in and incorporated into the structure of government; in particular, both the army and its food collection were regionally organized in the south. After 1665 Muscovy was unwilling to leave provisioning of its most valuable troops in this area to the mercy of market forces or to the vicissitudes of foraging while on campaign. An in-kind regional supply system was developed to meet these needs. Its limitations, however, led to new southern demands and to more military reform. Chapter 4 argues that, after 1683, growing provisioning demands, coupled with reforms intended to promote fiscal efficiency, led to the gradual incorporation of this regional organization into countrywide supply efforts. This incorporation was distorted, however, by concessions to local demands on the part of a relatively weak central government; at the same time, the needs of the army required that new pressures be put on the south.

Part II examines the impact of the supply system and accompanying military change in the south. The supply system created between the 1650s and 1700 was reasonably efficient, providing food primarily to officers and infantrymen on campaign. Chapter 5 examines two cases where the supply system was in use (Kiev, 1668, and Crimea, 1687) and indicates that the system improved in its ability to amass the needed quantities of grain and to provide the necessary transportation. Muscovy did not, however, extend its provisioning system to include cavalry forces, nor did it develop a solution to the ancillary problems of delivering supplies to a large army across the relatively unpopulated territories south of its frontier. These planning and technical failures help to explain the puzzling ineptitude of campaigns against Crimea in the 1680s.

Before and after the 1683 reforms, as discussed in chapter 6, the cost of supplying the army fell heavily on the garrison servicemen who defended the southern frontiers. The demands of these defensive duties should have limited the ability of these servitors to contribute their share to the supply system. In reality, the exigencies of frontier defense diminished for many garrison servicemen in the 1680s; with the southward movement of the frontier and a heavier reliance on artillery, their contributions to the supply system were increasingly emphasized. Similarly, campaign servicemen, their condition weakened by concessions they themselves had requested, were occasionally released from military duties after 1683 in order to contribute to supply. This was a significant transformation in a society where military service was a prerequisite of elite social status, and this change in function from active duty to supply made southern servicemen more akin to a taxpaying peasantry than ever before.

Finally, in the second half of the seventeenth century, the military and social elite of Muscovy endeavored to restrict access to its ranks. Part of the process was the imposition of explicit economic thresholds for elite military service between 1678 and 1682. Given the weight of economic demands on the military in the south, most servicemen there proved incapable of meeting the thresholds and thus were confirmed in their lowly status. As chapter 7 demonstrates, southern servicemen with small landholdings and little labor (odnodvortsy) fulfilled both taxpaying and military functions. The central government, however, failed to connect those responsibilities to a social status category, as Peter I's fiscal and military reforms later would.

Despite its successes, Muscovite provisioning in the seventeenth century was incomplete and inadequate for feeding a large and growing army. The inability of the state to extract sufficient amounts of food from the population, and the competing demands on its meager resources, helped to make the seventeenth-century army a "semi-standing, semi-regular force." Until the turn of the century many of its members continued to rely on landholding and the support that it offered them. Nevertheless, the impact of the provisioning effort itself was considerable, interwoven as it was with the ongoing process of troop reform. That impact was not only military; it had important economic and social consequences, leading to the dramatic redefinition of much of the southern elite.

1

MUSCOVY
AND ITS
SOUTHERN
PROVINCES

Imperial Russia emerged as an eighteenth-century power with a striking victory over Sweden at Poltava in 1709. Although, from a western European perspective, the Russian army had met with no comparable success in the preceding century, between the dynastic and social disruptions of the Time of Troubles (1584–1613) and Peter I's growing power after 1700, the army was nevertheless exceedingly active, in the field for about four-fifths of the time. By the 1650s Russia was pursuing an ambitious expansionary policy along its western and southern frontiers, a policy whose success rested not on spectacular victories but on the gradual transformation of Muscovy's military forces, described elsewhere as Russia's "gunpowder revolution."[1] Russia was shifting from a relatively disorganized, cavalry-dominated, feudal-style army to a larger, trained and salaried force, dominated by infantry proficient in the use of firearms, while regaining military parity with its European and Middle Eastern neighbors.

Muscovy had implicitly recognized the advantages of some European technological and organizational changes long before the seventeenth century. Russian copies of European artillery were produced in Moscow in the late fifteenth century; major fortresses were rebuilt to withstand the barrages European gunnery could now deliver.[2] By the late sixteenth century, regimental and siege artillery were commonplace; corps of harquebusiers and, later, musketeers were attached to the army; and Russia had launched the building of massive, modern fortifications at the western border town of Smolensk. These changes may well have been inspired by confrontations with other European states. During the Livonian War (1558–

1583) Muscovy had experienced the drawn-out warfare characteristic of new armies and had faced the troops of Sweden, whose forces had been considerably restructured, and Poland. These forces, though powerful, were not devastatingly so, and the changes Muscovy introduced by the end of Ivan IV's reign (1584) represented additions to, rather than a transformation of, its main military strength. The Muscovite army remained oriented south toward its traditional enemies, the Crimean Tatars; annual mobilization of feudal-style steppe cavalry, organized in five relatively unstructured corps, remained the norm.

Muscovy's seventeenth-century decision to embark on a substantial restructuring of its forces recognized a new calculus of power on its European borders—the rising might of Sweden and Poland relative to the Tatars and their Ottoman overlords. During the Time of Troubles, a period of extreme national disorganization and weakness, both Swedish and Polish forces occupied Muscovite territory; before it was over, Russia had lost its Smolensk fortress to Poland and its coastal Baltic towns to Sweden. Accordingly, when a restored Russian monarchy tried to recoup the loss of Smolensk between 1632 and 1634, half the troops it used were hastily recruited and trained modern regiments under the leadership of western European mercenary officers. In the interval, however, the Poles had had to deal with a newly reformed and much more effective Swedish army under Gustavus II Adolphus, and the Polish army had itself embarked (if somewhat unevenly) on a process of change.[3] Russia's failure to gain its ends at Smolensk did not immediately convince it to undertake military reform; on the contrary, the government dismissed its modern regiments and concerned itself with its traditional southern enemies for the next decade.

With the accession of a new tsar in 1645, however, Muscovy moved rapidly in the direction of a Europeanized army. Its modern regiments (which the Russians called the "new formation," or *novyi stroi*) were revived and expanded, new administrative units were added to direct them, new mercenary officers were hired to train them, and new revenue sources were tested with an eye to paying for them. This commitment to military reform proved steadfast through changes of advisors and tsars. Over the next half century, efforts to expand the new formations, to adapt older units, and eventually to merge them into the new persisted, no doubt encouraged by Russia's experience in the Thirteen Years' War (1654–1667) against Poland and Sweden, during which the new troops demonstrated their military advantages. However varied the methods and implementation, the goal of creating an effective Europeanized military remained, up to and beyond Peter I's accession.[4]

Although it undertook Europeanizing reforms, Muscovy's own fundamental structures derived from a different sociopolitical tradition. The autocracy reconstituted after the Time of Troubles in many respects resembled the pre-seventeenth-century model. The tsar ruled from his court, in consultation with his leading subjects; one of the principal vehicles for such consultation was the Boyar Council (*Boiarskaia duma*), whose members were men with records of outstanding service to the crown and close blood ties to the tsar or to prominent families of long standing. In the seventeenth century the council and other less formally constituted groupings of men from established families stood as a kind of counterpoise to an expanding administrative structure, which was embodied in a network of chancelleries (*prikazy*). Initially offshoots of the tsar's household, the chancelleries had a literate, trained staff that remained astonishingly independent of the social and political elite of the Boyar Council and the court. The seventeenth century saw new links across that divide; boyars and other members of the elite directed chancelleries, in addition to holding more traditional posts as army commanders or provincial military governors. At another level, lowlier military men undertook provincial functions at once bureaucratic and military.[5] This entire system was highly centralized and authoritarian, bolstered by the ideological support of the Russian Orthodox Church and a tradition of sacred kingship.[6] These ideological claims were in turn sustained by the public ritual behavior of Moscow's elite; foreign visitors were almost universal in describing these men as astonishingly subservient to the tsar.[7] Indeed, despite its hereditary status as Russia's ruling class, the sociopolitical elite was defined at least in part by the service it rendered the tsar.[8] Thus those members of the elite whose rank was commensurate with participation in the Boyar Council (*chiny dumnye*) or with a service assignment to the capital city (*chiny moskovskie*) can be seen as the upper reaches of a nobility in service to the crown, that is, an upper service class.[9] This centralized, autocratic system offered little framework for dealing with regional, social, and political differences.

A similar pattern of service to the state defined the outlines of the entire complex Muscovite social hierarchy. From the perspective of the state, the population fell roughly into two categories: those who paid taxes (*tiaglye liudi*) and those who rendered military service but paid no taxes (*sluzhilye liudi*). Each of these categories in turn comprised two strata. The taxpaying category was subdivided into (1) the more numerous agricultural workers (peasants, serfs), who were taxed on the basis of cultivated acreage, and (2) the free towns- and tradespeople (*posadskie liudi*), who were taxed on commercial transactions. The service category was subdivided into (1) a

lower service class, men who were recruited into service or who had contracted to serve (*sluzhilye liudi po priboru*) and (2) the more prestigious
hereditary service class (*sluzhilye liudi po otechestvu*), which included a
provincial or middle service class (*chiny gorodovye*) and the Moscow-
ranked upper service class already described (*chiny moskovskie*).

The two principal service strata were quite distinct in social prestige
and remuneration. Hereditary servicemen, for example, served on the basis
of estate ownership, either inherited (*votchina*) or received contingent on
lifelong military service (*pomest'e*); they were the backbone of the steppe
cavalry army. Hereditary service thus linked social status with economic
perquisites (the ownership of land and peasants) and military obligation.
Recruited servicemen, by contrast, were paid in cash and kind; they were
poorer, socially far inferior, and unlikely to have dependent labor. The
musketeers and artillerymen added to the army in the sixteenth century
were recruited servicemen as well as, for example, mercenary auxiliaries.
Even before the Law Code of 1649 (*Ulozhenie*) introduced legal prohibitions that rigidified the boundaries between strata, certain regularities
were observed, although the divisions between strata were often implicit,
rather than hard and fast. Thus peasants normally did not enroll in military service; entry into hereditary service required records demonstrating
that senior male members of the same family had already served in a hereditary capacity; the upper service ranks were generally inaccessible to
the rank and file of provincial hereditary service. The entire system rested
on the assumption of a hereditary elite in cavalry service, an assumption
that conformed poorly to the needs of a reformed bureaucratic army.

This quick sketch of the Muscovite social pyramid also hints at the
country's economic contours. Russia's was an unproductive agricultural
economy, where wealth and prosperity were measured by access to land
and the labor to work it. Since the Time of Troubles, labor had grown
more precious relative to land, which in many places remained abundant.
Institutional estates dominated the landscape, especially in the north of
the country. The tsar and his family were, of course, major landholders, as
was the church; the patriarch was nominal proprietor of vast and scattered
lands with over 6,400 peasant households (about 32,000 people) in resi-
dence in the 1640s. The great Troitse-Sergeev Monastery held more than a
half million acres at about the same time. The patriarchal holdings were
matched by each of the five or six greatest families, but men who served
on the Boyar Council averaged some 530 peasant households each. Much
of the land in these large holdings was heritable (*votchina*). By comparison,
other landholders—also hereditary servicemen—were more precariously
placed, more numerous, and typically dependent on land issued in return
for military service (*pomest'e*). Provincial hereditary servicemen at midcentury, for example, held lands with an average of five or six peasant

households each. All told, there were less than 200,000 such servicemen, about 5 percent of the population.[10]

Peasants on these estates (supplemented by cotters, or *bobyli*, slaves, and hired labor) produced cereals on their own and demesne lands, gathered forest products, and extracted minerals. A relatively small percentage of these products was marketed, except from the larger estates, in part because agriculture only produced yields between 1:2 and 1:5 (that is, for every seed planted, 2 to 5 were harvested; England's yield ratios in the 1600s were between 1:6 and 1:9).[11] Landowner dues and taxes paid on cultivated land were more common forms of resource extraction. Agricultural laborers made up the vast majority (80%) of the population.

Town populations and commercial activity decreased after the Time of Troubles before regaining strength a half century later. Only about one-third of urban residents actually fell into the town taxpaying category, but those taxpayers (13% of Russia's population) made disproportionately large payments into the state's coffers.[12] In short, the economic base of the country was unproductive and its tax system inefficient by comparison with some western commercializing states. Although difficulties in mustering financial and social support for military changes were predictable, the Muscovite autocracy afforded no obvious institutions for contending with the problems of military transformation.

As Muscovy embarked on military change, the country's southern and southwestern provinces served as a crucible for its progress. For most of the seventeenth century this frontier area was the locus of intense military activity; it faced Muscovy's traditional steppe enemy, the Crimean Tatars, and also bordered Polish Ukraine, which would be the site of conflict between modern forces in the latter part of the century. In geographic terms, the territory was bounded on the south by the limit of settlement—which in practice, for much of the century, was a fortified defensive line built through the town of Belgorod. On the east, the Don and Voronezh Rivers formed its border, as did the pre-1667 Muscovite frontier with Poland on the west. An older wall of fortifications through Tula separated the southern provinces from the central provinces to the north. The area encompassed was quite large—somewhat larger than the United Kingdom or the former West Germany. As this study will argue, these southern provinces had a particular regional identity relative to the rest of Muscovy; that identity was the product of their geopolitical location, the character of the southern population, and the demands made upon it by the state. The anomalous nature of this region, far from being eradicated by centralizing tendencies, was acknowledged by the central government for most of the seventeenth century.

Many of the south's unusual characteristics were connected to its geopolitical situation prior to the 1650s. The general decline in importance of the Tatar military threat in the first half of the seventeenth century has been described above, but evidence of that decline was not visible in the south, where the presence of the Crimean khanate hundreds of miles across open steppe lands shaped the lives of southern provincials well into the seventeenth century. The Russian south (like the adjacent part of the Polish Commonwealth) had long been subject to frequent raids from Crimea; the Tatars carried off booty—people, livestock, possessions—whose sale provided them with a substantial part of their livelihood. Toward the end of the sixteenth century Muscovy had extended its frontier defense system (which had been in place for nearly a century) to the southern provinces. Fortress towns with military garrisons acted as bases for wide-ranging steppe patrols intended to sight Tatar raiders before they penetrated deep into settled territories. Sightings were reported north to the line of connected fortresses that ran through the town of Tula and that marked the southern boundary of the more densely settled central regions. In case of a significant attack, the old-style steppe cavalry forces that mustered annually nearby could be called upon to confront the intruders. This system was principally geared to the protection of Muscovy's settled center and provided meagerly for southern residents, who did what they could to protect their property during raids and then took shelter in nearby fortified towns; for this reason, among others, southern Muscovy remained sparsely settled.

The defense system's failure in 1632, when the Tatars moved against Moscow unhindered by the army, which was preparing for the Smolensk War on the western front, presaged major changes for the south. After the war was over, the south benefited from renewed concern over Moscow's traditional Tatar enemies. Between the late 1630s and 1651 a series of new fortress towns was built several hundred miles south of Tula, near the edge of the forest-steppe zone. The fortresses were then connected by a defensive abatis line (cherta); innovations were introduced in the fortifications, probably with the aid of French Huguenot and Dutch military engineers.[13] The new fortified Belgorod Defensive Line (Belgorodskaia cherta), named after the major town of Belgorod near its center, proved very effective. From the late 1650s Tatar raids ceased to plague most southern provinces north of the defenses, a factor that encouraged settlement there.[14]

Despite this important change, the Tatar presence continued for the rest of the century to play an important role in military calculations involving the southern frontier. For one thing, raids did not cease altogether, and the Tatars remained formidable steppe warriors, however restricted their scope. Even though the cavalry army that had formerly mustered near Tula was no longer needed, the fortifications of the Belgorod line required continuous garrisoning; so did the fortress towns that appeared to its south as colonization proceeded. For another, the decline of the Tatar threat did not turn a frontier zone into a conventional political boundary. Military conflict among steppe peoples for the unclaimed expanse of steppe persisted. The Crimean Tatars were among the most organized players in this competition, backed as they were by their khanate; the Nogai Tatars and Kalmyks further east were equally skilled warriors with their own claims.

Another important factor was the various Cossack groups on the steppe, at first perhaps renegade Tatars but by the sixteenth century composed of increasing numbers of fugitive peasants from central Muscovy and Poland. Significant Cossack military encampments existed on the lower Don and lower Dnepr, with smaller groups elsewhere. These Cossacks lived by raiding on land and sea, in this respect resembling the Tatars; agricultural settlement intruded on this nomadic existence as the Cossack populations grew, particularly in the seventeenth century. Even before then, the steppe peoples were supplementing raiding and farming with another means of support—loose relationships with larger surrounding states. The Tatar khanate thus became a vassal of Ottoman Turkey. Some individual Cossacks or smaller groups (to whom I shall refer as "service Cossacks") were accepted into Muscovite or Polish frontier life; in return for cash or land, they settled down to become a loyal part of each country's frontier defense. The alliances of other Cossack groups were more explicitly mercenary; the group on the lower Don accepted occasional subsidies from Muscovy for service as auxiliaries to the Russian army, and Cossacks of the lower Dnepr were hired individually or in groups into local or Polish royal service. Such alliances, on the one hand, coexisted uneasily with the fierce independence of steppe encampments; on the other, the presence of registered Cossacks (a negotiated number of Cossacks receiving official subsidies) could arouse jealousy and cause internal divisions in Cossack camps. For these and other reasons, alliances did not always restrain the behavior of steppe peoples, and it was understood that the actions of such vassal-allies did not always correspond to the wishes of the overlord.[15] Using steppe peoples as buffers still occasionally drew the larger states into confrontations not of their own making. In this fashion, the steppe peoples became part of the new confrontation over the empty steppe zone among larger states with bigger armies and more resources: Muscovy, the Polish Commonwealth, and the Ottoman Empire.[16]

In Muscovy's southern provinces the persistence of steppe warfare required a regular commitment of men to anti-Tatar garrisons. Data on the size of these garrisons from early in the century are incomplete, but eight towns alone had 7,500 defenders in 1626; eleven towns, for which there is information, had nearly 14,000 troops nine years later; and beginning in 1651, about 17,000 southern men were enrolled exclusively in garrison or town service (*gorodovaia sluzhba*).[17] This kind of military service had a long history, having existed in a number of Muscovite border regions before 1600. It was by definition resistant to military reform; a population that manned garrison posts traditionally had no obligation to serve in offensive campaign regiments (such as those mustering at Tula). The character and local orientation of border warfare in which these men engaged provided little incentive to abandon traditional military techniques for modern training.[18] The social and economic arrangements prevailing in the southern provinces during the early seventeenth century, though unusual by comparison with most of Russia, were almost ideally tailored to the military requirements of a Tatar frontier. That they were so was neither entirely coincidental nor completely the result of state policy; an elaborate interplay of traditional military policies with existing conditions and developing regional demands produced a surprisingly felicitous result.

A brief excursus into the history of southern settlement, a process discussed in a relatively abundant literature, will clarify this point.[19] As mentioned earlier, migration into the region prior to the 1630s was limited by the very real possibility of frequent raids by Tatars or Kalmyks. Until then, most of the population clustered in two areas. First, there was settlement in the best-protected areas, around the fortress towns that marked Muscovy's slow expansion into the steppe. Towns as far south as Belgorod, Valuiki, and Putivl' were founded in the late sixteenth century. Despite their garrisons, the presence of these towns on the steppe's edge was precarious;[20] their existence and growth were generally supported by the Muscovite government with cash, supplies, and men. Landholders who had been displaced from western towns by Polish conquest during the Time of Troubles were thus relocated in steppe provinces, such as Briansk and Putivl'.[21] The population also grew because of the involuntary military relocation of men into southern garrisons; musketeer troops, some of them from Moscow itself, were transferred south and then remained as permanent inhabitants.[22]

Such officially sponsored settlement paled by comparison with unofficial migration. A trickle of population southward began in the sixteenth century, a movement of people escaping war, devastation, poverty, and enserfment. Some settled near southern fortress towns; others continued south into Cossack lands. The enticements of migration and settlement were twofold. First, moving south held open the hope of agricultural prosperity in spite of the threat of Tatar raids. With few exceptions, southern lands were exceptionally fertile, and even using extensive agricultural practices, the south's first settlers generally boasted of exceptionally high yields.[23] The cities and provinces that made up the southern regions were located on or near the central Russian uplands, whose soils were, and are, rich black-earth and gray-forest loam. The rainfall was normally abundant (30–36 inches per annum) and the growing season relatively long; the natural vegetation, still plentiful in the seventeenth century, followed soil types and rainfall. Most of the region was black-earth forest-steppe, upland forests alternating with valley grasslands. To the north of this parkland, a band of broadleaf forest stretched from the town of Riazhsk westward through Tula province then sharply south-southwest, characterized by heavier annual rainfall and gray-forest loam, slightly less fertile than the soil to the southeast. Much of the western part of the region lay in this belt; so did Briansk, one of the only southern provinces with less fertile soil.[24] The forests of this entire zone also provided some protection against Tatar raids, and most of the early fortress towns were located in this region. To the south of the forest-steppe was a parallel band, running from south of Simbirsk and Saratov southwest across the middle reaches of the Don. The fertile soils of this region, combined with hotter and more variable temperatures, supported only tall steppe grasses. Successful farming here was more difficult and protection from raids more problematic;[25] this open steppe remained virtually unpopulated.

The steppe and forest-steppe were also generously supplied with rivers, including tributaries of the Dnepr and the basins of the Desna, Donets, Oka, and Don, which provided water, mill power, and local communication. The first settlements spread out along rivers and creeks from the main fortresses. Water also provided relatively easy access for goods and people along a north-south axis, but the significance of this was largely military and administrative. The south had little commerce and few merchants in the period; the major Muscovite trade routes glanced along the region's eastern and western borders.[26]

In addition to good farmland, unofficial southward migration offered a second enticement, that of social advancement. During the early years military commanders in southern fortress towns often needed more servicemen for their garrisons; as a result, they enrolled men who presented themselves locally with relative disregard for the enrollees' rank and qualifications. Besides official and unofficial migration to the southernmost fortress towns, there was prior to the late 1630s an older, established concentration of population on large properties, particularly near the region's northern edge, where they were also relatively safe from Tatar encroachments. Hereditary servicemen of considerable rank and stature held large tracts near the older provinces, especially those close to the Tula defenses: Voronezh, Dankov, Elets, Karachev, Kursk, Mtsensk, Briansk, and Orel. The south also had extensive institutional estates belonging to the church, the state, and the tsar, not to mention the personal holdings of Tsar Michael's relative N. I. Romanov. Such properties often had significant peasant populations. As late as 1630, these peasant-cultivated lands, concentrated in the northern part of the district, probably outweighed those cultivated by any other hands.[27]

By the 1630s the combination of new migration and older established settlement had produced a regional population with an unusual social profile. First, the region as a whole had unusually large numbers of hereditary servicemen who had recently received small land grants contingent on military service (pomest'ia). Large estate owners along the northern borders were greatly outnumbered by petty servicemen living further to the south. For the purpose of defending against raids, this was highly desirable, as the Muscovite government already knew. Servicemen living and working on small land grants were active members of local garrisons, dedicated to protecting their own territory. As absentee landholders, elite and institutional landlords were less satisfactory in this regard. Second, the region's urban and peasant populations (the taxpaying segment) were unusually small. Towns in the south were overwhelmingly military, not commercial, centers, and few of the newly arrived servicemen had large peasant communities on their land. Although the government found it fiscally inconvenient to have so few potential taxpayers, the prosperity of southern servicemen was not in jeopardy, so long as they served in nearby garrisons and their land remained fertile.[28]

These characteristics were reinforced after the Smolensk War, when southern fortifications were extended (1630s–1651). The requirements of constructing the Belgorod Defensive Line contributed massively to the flow of population (both forced and voluntary) into the southern provinces. Two distinct problems presented themselves in this region. The first was finding the labor to build the garrison fortifications and defensive line and to protect the construction and the frontier while that process was under way. Military men brought in from further north protected the site and did much of the building; men of varied rank and status participated. Existing southern garrisons, nearby peasant populations, and any locals that could be found were conscripted for construction; by the 1640s the main army also began mustering near the new line. The second problem was finding permanent residents for the towns as they were completed. Existing southern garrisons were necessarily redistributed among the new fortresses, such that some older towns lost 30 or 40 percent of their population.[29] As before, many transferees became permanent residents. The new garrisons again accepted those individuals who presented themselves locally as fit for service; such men could include Cossacks, wanderers, and Ukrainians who had long lived nearby, but many were migrants and fugitive serfs from further north. The need for enrollees was so desperate that local commanders continued to disregard the usual status distinctions. Gradually, Cossacks and some wealthy Ukrainians entered service as the equivalent of hereditary servicemen; so occasionally did former peasants.[30] The more plebeian lower service class, which was made up of recruited contract servicemen (such as musketeers), drew heavily on local recruits with little regard for social origin. One scholar of the process has estimated that among southern musketeers and other recruited servicemen of the 1630s,

40 percent had been transferred and 60 percent locally enrolled, with up to 75 percent of the total coming from families with no prior military service.[31] As a result, by 1658 even the more elite members of new southern garrisons included runaways and migrants, as well as more legitimate claimants to various levels of service rank and status. Not surprisingly, retaining peasant populations on southern estates became increasingly difficult during this period. Southern peasants, too, moved on in search of new lands and higher status. The anomalous character of the southern population, in particular the predominance of petty servicemen and the relative absence of peasants, was strengthened in the 1630s and 1640s.

The central government was prepared to go to considerable lengths to preserve this regionally specific character. With the construction of the new defensive line, renewed national political debate over the allocation of scarce (peasant) labor focused attention on the southern provinces. The Smolensk War and subsequent decades saw the rise to prominence in Moscow of the middle service class; these were provincial hereditary serviceman (dvoriane, deti boiarskie) with limited lands and few peasants, rather than the Muscovite elite of hereditary servicemen with extensive lands, numerous peasants, and prestige at their disposal. Chief among the demands of the middle service class was the right, unlimited by time, to pursue and retrieve any peasant fleeing from their lands. The five-year limit to such pursuit that existed in the mid-1630s (when building in the south began) created an undeniable advantage for larger landholders. They had the resources and personnel to conduct extensive and immediate searches for their own missing peasants and, indeed, to conceal others' fugitive peasants on their lands for a few years. As is well known, the Law Code of 1649 (Ulozhenie) granted serfholders an indefinite period to pursue their runaway serfs, thus creating the legal apparatus for enserfment and meeting demands that scarce peasant labor not be permitted to redistribute itself from the less wealthy to the great magnates.

Construction in the south also confronted the perennial shortage of labor in Russian society. Local commanders complained bitterly of the need for men to build and defend new southern towns. But the issue here was not the transfer of peasant labor from one group of owners to another, although such transfers might have sufficed to build the new fortresses and defensive line. Rather, the south required an increasing number of servicemen who would be capable of defending the southern frontier over an extended period. Thus neither the five-year limit on the retrieval of peasants from the 1630s nor the ten-year limit instituted in 1642, nor even the unlimited right of pursuit after 1649, corresponded to the defensive needs of the south or to the wishes of southern servicemen. What had already taken place there was the transfer of manpower from the category of taxpaying peasants to the category of free servicemen. It is difficult to imagine anything but hostility toward this transfer on the part of the Russian service population: it challenged their status while exacerbating the labor problem about which everyone complained. It is worth pointing out, therefore, that the central government (waveringly) upheld the interests of southern servicemen and the regional requirements of southern defense, rather than the interests of either central Muscovy's provincial servicemen or the capital's elite.

The government first winked at the continued enrollment of peasants (and other socially indeterminate or inappropriate persons) into southern garrisons and then explicitly encouraged it. In 1635 garrison commanders were ordered not to return any fugitive peasant discovered in southern garrison service without special orders from Moscow, an unusual intrusion by the central state into essentially routine local administration. The following year, servicemen who had been reduced to the peasantry or other lower social status by poverty since 1613 were invited to regain their former status by enlisting in southern towns.[32]

These actions flew in the face of the growing influence of the middle service class in the capital and the interests of southern magnates who were losing peasants to the frontier. Outraged protests from serfholders slowed the enrollment, as local commanders were ordered to be more cautious in checking enrollees' background and to ensure that new servicemen not be enrolled in one town at the expense of another.[33] But complaints and protests were not allowed to change the policy nor to reduce significantly the flow of men. During the 1640s peasants on southern magnates' land were freed and enlisted in dragoon regiments for garrison defense. The new servicemen retained their former owners' confiscated land as a means of support. This had the added effect of eliminating the problem of peasant flight so intolerable to prominent landholders, while adding to the number of settled defenders in local garrisons.[34] The process continued even after the Law Code of 1649 was promulgated. A government order in 1653 mandated that fugitive peasants discovered in southern service not be returned if they had been serving for at least seven years. By 1656 three years of service rendered a migrant, who in this case had fled since the new laws on pursuit, immune to return, "so as not to empty the defenses of people." Such exemptions were then periodically renewed.[35]

It would be easy to perceive in this wavering but persistent thread simply the desire of the state to allocate adequate manpower to the south for defensive purposes, and this motive was unquestionably present. But the entire process was more complex, an elaborate quid pro quo between southern defenders and the central government. That is, successful defense of the south required cooperation from southern defenders and therefore a genuine attempt to heed the voices and complaints of southern servicemen. Building the Belgorod line's earthen fortifications, mounting its stockades, and constructing its towers was tedious, time-consuming work that could take southern servicemen from their fields for weeks at a time. Resettlement to new fortress towns meant that families abandoned cultivated fields, often to settle on new or uncultivated lands. Some servicemen complained bitterly about the poverty and hardship that resulted; when their complaints went unmet, some deserted and fled further south. The authorities were clearly concerned about losing crucial workmen and defensive troops—concerned enough to redress some of their varied complaints.[36] Such concerns went beyond resolving individual complaints to preserving the integrity and well-being of garrisons themselves. For example, landholders from Chernigov, after losing their Chernigov lands, were resettled in the town of Putivl', but without land. When arrangements were made in 1646 for them to receive estates near a newer fortress further south, the established landowners of Putivl' petitioned for the newcomers to stay, arguing that their departure would deplete their town's defensive forces and cause the local agricultural market to collapse. Investigation concluded that the landowners were exaggerating, but the petitioners were successful nonetheless.

The 1646 incident was part of the capital's larger preoccupation with preserving the inviolability of southern service cities for defensive purposes. Moscow invoked the earlier notion that cities should be garrisoned by local landholders but was forced to modify its application to southern fortress towns in order to conform to the southerners' own ideas. In principle, provincial servicemen in a service city were constrained to hold land only in their garrison's province. Thus, when collective petitions from the south accused outsiders of displacing garrison servitors, the government decreed in 1634 that provincial hereditary servicemen could hold land only in their home provinces. This decree proved inconvenient to the most prosperous members of southern garrisons because they wanted land in adjacent provinces, and so, although this order would be repeated in subsequent years, it was persistently ingored.[37] On the other hand, service city arrangements implied that outsiders from the capital also could not hold land in a garrison's province. This concept was embodied in a decree of 1637, which forbade members of the capital's upper service class to purchase land in any one of twelve named southern provinces or those further south; this prohibition was quite successfully enforced into the 1650s and 1660s.[38]

At the same time, the central government moved to acknowledge the south's importance and cohesiveness by partially consolidating that region's institutions of rule. Local government in Russia before midcentury was typically fragmented. Each chancellery communicated with its local representatives directly about its particular tasks; on the frontier, each town's military governor (voevoda) was in direct contact with Moscow. As building of the southern fortifications proceeded, the Military Chancellery (Razriad) in Moscow began to consolidate the southern command. The unification of all southern military activity in the hands of Prince N. I. Odoevskii, in anticipation of a Tatar attack in 1646, created a regional military command hierarchy throughout the south, while leaving older jurisdictional arrangements in place.[39] In other words, for a variety of reasons including defensive needs and southern service demands, the anomalous conditions of southern life were to some degree protected legally and institutionally by the central state.

After completion of the Belgorod Defensive Line in the early 1650s, three fundamental changes called into question the special arrangements characteristic of the south. First, Russia's entry into a war with Poland over the fate of Ukraine made the southern provinces not only a defensive arena against the Tatars but also a staging area for offensive campaign forces. Second, the old cavalry was gradually replaced by new formation troops, a process that pitted the central state's military needs against southerners' social and economic expectations. Finally, a new regionally based bureaucratic structure was introduced in the south. The region then had to confront the impact of these evolving pressures on its atypical service population, even as Muscovy as a whole experienced the military revolution.

As work was being completed on the southern fortified line through Belgorod, the new government of Aleksei Mikhailovich (1645–1676) was drawn into war with Poland. The Thirteen Years' War (1654–1667) took place at least in part because of events in Polish Ukraine, where steppe animosities flared into open conflict. Under the leadership of Bogdan Khmel'nitskii, the Cossacks rebelled against Polish encroachments on their liberties in 1648. When the Cossacks were losing ground against Polish forces in 1650, Khmel'nitskii sought Muscovite protection for Ukraine. Moscow was reluctant to enter the fray, although war with Poland seems, in retrospect, to have been all but inevitable. Such a war offered the rich reward of Ukrainian territory and the possibility of regaining Smolensk and perhaps some Baltic lands from Muscovy's longtime enemy, Poland. Furthermore, Muscovy's opportunities for expansion in any other direction were slim; the Ottoman Empire was too distant, and Sweden remained a rather formidable foe. Russia thus consented to the absorption of Ukraine, an action formalized by the Union of Pereiaslav, signed early in 1654.

The opening of hostilities in 1654 hastened the process of military reform; all along the Russo-Polish frontier, new formation troops (commanded by western European mercenary officers) were expanded and rushed into action alongside the older-style army. The war proved an exceedingly costly one, despite some early successes in the north. The inability of the old-style cavalry to arm, feed, and maintain itself through

prolonged conflict necessitated the continued expansion of the new formations, and major losses in the 1660s required constant levies of new men
from all over the country. By 1667 Poland and Russia had exhausted one
another; they signed the Peace of Andrusovo.

During this period the southern provinces became a source of recruits
for both the garrison forces already mentioned and campaign troops (*polkovaia sluzhba*), who served for extended periods at distant fronts. The levy-
ing of campaign regiments from the southern population began in earnest
in 1653, when 8,000 servicemen were called to muster at Iablonov, a town
east of Belgorod on the defensive line, and continued in 1658, when a campaign army corps of nearly 20,000 new and old formation troops met at
Belgorod.[40] During the war the brunt of such demands for both defensive
and offensive military manpower was borne by beleaguered border territories, like Novgorod, Smolensk, and Belgorod. Elsewhere, in central Muscovy and Siberia, the old rule continued in force: either campaign service
or border defense duties, not both.[41] In the relatively sparsely settled south
the combination of military requirements, astonishingly, enlisted the services of as much as 5 percent of the population.[42]

These military burdens imposed on southerners proved not to be a
short-lived wartime measure but persisted for the rest of the century.
There can be no doubt that the Thirteen Years' War (1654–1667) resulted
in repeated calls to military service throughout the country, but the demand for southern campaign regiments continued after 1667. Factional
disputes in Ukraine emerged even during the war. Upon Bogdan Khmel'-
nitskii's death, Ukrainian territory on the right bank of the Dnepr rejoined
Poland, while the left bank, under different leadership, retained its Muscovite allegiance. Although the Peace of Andrusovo confirmed this new arrangement, internal Cossack disputes and open rebellion against the terms
of the peace not only prolonged the fighting but extended it to both the
Tatars and Ottoman Turks, who entered the fray against Moscow. After
1667 Muscovite troops fought Cossacks and Tatars, took up stations in
left-bank towns, and supported Muscovy's adherents. Several regions contributed campaign regiments to these efforts, but forces from the southern
provinces were a constant element because they were so close by. Very
much the same thing happened during the rebellion of Stenka Razin
(1667–1671) along the lower Don and Volga. Troops from all over Muscovy
contributed to his defeat, but the southern provinces dispatched nearly all
of their campaign troops to confront him along their southeastern frontier.[43] In sum, although the character of military demands on the southern
provinces was not unusual for some border territories during the Thirteen
Years' War, the location of the south and its relatively sparse population
meant that such demands were high by comparison with the rest of Russia, and they persisted after the Thirteen Years' War had drawn to a close.

The possibility of meeting these demands was at least partly contingent on continued growth of the southern population. Completion of the Belgorod Defensive Line made southern settlement a more attractive proposition; the central provinces of the south acquired population gradually over the rest of the century. Increased migration and new settlement pushed the frontier southward. Ukrainian settlers, in particular, were encouraged to establish themselves south of the defenses with promises of land grants, tax-free trade, and other privileges; they were not, however, as welcome in the provinces along the defensive line or to its north.[44] Especially during periods of fighting in eastern Ukraine between 1667 and 1681, waves of migration populated Slobodskaia Ukraina, a territory south of Belgorod, much of which would later be enclosed by the Izium Defensive Line. In addition, Muscovite peasants and others fled south much as before. All told, the number of inhabitants in the area rose by a factor of four over the second half of the century, as indicated in table 3 of the appendix. Additional campaign regiments were quickly formed from this population.[45]

New settlement did not alter the anomalous character of the southern population. The high proportion of servicemen in the population still distinguished the south from much of the rest of Muscovy. For the next decades, between one-third and one-half of southern families had one or more men in active military service.[46] As before, the hereditary servicemen among them were relatively poor petty servitors with little land and inadequate labor at their disposal. By 1700 the south averaged only two or three serf households per serviceman, rather than the five or six typical earlier in the century.[47] As before, the region contained few taxpayers. Most serfs lived in the northern parts of the region and were distributed among relatively few landholders. The service population elsewhere in the south retained little, if any, serf labor. Many of the older southern provinces nearest the frontier experienced a net loss of serfs between the 1620s and 1700.[48] In an agricultural economy where prosperity depended on the acreage of land under cultivation, servicemen without serfs faced significant economic problems if they were required to meet the new demands for campaign service.[49] Towns, on the whole, remained small.

The new military demands placed on southern residents were not just onerous but socially disruptive because the military system throughout Muscovy was simultaneously adjusting to the presence of new formation troops, that is, those trained and organized like European standing regiments. For most of the seventeenth century, the traditional hierarchy of military service throughout Muscovy fell into the two broad categories already mentioned: old-style military service by those with hereditary status (sluzhilye liudi po otechestvu) and recruited contract servicemen (sluzhilye liudi po priboru). Traditionally, hereditary servicemen could be further divided into two broad categories: the upper service class and the middle service class. The former were Moscow-ranked and included the uppermost levels of Muscovite society. Access to this category depended upon individual and family advancement up the social and military hierarchy. Except in the region's northernmost provinces, upper service class families were not represented in the south after the land transfers of the 1620s and 1630s. Where they were present, they were not typical of southern service and will not be discussed further here.[50]

Southern hereditary servicemen were part of the middle service class serving from provincial towns (*dvoriane* or *deti boiarskie, sluzhilye liudi po gorodovomu spisku*). Traditionally, men of the middle service class acted as cavalrymen in the old-style campaign regiments, which were closed to those of lesser rank. For a provincial hereditary serviceman, his service duties and economic resources, along with his family's status, were factors that determined his advancement from novice upward through three successive social echelons of provincial service (*gorodovoi, dvorovoi,* and *vybornyi*). Periodic military initiations (*verstan'ia*), which sometimes took place simultaneously with army musters or reviews (*razbory*), were occasions on which military appointments were made and a serviceman's social status recognized and recorded. At this time, he would be assigned an entitlement (*oklad*),[51] consisting of a sum in cash and an amount of service land; the amount reflected a hereditary servitor's right to service land and established the maximum he could claim (until he was reevaluated). Notwithstanding the general orientation of this system toward campaign service, hereditary servicemen in the south prior to the 1650s were usually assigned garrison duty in nearby fortresses, where they served as mounted patrolmen, long-distance couriers, or defenders of distant fields and outposts.

In the provinces the size of entitlements depended not only on the serviceman's status and duties, and his family's standing, but also on the importance and age of the province whence he served. That is, entitlements were generally smaller in newer provinces (such as those in the south) than in older ones (such as those in central Russia) and smaller for garrison service than for active campaigning.[52] For southern hereditary servicemen in the first half of the century, given the pattern of southern settlement, land entitlements tended to be relatively small; furthermore, local conditions made attracting and retaining serf labor most unlikely. Although the presence of serfs on hereditary service land was certainly not guaranteed in the south or elsewhere, it was broadly a perquisite of hereditary status; peasant or other labor kept an estate economically viable. In principle, a hereditary estate was intended to produce the surpluses needed to feed, mount, clothe, and arm a serviceman while on campaign and to support him while at home. In practice, monetary supplements were paid to the poorer cavalrymen to eke out the products of their estates. Finally, hereditary servicemen in the southern provinces, for lack of labor, easily accessible good land, or the time to claim it and clear it, often claimed and farmed as little as half their land entitlements.[53] These phenomena were factors in the generally low level of prosperity among southerners. Thus even the elite of southern servicemen included a sizable contingent of men who held small plots of land and whose families had little or no labor beyond their own. In the seventeenth century such servicemen were called *odnodvortsy* (smallholders, hereditary yeomen farmers with only their own labor), and the southern provinces had increasing numbers of them after 1635.

Other southern servicemen were members of the lower service class; this group tended to be a minority of southern garrisons before 1650. Elsewhere in Muscovy, membership in this service group, whether as a musketeer, harquebusier, Cossack, or artilleryman, might imply birth into a humble service family. Even so, this service was often filled by recruitment and conscription from the free population. In the south a majority of these servicemen probably came from families with no previous military status. Contract service was remunerated in cash and grain allowances, such that maintaining a recruited garrison at full pay could be quite costly.[54] In the seventeenth century land allotments increasingly became part of the payment offered. The land allotted was in principle smaller than that to which a hereditary serviceman was entitled,[55] and serfholding was improbable for the lower service class. Most frequently, a southern city's lower service class lived within or near its walls and held garden plots or fields nearby. Arable land was often granted as a parcel (*nadel*) in a group holding.[56] For example, a company of Cossacks sent to Belgorod would receive lands near the fortress, from which an individual Cossack would receive his personal allotment of 12 *chetverti* (about 16 acres). If the individual Cossack or his group were transferred to Elets, he or they lost the Belgorod allotments and subsequently received a similar acreage in Elets's Cossack holding.[57] In addition to family origins, recruited servicemen were traditionally distinguished by such collective holdings. Individual land allotments were rarely issued to members of this group. Excluding recruited Cossacks and a few musketeers, servicemen in this category were not cavalrymen but infantry.

The new formation regiments that Muscovy began introducing in the 1630s were in many respects profoundly incompatible with the old order of military service. That is, the old system implicitly linked status to wealth, service, and family; it rewarded cavalry over infantry service and valued remuneration in land over cash. In some fundamental ways, it was a system of status categories first and military appointment second. Ideally, the new regiments were hierarchically organized and promoted men on merit, not heredity; the men were to be regularly paid and supported by the state, which made them into standing troops and obviated the need for personal wealth. Finally, the style of warfare to which new regiments were best suited placed a premium on well-trained, numerous infantry regiments with standardized firearms.[58]

The first new formation regiments in the south were nevertheless quite easily fitted into the older system. Some peasants on private and court lands in southern provinces were taken into military service as free men (militarized) in the 1630s and 1640s; the resulting special dragoon regiments were treated much like other members of the lower service class. They were provided with arms and mounts by the state if poor, were supported by collective lands, and served as part of the defensive force in the local fortress. Although the peasants' former owners may have objected, this conversion was evidently broadly acceptable to most servicemen, drawing from a single social stratum to create a traditionally recognizable service population. Similar levies were widely used during the Thirteen Years' War in other parts of Muscovy, bringing over 100,000 men into infantry regiments.[59]

As far as the south itself went, the transition from peasant to recruited servicemen was common enough locally, however much it may have lowered the status of infantry service, but the continued drafting of peasants into the new formations was not viable, and alternatives were quickly found. The south's few peasants were needed on the land, and the draft put financial pressure both on peasant economies and the state's resources. The 1653 muster at the southern fortress of Iablonov, mentioned earlier, represented an attempt to draw on different social strata to create new formation infantry. While some men volunteered for the four new regiments, one-half of the adult male relatives of southern garrison servicemen were drafted to fill out their ranks. These men had not themselves, by definition, served previously, but family standing and their relatives' service justified certain traditional expectations, especially for those of hereditary service background. Any such expectations were given short shrift. The troops received a cash food allowance (*kormovye den'gi*) in return for service, as appropriate for a standing infantry. But cash payments resembled the salaries usually paid to recruited servicemen, rather than the land received by hereditary servitors, and the new reinforcements' duties in four southern garrisons were similar to those of the unmounted lower service class. Because the distinction between recruited and hereditary servicemen was less pronounced in the south than elsewhere, however, especially as regards social origin and wealth, southern soldiers apparently acquiesced to new formation service. At least by remaining in garrisons, the new soldiers were not forced to serve alongside still lowlier peasant regiments.[60]

The implicit incongruity of traditional status and new formation service resurfaced quickly. The superior mobility and availability of the new infantry meant the four southern regiments were quickly pulled from their defensive functions in garrisons. In 1655, when a Muscovite field army was sent to Ukraine to support Khmel'nitskii's claims against Poland, both the new infantry and the new dragoon regiments served alongside troops from other regions. Furthermore, given the expense of keeping a large army in the field, Muscovy was reluctant to pay any serviceman not on active duty. Reverting to an older pattern, it sent some of the new soldiers back to their families for the winter months. After serving a number of years, some soldiers requested their own lands. Financially, granting them land was a providential solution, but the crucial question of remuneration and its status implications awaited response. Were the holdings to be the collective ones of the recruited services or the individual lands of the hereditary servitors?

The question was complicated by the changing scale of military operations. In 1658 a massive review of southern military servicemen from thirty-eight cities was undertaken with a view to organizing the Belgorod Army Group (*Belgorodskii polk*), campaign forces to be drawn only from the southern provinces. The very contemplation of that army predicated military and administrative reform. After the review the Belgorod military commander was put in charge of all the region's military, expanding upon Prince Odoevskii's responsibilities in 1646. In order to maintain those forces, the commander's jurisdiction (and the Military Chancellery's) was gradually broadened so that a species of incomplete regional military government developed.[61] At the very least, the Belgorod command now included about 17,000 garrison forces, as well as field or campaign forces of nearly 20,000 men, and the commander was given the authority to provide for them. Specifically intended for use in the Thirteen Years' War, the field troops were also the first significant numbers of new formation forces to be introduced into the south. The Belgorod Army Group was composed of two new-style cavalry troops, four dragoon regiments, and six infantry regiments. The old-style forces were in the minority: 2,000 cavalrymen (*sotni*) and 600 members of a musketeer unit (*prikaz*). At the same time, garrison forces continued to defend southern fortresses. This coexistence created competing kinds of military service for southern men: town or garrison service (*gorodovaia sluzhba*) and campaign or regimental service (*polkovaia sluzhba*). To fill both also required the mobilization of southern men from an already labor-short economy. Significantly, there were now 16,600 new formation servicemen in the southern provinces, and their place in the traditional social structure remained unresolved. This last problem was not in any way exclusive to the south; with the war continuing, new formation troops being raised throughout Muscovy generated similar status questions.

Apparently, no attempt was even made to feed, arm, and pay all these new formation men in a way parallel to efforts made with the earlier infantry regiments. Instead, older forms of remuneration were tapped; these also preserved older status distinctions and can be seen as a kind of accommodation to servicemen's expectations and requirements.[62] The result was a complex but flexible mixture of old and new, whose implications would still plague Peter I in the eighteenth century. Broadly speaking, the new formation cavalry (cavalry and lancers; *reitary* and *kopeishchiki*) was treated like the old cavalry (*sotni*). These men were generally of hereditary service origins; thus they could aspire to holding service lands and could provide for themselves while on duty—a horse, firearms (carbine and pistols), armor, food, and fodder while on campaign. In practice, the questionable social origins of some southern hereditary servicemen and their relative poverty made both these expectations somewhat questionable. Just as broadly speaking, infantrymen and dragoons were conceived as similar to the lower service class; although many held land, it was often held in common tenure for peacetime and off-season sustenance. The infantry, however, was not expected to support itself on campaign; arms and money for food were provided.

Again the south proved somewhat exceptional. Southern infantry regiments simply contained more putative hereditary servicemen than their counterparts elsewhere; furthermore, some soldiers, especially of the 1653 levy, held personal service lands, albeit small and tenantless ones.[63] In the south the degree of accommodation to old standards of status and service involved in the fledgling new formations can be readily seen even in early records of military reviews and initiations into these regiments. Inventive use of these ceremonial processes permitted hereditary servicemen and men of the recruited service to coexist in similar regiments without entirely losing sight of the status orientations so central to Muscovite society. This arrangement was similar throughout the country, though the level of permissiveness exercised with both old and new rules was less flagrant in those parts of the country that did not share the south's particular military requirements and anomalous socioeconomic structure. In general, at a military review or inspection (such as the one in 1658 creating the Belgorod Army Group), a hereditary serviceman would undergo initiation (*verstan'e*), just as he would have prior to 1653. This process recognized his social origins, acknowledged his economic and social status, and established his entitlement; he was then demonstrably a potential serfholder and recipient of service land, and his hereditary service status had been recorded. In the south alone, certain settled southern Cossacks and their commanders (*atamany*) also had the right to service land, and they went through initiation as hereditary servicemen.[64] Once initiated, in the south as elsewhere, a serviceman would be assigned a military position in accordance with his relative wealth, training, standing, and possessions. The most prized, both for social exclusivity and prestige, was an old-style cavalry unit (*sotnia*); only about 10 percent of the Belgorod Army Group was *sotni*.[65] However reluctantly, hereditary servicemen and their offspring entered, or were forced to enter, other forms of service.[66] Lancers and cavalrymen received higher entitlements and were in general more prosperous than soldiers in the infantry. These implied economic distinctions were also functional; cavalrymen were expected to use their land entitlements and occasional cash payments to provide for themselves. Soldiering was the least prestigious of services for hereditary servicemen and their relatives, and they accepted their assignments with reluctance, but at least the inspection and muster process confirmed their hereditary status. In addition to the branches of regimental service, hereditary servicemen in the southern provinces could also be appointed to garrisons, as before. The southern provinces were one of the few areas in European Russia in which town service remained an active service category for members of all service classes even after the introduction of new formation troops.

These arrangements, which neatly accommodated the south's special needs, had considerable flexibility. If a serviceman's changing circumstances permitted it, he could move from campaign to garrison service, from soldier to cavalryman.[67] Promotion within a service (to officer, or up the chain of command) was probably also accompanied by social and economic rewards.[68] It was even possible to advance socially (from *gorodovoi* to *dvorovoi*) without serving in the most select regiments, which also required the greatest financial resources of their members.[69] Those who were not hereditary servicemen also attended reviews and musters. Such men could be drawn into both regimental and garrison service and at similar rates of recruitment. When on active duty, infantrymen, whether of hereditary service origins or not, received comparable allowances; some recruited servicemen even received land. In short, the two types of servicemen served in similar regiments, but they were not both initiated. This distinction was embedded in procedure; at a muster, hereditary servicemen were reviewed first as a group, in descending order according to social echelon and branch of service. Other servicemen then followed separately by branch of service and regiment.[70]

The interlocking of the new system with the old also extended to army organization. Despite the new regiments, the army retained its overall prereform structure.[71] Only foreign-born new formation officers and men were not embedded in this labyrinthine network of unstated rules that linked military service, social status, and economic condition and that adapted old expectations to newer military conditions. As a result of this accommodation of old and new, and of the greater demands made on the troops, the military in the southern provinces displayed certain features peculiar to that area. First, the creation of campaign forces, and especially new formation troops, far from resolving the anomalies of the southern provincial population, produced newly atypical results. That is, except for a very limited number of well-to-do hereditary servicemen whose credentials and economic circumstances permitted them to join old-style cavalry regiments (*sotni*), the southern provinces were disproportionately populated by two groups: recruited servicemen and relatively poor hereditary servitors. The complex, implicit calculus that combined family history, wealth, and military service, which was used by much of the rest of the country to determine status, did not produce the same clear distinctions between the two groups in the south as elsewhere; little effort was invested in reinstating them. Thus different emphases on status and service separated southern servicemen from much of the rest of the country. In addition, questions about the support of new formation forces took an unusual form in the south. Even in its whittled-down form, a new formation army created enormous financial pressures on Muscovite society. In cash terms, because of its relative lack of taxpaying subjects, the south existed at the expense of the rest of the country.[72] The south was asked, however, to provide its infantry with food, which was impractical to bring in from elsewhere, but the absence of large-scale serf agriculture on the southern frontier suggested no obvious answers and required special adjustments.

Again the central government acknowledged the anomalous conditions of the south, most obviously by introducing new organizational forms. The Belgorod Army Group (*Belgorodskii polk*) formed in 1658 was part of a new pattern of government developing along Russia's western frontiers. Its creation gave the Belgorod army commander unusually concentrated local administrative powers; he then reported to the Military Chancellery (*Razriad*). As the territory supporting the army group was formally transformed into a military-administrative region (*Belgorodskii razriad*) in 1663, Belgorod and the Military Chancellery acquired still more control over the territory. The pattern proliferated in the south: Belgorod's western provinces separated to form the Sevsk Military-Administrative Region (*Sevskii razriad*) in 1665, and the eastern provinces formed the Tambov region (*Tambovskii razriad*) from 1679 to 1681. This form of local military administration was expanded to encompass most of the country and may have acted as a model for Peter I's *gubernia* reforms in 1708,[73] but the degree of regional autonomy and the relative absence of overlapping chancellery jurisdictions remained peculiar to the south. This format permitted the development of regional responses to regional problems. The interactions of the Belgorod regional and the central governments with the southern population over the questions of food supply and sociomilitary status in the broader context of army reform are the subjects, respectively, of parts I and II of this book.

PART
I

2

FOOD
AND THE MILITARY
BEFORE 1663

In the seventeenth century, grain products were Muscovy's principal food. In the north, rye, barley, buckwheat, and oats were grown, with supplementary plantings of peas, millet, and beans added for the peasant diet. Further south, winter plantings were of wheat, rye, and millet. The summer plantings of oats fed horses, oxen, and other livestock, as well as their owners. Except for buckwheat, these were the same crops that had fed Kievan Rus', Novgorod, and Tver', long before Muscovy's rise to power.[1]

There are ample signs that gruel, groats, and various breads were the staples of most diets. Large water-powered mills ground various grains into an enormous variety of flours. In remote or poorer areas hand mills substituted for water-powered grindstones. Though baking could be done at home, big-city markets teemed with specialized bakers.[2] Plain bakers sold the heavy rye loaves that fed most Muscovites; these breads weighed as much as sixteen pounds apiece. Up to three pounds of such a loaf fed a hard-working man for a day.[3] Bread could also be dried and preserved for later use as hardtack (*sukhari*). Other stalls sold wheat bread to the more prosperous; there were sweet breads and holiday loaves, small pastries filled with meat, cheese, or vegetables (*pirozhki*), pancakes (*bliny*), meat and fish pies, dough filled with groats and vegetables. But always, and above all, there was bread.[4]

Muscovites not only ate grain products; they drank them, too. *Kvas*, a popular kind of near beer, was made of rye, oat, and barley malts with oat flour. A single distilling of fermented grain, usually rye, was called "wine" (*vino*); double-distilled grain liquor, or "double wine" (*dvoinoe vino*), was what we would today call vodka. Both products were relatively recent arrivals in Muscovy in the seventeenth century, but excise taxes on them already generated a considerable proportion of Muscovy's cash revenues.[5] Among the common alcoholic drinks, only mead was not grain-based; it was made mostly from honey.[6]

Such dependence upon grain and grain products as a dietary staple made grain and its availability a matter of intense concern to consumers and rulers alike. Peasant producers were always vulnerable to the vagaries of weather, pests, or other farming difficulties. Low yields, early frost, nearby military activity, and disease could reduce most of a province to the brink of starvation. Large granaries, built adjacent to peasant homesteads, stocked foodstuffs produced in a good year as insurance against the inevitable coming of bad crops and low harvests.[7]

Those who lived farthest from the land, in Muscovy's urban centers, were often more vulnerable than the peasantry to changeable harvest conditions. Many residents of even the larger towns had suburban farmlands or small garden plots. Others lived in the tax-free suburbs of some great monastery or wealthy landholder and could therefore rely on the estates of their overlord, as well as their own gardens, for food. Much of the tsar's court in Moscow was supplied from granaries filled with the harvests of court lands far distant from the capital. Nevertheless, some urban dwellers depended on purchased foodstuffs to supplement their diets; still others purchased most of their food.[8] When crops failed in the nearby countryside, cities received less grain, prices rose, and serious hunger could threaten both town and countryside. Widespread shortages or major famines occurred in Russia in 1639, 1645–1646, 1648, 1650–1652, 1674, 1677, 1690, 1696, and 1704; numerous other agricultural disasters affected only a province or two.[9]

Because the availability of grain was such an important matter for much of the population, it was also a major concern of the Muscovite government. Severe shortages caused flight, unruly behavior, and sometimes violence. The political difficulties of the Time of Troubles were infinitely complicated by consecutive crop failures from 1601 to 1603, resulting in mass exodus to the borderlands and outrageous grain speculation in urban markets. These kinds of events emphasized the importance of a steady food supply in preserving public order;[10] moreover, government dependents were among the potential victims of disrupted food supply, thereby further endangering civil order during grain crises. In the cities, chancellery employees who were paid salaries for their services, rather than granted land, were at risk during periods of shortage and high prices; recruited servicemen, who were stationed in towns and granted little land, were also affected.

There is abundant evidence from the period prior to 1650 that Muscovite leaders were conscious of the vital importance of food availability for the smooth functioning of their society. In the sixteenth century the government issued grain allowances, food gifts to clergy, and bread as charity.

Such distributions began as infrequent and intermittent payments from the tsar's household to individuals. By the early years of the seventeenth century, however, grain distribution had acquired a more organized and predictable character. Much of the bureaucracy was fed regularly from the tsar's own holdings, for example. Members of the lower service class, especially the musketeers, received payments intended for food purchases; so did the officers first hired to lead new formation regiments. A limited number of supply wagons, often filled with grain from the tsar's own lands, followed troops on campaign so that men with cash allowances could purchase food. The tsar's private granaries also distributed some food in the capital city during emergencies, such as during the 1601–1603 famine. And finally, the government frequently fixed grain prices on certain delimited markets.[11]

These efforts remained quite small in scope, sporadic, and decentralized well into the seventeenth century. The bureaucracy and the musketeers were still limited in size during the early 1600s, the army prior to midcentury was in great measure self-supporting, and urban populations had actually declined from their pre-1600 size.[12] Even when army reform under Aleksei Mikhailovich began to create a larger dependent population, the Russian government did not immediately recognize the need to organize additional provisioning. Only when the size of its army had doubled and the numbers of new formation troops vastly increased did supply become an important element of the military reforms.

Despite its military and strategic importance, little is known about provisioning after 1660. To some extent, this lacuna results from the concentration of research on the beginnings of reform in the 1640s and 1650s. In addition, research about this crucial issue is hampered by Muscovy's generating few, let alone centralized, new institutions of supply, even after 1660. Instead, Russia built upon older mechanisms that were administratively diverse; there were local and regional collections and also purchases and disbursements that supplied the troops for only part of the year. Until the 1680s, the agencies of collection and distribution could be separately subsumed in the jurisdiction of different existing chancelleries, which obscured their new importance and impact. Not until the eighteenth century did Russia establish a permanent national institution to coordinate and supervise military supply.

Thus, when historians discuss seventeenth-century military supply at all, they are inclined to assume continuity rather than to look for change in the way armies were fed under Ivan IV and one hundred years later under Fedor.[13] Such a perspective not only ignores the new quantities of food produced by supply networks in the late seventeenth century. It also fails to recognize the different needs and impact of supply on a small, largely cavalry army of the 1580s and on the massed infantry and cavalry

regiments of Muscovy's late-seventeenth-century military. Finally, it ignores some very real successes at large-scale, coordinated supply. Even
after decades of fighting in Ukraine, Muscovy mustered and dispatched
two expeditionary forces toward Crimea in the 1680s—forces of more than
100,000 men each, supplied with arms, ammunition, horses, and followed
by barges and carts laden with grain, fodder, and hardtack (sukhari). Such
successes were key to the survival and continuation of military reform.
The impact of provisioning was outstandingly visible in the Russian
south, where supply was a particularly important element in producing
and supporting new formation troops on campaign.

Given the evolution of late-seventeenth-century supply, however, it is
particularly important to understand the earlier systems and institutions
upon which it was founded. The material that follows discusses provisioning as it existed in the early seventeenth century, with particular reference
to the Russian south. Prior to the 1650s grain collection and distribution
in the south was regional, intermittent, and intended for emergency and
occasional supply, not troop provisioning. The frontier contributed little
to such national collections as existed, and the central government was,
in this context as in others already discussed, tolerant of regional peculiarities, treating periodic shortfalls with doses of benign neglect.

The availability of food for the southern defensive forces early in the
seventeenth century was a particularly troubling problem. The general
principle, that "the land supports the army" (zemlia soderzhit voiska),
here proved especially inadequate. Peasant labor was in short supply; military men often had conflicting obligations; and the southern market in
grain was a relatively meager one. Some provisioning arrangements, if only
for emergency purposes, proved necessary to the settlement and defense of
isolated frontier towns. Gradually, these simple arrangements became the
basis of a major southern contribution to the changed military of the later
seventeenth century.[14]

Before 1650 a welter of local obligations in kind emerged as a part of
southern servicemen's responsibilities. Few of these dues and taxes were
unique to the southern provinces. Indeed, they existed for a number of
purposes and in a variety of regions in Russia, but their collection and
distribution was local, and regional needs and abilities were observed.[15]
Generally speaking, archival records show that the grain collections desiatinnaia pashnia (arable tenth) and otsypnoi or posopnyi khleb (tenth-grain)
were often irregular sources of supply. In the south, all three of these collections were used as emergency supplies for garrisons. Occasional and
local requisitions, as elsewhere, provided supplements for local servicemen. These collections sustained the south, despite the existence of at
least one larger-scale provisioning system, streletskii khleb (musketeers'
grain). A regular tax, intended to provide regular musketeers' salaries and
dating from the early years of the seventeenth century, musketeers' grain

was collected throughout the century and most of Muscovy, including the southern provinces.

MUSKETEERS' GRAIN

In the first half of the seventeenth century the Musketeers' Chancellery (*Streletskii prikaz*) ran the only national organization attempting to assure a regular supply of food to Muscovite troops.[16] The organization's scope was limited; musketeer regiments were supposed to be its only clients. Nonetheless, it represented a new kind of effort at military supply in Russia. First, it was intended to provide regular, year-round supply rather than emergency provisions or special supplies for the duration of a campaign— both of which had been attempted on a small scale before. Second, it paid out actual grain—anything from 162 to 810 pounds (1 to 5 issuing *chetverti*) of various cereals a year per musketeer.[17] Because conditions in Russia, especially when troops were on the move, could not guarantee the availability of adequate or reasonably priced grain on the market, these grain payments were at least occasionally more effective than salaries or food allowances paid in cash, the expedient tried during and after the Smolensk War. Finally, it drew on a large national source (taxes) rather than on a semiprivate one, such as the tsar's demesne lands.

The musketeers' system, although deeply flawed, persisted through the seventeenth century; indeed, its many shortcomings may well have helped prompt Russian authorities to reject a national, year-round, in-kind military supply system, and to choose instead a decentralized supply system based on cash salaries, emergency supplies, and campaign provisioning. Whatever the reason, musketeers' grain failed to become the basis for a national military supply system until the eighteenth century.[18] Its impact in the southern provinces reveals some of its problems.

Founded in the sixteenth century, the musketeers were Muscovy's first regular troops. Their numbers multiplied quickly from 7,000–10,000 at the end of the sixteenth century to 33,775 in 1632 and 65,000 in 1663 before declining. By 1681 reforms and reorganization had reduced their ranks to 55,000. Some of these troops were initially garrisoned in the capital and were thus Moscow-ranked; the remainder, deployed in provincial cities, were of lesser status.[19] Their support, including uniforms, firearms, food, and salaries, was ostensibly the responsibility of the state. As their numbers grew, paying musketeers' food allowances and cash salaries became an expensive undertaking. By the early years of the seventeenth century, a regular tax helped to meet the costs; the northern provinces of Muscovy, in particular, contributed cash. A companion or supplementary tax, called "musketeers' grain" (*streletskii khleb*), appeared in 1613–1614.

Broadly speaking, musketeers' grain accumulated either grain or money with which the state would later buy grain (*khleb, ili za deneg khleb*) from the taxable population (*tiaglye liudi*). The peasantry and townspeople (*posadskie liudi*) were assessed collectively, so that a set tax was due either from a certain number of households or from a given acreage of land. In general, peasant cultivators paid in kind and urban residents in cash.[20] Although the Musketeers' Chancellery did not itself administer the cash and the grain collections, the proceeds of both usually came from all over the country to Moscow, whence the Chancellery paid musketeers' cash salaries and food allowances in kind.[21]

The musketeers' food distribution system, which represented Russia's first effort at supporting regular troops, remained remarkably unchanged until the tax and military reforms of 1678–1682. Although a levy of the grain tax took place somewhere in Muscovy for every year after 1613, musketeers' grain may not at first have been a regular annual collection.[22] By midcentury, when both demand and collection were regular, the annual assessment was grossly inadequate to pay the growing numbers of musketeers. There simply were not enough taxpayers paying at a high enough rate. Only in 1680, after the reform and consolidation of the tax system and a significant drop in the musketeer force, did musketeers' grain come near meeting demand, but even then actual collections fluctuated considerably below assessments. In any case, the musketeers had by 1680 ceased to be Muscovy's only standing troops, and grain collected on their behalf was being heavily diverted to other purposes the government perceived to be more important, including the payment of new formation troops.[23] The result was hardly an advertisement for the benefits of regular national supply.

Alternative arrangements that provided off-duty musketeers with peacetime income remained acceptable in the seventeenth century because they reduced the salary requirements of the musketeers. Trading privileges or small plots of land were granted to musketeers as substitute compensation; these devices helped maintain the regiments but undercut their status as standing troops. Such arrangements were particularly likely for provincial musketeers, who rarely received their share of the tax. Food allowances for musketeers outside of Moscow, when they were paid at all, became a drain on other resources.

The south, in particular, did not lack for musketeer troops. There were some 1,200 musketeers in the larger garrisons in 1626. While the defensive line at Belgorod was under construction in the 1630s and 1640s, more musketeers enrolled in local garrisons or transferred south. There were 3,400 musketeers on the Belgorod Defensive Line in 1651 as well as a detachment of 600 Moscow-ranked musketeers in the Belgorod Army Group muster of 1658. Musketeer regiments in southern towns numbered about 5,800 between 1663 and 1678.[24] Even after 1682, musketeers remained in Sevsk, Kursk, and other southern towns; some garrisoned Ukrainian cities;

and former musketeers dominated several infantry regiments of the Belgorod and Sevsk armies.[25]

Part of the visible failure of musketeers' grain as a supply system derived from its inability to deal organizationally and otherwise with the manifold institutional intricacies and shortcomings of Russian economic organization. For example, the amount of cash and grain collected from the southern provinces to support the musketeers before 1680 was, on the whole, small. There were two reasons for this. The first was jurisdictional. The consolidation of military command in the south created unusually complete control over a contiguous territory for the Belgorod commander,[26] although many older jurisdictions, including that of musketeers' grain, remained in place. The superimposing of new spheres of authority on top of older ones was characteristic of Muscovite (and other ancien régime) bureaucratic reform. At least until 1681 southern musketeers' grain was paid almost exclusively by southern provinces predating the Belgorod line.[27] This multiplicity of jurisdictions hardly made for efficient administration.

There was a practical, regional, and economic reason for not changing the established jurisdictions in this case. Collective assessments require detailed tax rolls. The censuses undertaken by the Military Chancellery after 1646 were inappropriate for the musketeers' grain collections because they counted households rather than cultivated land. Abandoning the older jurisdictional framework to add to the musketeers' tax rolls, in other words, would have required a major population recount. There was no reason to undertake such a massive project. Musketeers' grain payments came from peasant cultivators (and the cash from townspeople). The south had few of either group, who in any event tended to be concentrated in the older towns where they were probably already paying *streletskii khleb*.[28] One might easily argue that the costs of introducing the musketeers' grain tax more broadly in the south would have outweighed the return, as well as infringing on established bureaucratic procedure.

Thus the southern provinces together contributed only small amounts of grain to the musketeers' support, probably about 405 tons (3,750 deposit *chetverti*) annually before 1672.[29] This amounted to less than 6 percent of potential musketeer needs in the area. Quite large provinces paid very little. From Belgorod 1,500 households contributed grain for various military purposes in 1668, but only 145 of them paid musketeers' grain, and that at a relatively low rate. Their annual contribution amounted to a rather paltry total of 16 tons (148 deposit *chetverti*) of rye and oats together. Putivl', in the Sevsk region, contributed an almost identical amount.[30]

After 1672, when a new military census was completed, the tax shifted to household assessments. Despite the subsequent doubling of payment rates, southern contributions to musketeers' grain remained low. Though the tax was then compatible with other southern dues, all of these southern assessments were inconsistent with other national figures until a general household census was taken in 1678.[31] Far from being an efficient local model for year-round supply, the musketeers' grain tax represented a net outflow of some 400 tons of grain from the south's few peasant cultivators to Moscow.

The organizational and economic problems of this collection system were exacerbated in distribution. Southern proceeds from these collections (as from most of Russia) were taken to Moscow for distribution, a process both elaborate and costly to the taxpayers.[32] In fact, although some money for southern musketeers' salaries was issued by Moscow, neither the grain paid locally nor adequate cash to pay southern musketeers was forthcoming. This does not mean that these regiments went entirely unpaid. Supporting musketeer troops, who perhaps played a more significant role in garrison defense and local policing along the southern frontier than in most other regions, was a relatively high priority in the south from the 1620s on. Responsibility for their provisioning devolved onto local garrisons or onto the southern provinces as a whole.[33] To judge from the results, these demands were instrumental in the development of a substitute, regional supply system there after midcentury. Thus local surpluses stored in emergency town granaries were often inadequate to the payment of southern musketeers. For example, an extra 1,728 tons (16,000 deposit *chetverti*) of grain had to be bought locally to pay southern musketeers in 1643; this purchase was nearly equivalent to all southern emergency reserves for the preceding year.[34] In an effort to minimize the impact of these burdens, some well-tested stratagems were used in the south. After 1643, musketeers in some southern cities were given land parcels (*nadely*), usually 33 to 42 acres (8–10 *chetverti*) of farmland, with additional acreage for orchards and haying.[35] Land grants continued into the 1670s, but appropriate land near fortress towns was in high demand, and the Military Chancellery could not avoid grain payments by settling all the musketeers it would have liked to. Despite some variation from town to town, remaining unlanded musketeers nominally received similar yearly salaries throughout the last decades of the century: 2 rubles and from 486 to 1,944 pounds (3–12 issuing *chetverti*) of grain, half rye and half oats, for the rank and file; 3 or 4 rubles and up to 1.2 tons (13–15 issuing *chetverti*) of grain for the officers, excluding the highly paid heads (*golovy*) or colonels (*polkovniki*).[36] Thus musketeer support remained a major local expense for the southern provinces.[37]

In short, Muscovy's first attempt at a national, year-round, in-kind food supply for standing regiments in its armed forces, the musketeers' grain tax, proved a considerable liability at the local level in the southern provinces. The tax collection and distribution system was ill adapted to the unusual demographic and economic circumstances of the south; nor was any real attempt made to cut through the jurisdictional obstacles to its effective functioning. While it is unclear to what extent these problems instigated the subsequent creation of a regional supply network in the south, it is clear that these failures increased the local need for some assured source of food supply in the first half of the seventeenth century. Not only did isolated garrisons need emergency reserves, but musketeers in southern garrisons had to be fed.

EARLY SEVENTEENTH-CENTURY PROVISIONING IN THE SOUTH

By comparison with the organization and purposes of musketeers' grain, sources of food available for southern servicemen were primitive indeed in the first half of the seventeenth century. There was no system designed to assure payment of regular food allowances in kind. This was not due to a lack of interest in supply either locally or at the Military Chancellery; on the contrary, tsar's granaries (*gosudarevye zhitnitsy*) with reserve stocks of grain began appearing in the new fortress towns shortly after their founding. These granaries, however, served primarily to supply emergency military needs by controlling extreme fluctuations in local supply; at least initially, their capacities were limited and their clients and contributors local.

In the early 1600s hostile neighbors frequently attacked isolated fortress towns. The inhabitants needed food, water, and military supplies to survive. As late as 1650 the military governor of Boboriko, a fortress town in the extreme southwest, wrote to Moscow: "Boboriko should have supplies for its needs and for siege time, for Boboriko gets many reports of hostilities and I myself have sat, besieged. The town is close to the border and during the next siege people might die of hunger." Emergency supply was a matter of military preparedness, a reserve in case of attack. The tsar's granaries accordingly stood within the earthen walls surrounding urban living quarters; on occasion, they even lay behind the wooden stockade walls that were the best fortifications Muscovy had to offer in the region. Their contents were by no means intended for regular use. Members of a southern garrison normally fed themselves by farming; musketeers, where they had been issued land, were also expected to conform to this standard.[38]

For military and other reasons, the granaries also were used to manage the flow of necessary food supplies in remote towns. Personal reserves were often inadequate to maintain small southern communities. "Boboriko stands far from other Russian towns," the governor continued, "and its residents do not have much grain of their own. They purchase grain in various cities and have only small supplies. Grain supplies are needed in this new town."[39] Boboriko's situation was common enough in the southern provinces. Small towns, distant from any trade that regularly brought them grain, themselves produced little. In the first years of settlement the opening of steppe and forest land was arduous, and most of the new farmers were also military men, whose farming time was limited by their military duties. Their plots of land were often small, and they frequently had little labor besides their own with which to work it. Even after the lands were open, bad harvest years were frequent, and farms that lay outside the fortress's walls were vulnerable to hostile attack. Local communications and military escort could not ensure the arrival of outside supply, even if town residents could afford to purchase grain.[40] Thus local granaries acted as emergency grain banks. Residents occasionally received food loans in times of bad harvests; more frequently, seed grain was given out in an effort to encourage local agriculture. Contributions to the support of military servicemen (zhalovan'ia) and ecclesiastical personnel (rugi) were also issued according to local and individual need.[41]

Maintaining reserves adequate to these limited functions was not always easy. One frequently used device was an adaptation of arable tenth (desiatinnaia pashnia) to frontier conditions.[42] Insofar as one can generalize about such local arrangements, arable tenth elsewhere in Muscovy usually meant that peasants living on court lands tilled demesne land for the tsar as well as their own fields, roughly one desiatina of demesne land for every vyt of their own fields—that is, proportions of 1:8, 1:10, or less. The situation differed substantially in the south. The local military governor (voevoda) took charge of court lands in his province. In the absence of a peasant population, he drew work parties from the men of his garrison, who not only farmed but provided whatever equipment and transport was necessary and who also stood guard over the farming parties. Seed for sowing came from the town granary, or from a nearby town's, and the harvest was returned there after threshing and preparation. As they farmed such land, early southern garrisons thus provided themselves and their community with an emergency reserve. To maintain this supply, new towns founded in the 1640s were also provided with arable tenth (desiatinnaia pashnia) to fill their granaries.[43]

The labor requirement of working these fields was treated in the south as a military obligation and therefore a demand appropriately made of any garrison servicemen. Servicemen were nonetheless reluctant to undertake it, having their own farms to attend during the agricultural season. In desperation, some military governors used nearby peasants, militarized or not, as an organized and compliant substitute. Servicemen's reluctance thus reinforced an implicit equation between this farmwork by southern garrisons and the arable tenth plowed by peasant labor in other parts of the country.[44]

Not only was arable tenth differently organized on the southern frontier. The grain was also differently used for emergency supply. In central Muscovy the tsar might sell the grain raised by his peasants on demesne fields or bring it to Moscow, where it would feed both court and bureau-cracy; such grain could also follow armies on campaign.[45] In the south, however, there were difficulties in using arable tenth as a source of local supply. Low agricultural return, the reluctance of labor, and the timing of military emergencies often meant that the arable tenth went un- or under-sown. Furthermore, even with compliance, there was simply not enough land available for this particular use or the labor to work it. Not all for-tresses had government land, and the amounts produced by those that did were both irregular and inadequate. Even towns with court lands had to rely on purchases, transfers of grain from the granaries of nearby towns, emergency levies, and requisitions to maintain their supplies.[46] Yet the system was not an entirely unproductive one. Ten towns with arable tenth recorded granary stocks of 2,484 tons (23,000 deposit *chetverti*) of grain in 1642.[47]

The inadequacies of arable tenth as a source of emergency supply led to its gradual replacement by something resembling a collection of dues in kind. This was by no means an abrupt transition nor one that took place simultaneously throughout the south. There were no decrees explicitly recommending its general replacement; nevertheless, arable tenth gradu-ally disappeared. Because court land was frequently good agricultural land near a fortress's walls, it was often distributed to newly arrived military personnel as parcels in a communal land grant (*nadel*) or as personal ser-vice land. In order to keep the granary full, then, farm labor obligations were commuted to nearly annual payments in kind, called "tenth-grain" (*posopnyi* or *otsypnyi khleb* and, at least on one occasion, *desiatinnyi khleb*). The southern towns of Kammenoe, Kursk, (Staryi) Oskol, Briansk, Karpov, and Voronezh made this shift by the 1650s; others followed soon after.[48]

Tenth-grain was usually assessed on a province as a whole. For example, in 1646–1647 all Oskol service households, lower and middle ranks to-gether, began paying 43 tons of rye and oats (200 deposit *chetverti* of each) into the town granary rather than working arable tenth. There is little indication of how the responsibility was divided except in Kursk, where payments were apparently divided among most of the province's residents approximately in accordance with their ability to pay.[49] Throughout the south some flexibility is indicated by fluctuating levels of actual payments and the apparent indifference with which shortfalls were treated. What-ever the other conditions of payment, these local collections did not in-volve the task of carting grain contributions over long distances. The col-lections seem to have preserved the principle of service dues: the local garrison (or part of it) paid into its own granary to support itself in emer-gencies. There were exceptions, of course. Some provinces began to assess their collections equally on every eligible household. In Belgorod and Sevsk provinces, where militarized peasants were living on court lands, tenth-grain payments became the former peasants' responsibility, while the remaining service population was exempted. A few cities kept the labor obligation after the 1660s or transferred it to the cultivation of more distant government lands.[50] Generally speaking, in the decade or so following its introduction, tenth-grain probably yielded slightly more than arable tenth at its peak because more towns were involved and compliance was probably greater. This volume declined in the following years when these exactions were reduced or eliminated in favor of other collections.[51]

Siege grain (osadnyi khleb) was a name commonly given to the collections that supplanted grain purchases, irregular collections, arable tenth, and the payments replacing it. Siege grain collections were innovative in that they systematically used households as the basis for assessment. This assessment was still relatively new in Muscovy; in the south it was primarily used as a basis for military service lists. Siege grain collections were also unusual because they failed to distinguish among contributors by size of assessments or in any other manner. All provincial households paid equally, whether the head of the household was a middle-level servitor (syn boiarskii), a lower-level serviceman (musketeer or Cossack), or even occasionally a peasant cultivator. Given the similarity of the siege grain assessments to service lists, these collections (like their predecessors) resembled local military dues rather than a conventionally organized tax, and they did not share the possible stigma attached to arable tenth labor.[52] These dues supported granaries in fortress towns that had never had court lands or arable tenth. Records suggest that collections were still on demand rather than automatic and annual. The first reference to siege grain appears in 1649. Other collections took place in 1650, 1651, 1652, 1654, 1655, 1657, and 1659.[53]

As local collections grew more regular, one might have anticipated that the expansion and reorganization of the military would put new pressures on provincial granaries' supplies. The population and total number of southern towns increased rapidly with the building and manning of the Belgorod Defensive Line. Tatar diversionary attacks and raids on the fortifications required defensive readiness from new and old garrisons alike. With the line complete and the Russo-Polish War about to begin, new formation infantry regiments were drawn from the southern population in 1653, even as siege grain was being collected.

The activities of southern granaries in the 1650s do not at first appear much different from their predecessors'. Disbursements still helped control the impact of local agricultural and military conditions. The granaries loaned grain for seed or food to local residents, and especially to newly arrived settlers, in case of hardship; they issued several hundred pounds of grain annually to convents, churches, and nearby monasteries; and they retained their siege functions. The overall impression is still that these provincial granaries were very loosely connected; most transfers and releases of grain, and even new collections, required specific local instructions.[54]

Nevertheless, in administrative terms, the collection of grain from southern households was taking on a more regional character, bringing local demands and sporadic collections into a regularized system. Record keeping moved to the regional level as the Belgorod army formed; thereafter, its commander was aware of the reserves available in southern granaries. Collection gradually became more standardized and widespread. By the late 1650s at least twice as many towns reported granary transactions to the Military Chancellery as a decade earlier.[55] In appearance only, payments equalized across provinces; households often contributed one *chetverik* of rye and one *chetverik* of oats. In Moscow, a *chetverik* of rye weighed 36 pounds, but unfortunately across the south, the *chetverik* could vary in size by a factor of as much as eight.[56]

Granary responsibilities, too, gradually acquired regional characteristics in the late 1640s and 1650s. For example, as musketeers, Cossacks, and other members of the lower service class who received some grain payment moved into southern towns in greater numbers, their food salaries appeared in local granary records. These payments strained the granaries' abilities; they had been organized to collect small amounts periodically and hoard them for emergency use rather than to collect and pay set quantities annually. In any case, the amount needed for lower service class salaries was large; had they all been paid, the 4,300 musketeers alone would have absorbed nearly 1,900 tons of grain.

When new formation troops were formed in the south in the 1650s, the granaries did not contribute much grain to their support. There is no evidence that year-round, in-kind supply was considered for those troops. As for the granaries, the volume of grain they carried was probably inadequate to that purpose in both quantity and regularity. The infantry and dragoon regiments of the Belgorod army in 1658 would have used nearly two-thirds of the collected granary stock for one short summer campaign; that in turn would leave little for the officer corps, emergency supply, the musketeers, or winter supply. Instead of exhausting granary stocks, troops were supported by cash salaries and food allowances during the summer; for peacetime and off-duty months, the government quickly reverted to land grants. In any case, payments in cash or grain to new formation troops were not at this period entirely within the jurisdiction of the Military Chancellery, which oversaw the granaries. Payments to the new formation drew on a variety of administrative sources, including the Foreigners' Chancellery (*Inozemskii prikaz*) for officers, the Dragoon Chancellery (*Prikaz dragunskogo stroia*) for dragoons, and so on.[57]

This does not argue that the army and its new formation regiments had no food supply system at all. Limited quantities of food followed the army on campaign, as they long had; some food could then be issued in kind on campaign or purchased with food allowances. As a result, individual purchases of food on the market and foraging remained important sources of supply. The grain that paid or followed the army on campaign drew on a variety of collections, some of them ad hoc. Although the sparse settlement and relative poverty of the southern provinces until the 1640s made them relatively ineffective resources, special collections there did occasionally amass grain for specific purposes.

As granary collections became regularized, however, special collections began to draw directly on the accumulations in southern granaries. The most significant instance of this involved payment of the Don Cossacks. Throughout the seventeenth century, Muscovy paid cash, munitions, cloth, and grain for Cossack aid in protecting the southern border against Crimea and the Ottoman Turks. Early in the century some of this grain was purchased and some was the product of small special collections from Don River towns within and outside the southern region. After the Cossack occupation of Azov in 1637, the shipments originated in the south, at the Don port of Voronezh. The grain component of that shipment was at first small and irregular; from 1649 on, as southern granaries began to make regular contributions, the size of the grain shipment stabilized at about 216 tons (2,000 deposit *chetverti*). Similarly, the town of Valuiki began to supply southbound emissaries, using grain from Belgorod province.[58] For these purposes, southern grain stocks were used in limited volumes, which allowed the granaries to persist in their original functions.

Supplying new formation regiments and military campaigns from emergency granaries continued to be impractical, at least until 1663, and this use would only later acquire importance in the south. Until then, occasional food for the army came from northern court lands, special collections in other regions, and from musketeers' grain. The southern granaries had neither the volume of grain nor the organizational form to contribute easily to this purpose, and their other uses (musketeer payments, emergency food and seed loans, siege grain, and Don Cossack contributions) were too important to sacrifice.

Prior to 1663 Muscovy had no supply system assuring regular provisions of food for its army. This was not because Russians failed to recognize the political and military significance of such supplies. On the contrary, there is ample evidence of attempts to provide food at crisis periods to critical populations. One grain collection system, musketeers' grain, even attempted to provide regular in-kind payments to Muscovy's first modern infantry, the musketeers, in the early seventeenth century. That system, however, was unsuccessful, defeated by jurisdictional and organizational problems and by the daunting economic conditions facing Muscovy's established grain payers, who were simply unable to supply adequate volumes of grain. Moscow apparently conceded the system's failure, making no effort to adapt year-round, in-kind supply to regional, economic, and jurisdictional conditions.

Instead, as the south gathered military and defensive significance in the first half of the seventeenth century, numerous local emergency granaries emerged in the region's fortress towns; their sources of supply matched the local population's economic and social circumstances. By 1650, however, the requirements of military provisioning were substantially transformed by work on the Belgorod line and by Muscovy's move toward a regular army. Granaries began to take on regular and regional responsibilities, reflecting the new regional importance of the south. In the mid-1650s regular responsibilities included shipments to Don Cossacks and payments to musketeers and other lower service class troops, in addition to providing emergency supplies. Such payments nonetheless bore the stamp of their military service origins. Southerners contributed grain to supply their own garrisons and to support the Don Cossacks as auxiliaries to the Muscovite army; notably, campaign and other new formation supply came neither within their purview nor within their capabilities. On the contrary, musketeers' grain and other peasant collections from outside the south partially fulfilled these functions. After 1650, as before, southerners in the campaign army and in the garrisons remained primarily servicemen, staffing the regiments rather than stocking the regimental cupboards.

In the 1660s, however, a regional consolidation of supply would take place in Muscovy's southern provinces. It would draw on a new annual grain collection from the towns of the Belgorod Military-Administrative Region. With the greater volume of grain this system produced, new military functions would be added to granary activity.

CHAPTER

3

ARMY REFORM AND REGIONAL CONSOLIDATION, 1663–1682

Muscovy's concern for providing food to its military forces changed quite abruptly in the 1660s. Until then, provisioning was not an important component in the creation of the modern army launched after 1645, and it proceeded in the old ways. Regular supplies in kind were available only to a limited number of Moscow-based musketeer regiments; other musketeers, cavalrymen of both old (*sotni*) and new formation regiments (*reitary, kopeishchiki*), and other servicemen with access to land or old-style cash supplements were expected to fend for themselves at home and on campaign. Before the 1660s, the emphasis was on cash salaries for new formation officers and infantrymen; as before, musketeers' grain and other collections irregularly contributed supplies to the front.[1] As the army grew after 1660, that focus changed. In the early 1660s supply in kind to officers and infantry at the front became a new and major preoccupation of army reform.

The new emphasis was signaled by the creation of a Grain Chancellery (*Khlebnyi prikaz*, 1663–1683) at the national level. Its task was apparently the provisioning of infantry troops at the front from escheated and confiscated as well as court lands, but extraordinarily little is known about this chancellery and its functioning; it appears in principle to have been similar to existing provisioning from court lands in the central provinces.[2] Other new grain collections came to be employed at approximately the same time. Extraordinary grain taxes, that is, occasional, special-purpose ones, were more frequently used to supply particular campaigns. But these were extensions of older provisioning systems, which fed campaigning troops on the agricultural surpluses of large, or peasant-tenanted, estates of the central provinces.

More significantly, the Military Chancellery initiated in-kind collections in 1663 from its new Grain Department (*Khlebnyi stol*) for some of the military-administrative regions (*razriady*) it controlled. Annual, or nearly annual, collections of grain began in the Oka River towns and in the Novgorod, Belgorod, and later, when it formed, the Sevsk Military-Administrative Regions. The collections took their name from the *chetverik*, a dry measure equivalent to one-eighth *chetvert'* or about thirty-six pounds of rye; the collections are hereafter referred to as "eighth-grain" (*chetverikovyi khleb*).[3]

Unlike musketeers' grain, special-purpose, and emergency collections before it, eighth-grain was collected primarily for the benefit of new formation troops on a regionally adjusted basis. That is, payers, collection and distribution systems, and exact uses varied according to region and, as a consequence, so did the eighth-grain's impact.[4] In essence, the new collection system proceeded from an altogether different principle. Rather than redistributing a countrywide collection to provision troops as determined by the Moscow-based chancelleries, eighth-grain had the population of a given region support its own troops. Thus Belgorod army regiments (members of the *Belgorodskii polk*) took their sustenance from contributors living in the Belgorod Military-Administrative Region. Like most best-laid plans in early modern Muscovy, the new system was not uniformly applied; its importance was greatest in the southern border regions, where the Military Chancellery held greatest sway and where unusual population configurations made previous arrangements the least workable. Elsewhere, older devices persisted or were resorted to in cases of need.[5] It is tempting to see in these experimental systems the prototypes for military-regional reform in 1680 and for Peter I's local-level provisioning of his troops.[6] This conclusion is also somewhat misleading; the efforts of the 1660s depended upon and reinforced regional characteristics, while the Petrine reforms attempted to create centralized uniformity. Beyond such general statements, little is known about the eighth-grain system as a whole or locally. What follows is an investigation of the structure, goals, regional peculiarities, and impact of the southern supply system in the regions of Belgorod and Sevsk during the period between 1663 and 1683, when the influence of military change was increasingly widely felt.[7]

The basic causes for increased concern over supplying food in kind are quite apparent.[8] Not only did the army grow after 1660, but the proportion of new formation forces in the army rose to and exceeded 80 percent, while the relative strength of the infantry (the sector most dependent on state payments) grew within the new formation. Of the 40,000 men led by V. B. Sheremetev into Ukraine during the Thirteen Years' War, a force which was not an unusual size for Russian armies in the late sixteenth and early seventeenth centuries, 11,000 were infantrymen. A short three years later, Muscovy claimed 98,000 men under arms, including 31,000 infantry soldiers and officers.[9] As of that date, the rank and file of the army alone should have been paid nearly 725,000 rubles annually, of which the Belgorod army's share came to more than 125,000 rubles; separate food allowances and the highly paid new formation officer corps cost still more.[10] Muscovy strained to meet its growing financial obligations. To pay military salaries after 1654, which it would have otherwise been unable to do,[11] Muscovy had devalued and then massively debased the silver ruble with copper. Inflation set in quickly; the army may have had money, but the men could buy little with it, including food. As prices began to rise, the grain trade came to a virtual standstill.[12]

The effects of the coinage debacle were strongly felt in the south and wherever forces were concentrated along the frontier. About one-fourth of the reminted coins were sent southward to pay officers at Briansk, and by 1662 Belgorod army troops under Prince G. G. Romodanovskii's command had received some half million copper rubles in salary payments. As elsewhere, food prices skyrocketed. The distress and anger are almost palpable in contemporary documents. Four of the thirteen colonels in the Belgorod Army Group applied to return to their western European homelands.[13] As a temporary measure, the militarized peasants of the Komaritskii district (volost') near Sevsk provided grain in kind for troops on campaign. Similarly, using granary records to identify likely contributors, special collections in 1655, 1656, and 1657 levied grain from the southern provinces.[14] The inflationary cycle was ended by the "copper riots" in Moscow in 1662 and by the government's commitment to return to the silver ruble.

The Thirteen Years' War was not yet over, and the army had still to be paid and fed in 1663. The state's attempt to shift more of its troops away from reliance on cash and market supply and to pay them food allowances in kind can thus be seen, at least in part, as a fiscal expedient. It had the convenient effect of reducing the amount of cash required to keep the new army solvent. The idea was hardly original. Musketeers' salaries had been quoted in grain as well as cash for over half a century, and a number of new formation regiments had occasionally been paid in kind. In the context of general army growth and, in particular, the recent addition of the 20,000-man Belgorod Army Group, the matter was pursued with new concentration and significant organizational resources. Although the activities of the Grain Chancellery (Khlebnyi prikaz), created at the national level in 1663 and expanded in 1665, had little direct impact on the southern provinces,[15] matters were put in train to consolidate a southern regional supply network under the aegis of the Grain Department (Khlebnyi stol) of the Military Chancellery, which was acquiring new powers there.

In October 1663, a special collection was ordered throughout the southern provinces "for food for the military, as previously, [and] above all previous collections." A relatively complex system of grain collection and storage was used to move foodstuffs from the southern provinces to troops in Ukraine. Forty cities participated in the levy; each contributed between 108 and 216 pounds (1/2–1 *chetvert'*) of grain per household, using a process already familiar from siege grain and other local collections. Contributors from the northwestern parts of the region themselves carted their grain to the northern city of Bolkhov; those from the northeast delivered grain to Voronezh on the Don River, whence it was shipped to the Don Cossacks. Most provinces, however, carted their grain either to Belgorod (from the south and southeastern towns) or Sevsk (from the center and west), where it was to be turned over to departing troops. The collection proceeded punctually; by the deadline of 25 May 1664 the levy had reached 87 percent of its expected volume from thirty-four cities, with only six cities failing to report. In short, the first large regional collection organized by the Military Chancellery in the south used and augmented the existing granary system to amass large volumes of grain (about 2,205 tons of supplies) to feed new formation campaign regiments.[16]

This use of an extraordinary collection to fulfill new needs was not entirely satisfactory; southern garrisons wishing to use local stores found the cupboards bare. In particular, musketeers who had little or no productive land complained bitterly of their plight. Border garrisons, like Belgorod, Sevsk, and Putivl', reported themselves unable to issue any rye to their musketeers, "even taking all old collected grain together." Some granaries, emptied of rye by the special collection, substituted barley and less expensive oats; others borrowed grain or paid them in money instead.[17]

Because a collection that fed the infantry at the expense of the garrison forces was unacceptable to the Military Chancellery, in 1664 the special collection was transformed into a regular annual levy that took these concerns into account. The granary collections became a formal, annual process directed from the new Grain Department of the Military Chancellery (*Khlebnyi stol Razriadnogo prikaza*), headed by Fedor Oboianikov and three younger clerks. Local granary personnel were identified and their activities monitored from the Grain Department. A record-keeping process was also clearly defined. Each province was to list how many households contributed grain to the granary, what rank the heads of those households held, how much had actually been received and disbursed, and how much stock remained in the granaries. The resulting lists were then collected at a central point, usually in Belgorod. The amount of grain typically paid per household was one *chetverik* each of rye and oats. This system was to provide grain for three distinct purposes: "for military salaries and food allowances, reserves for the towns, and grain to ship down the Don (to the Cossacks)."[18] As the most rapidly changing variable and the single largest quantity, military salaries were the primary use of collected grain.[19]

From 1663 to 1682 this first collection of eighth-grain (chetverikovyi khleb) remained the prototype. A set and equal amount of rye and oats was levied on each eligible southern household, except in the Don cities, where collections were gathered in rye flour to simplify food preparation for the Cossacks and other recipients. Records of provincial payments (and arrears) were compiled each time a collection was undertaken, usually in Belgorod. The grain collected was either stored locally in provincial granaries or carted by the contributors to selected regional depot granaries, as was the case during the special collection of 1663.

As the first collection orders suggest, the new eighth-grain collections did not function primarily as a cash substitute. The practice of taxing in kind, which had shown signs of waning in favor of cash taxes in the early seventeenth century, had persisted in many areas and been revived in others.[20] Obviously, grain collected in kind had a direct monetary value and brought the money equivalent into Muscovy's coffers;[21] the government could, and did, occasionally offer grain as a substitute for cash, although other payments in kind, such as furs, were preferable.[22] It seems highly doubtful, however, that these expedients were the primary purpose for the existence of southern grain collections. Southern grain made no extraordinary contribution to Muscovite revenues. Based on the Muscovite state budget of 1680, the single complete record of late-seventeenth-century fiscal administration, southern grain collections could at most have contributed 1 percent of revenues. As a share of total grain income, the south's contribution was approximately proportional to its population: the southern population of 875,000 in 1680 represented about 9 percent of Muscovy's inhabitants, and the southern provinces contributed on the order of 9 percent of all the grain assessed in 1680. This contribution might be reckoned something of a triumph for tax collectors, given the frontier aspects of southern life and the relatively recent acquisition of the territory, but the grain's monetary value remained small. Furthermore, from the sketchy price data, it appears that southern grain prices were stable or even declined after 1665 and that they were in any case lower than prices in central Russia;[23] this could only have diminished the contribution of southern collections to overall revenue.

Instead, the evolution of southern collections leaves little doubt that the government's first goal was to establish a regionally based, efficient, and predictable system to supply new formation troops beyond the Muscovite borders. Between 1663 and 1683 Russia's relations with its most powerful immediate neighbors—the Polish-Lithuanian state, Sweden, and the Ottoman Empire with its client, the Tatar khanate of Crimea—continually erupted into open hostilities, creating conditions of extreme

military pressure. While the western borderlands of Muscovy were generally troublesome, the shifting allegiance of successive Cossack leaders in
Ukraine made the southwest a principal focus of dispute. Russian efforts
there in the Thirteen Years' War would prove relatively successful, since
the Peace of Andrusovo in 1667 divided Ukraine between Poland (which
retained right-bank Ukraine) and Russia (which gained left-bank Ukraine
and the city of Kiev). Poised between Muscovy, Poland, and Ottoman Turkey, Cossack leaders on both the left and right banks wavered in their
commitment to any one state. The election of Hetman Peter Doroshenko,
who favored the Turks, was only the beginning of renewed struggles over
Ukraine, which were to last for the rest of Tsar Aleksei's reign (d. 1676),
throughout Tsar Fedor's (1676–1682), and indeed into Sophia's regency
(1682–1689).[24] More specifically, even after the close of hostilities in the
Thirteen Years' War, the Russian south mobilized its army (and the new
formation troops dominating it) against Hetman Doroshenko and his allies
(1667–1669) to support Doroshenko's rival, Ivan Samoilovich, in the early
1670s, to fight in the Russo-Turkish War (1676–1681), and throughout this
period to garrison Kiev and left-bank Ukraine.

After 1663, then, the expansion of the granary system was clearly related to the repeated and growing demands made by Belgorod's new formation troops on campaigns and in forward garrisons. Over the decade and a
half following the introduction of eighth-grain, the amounts of grain demanded by annual collections increased by a factor of ten, and rising yields
reflected an increase in the number of settled households in the south as
well as an increase in the amount of grain extracted per paying household.
By the late 1660s eighth-grain was paid by more than 34,000 households.
Most of the contributors lived in the much larger Belgorod Military-Administrative Region, which contained 20,885 assessed households in 1670,
21,033 in 1673, and 43,208 in 1678. The doubling of population resulted
mainly from the addition of the territories south of the Belgorod line,
which were being settled by Ukrainian migrants. (These vulnerable garrison towns would eventually be linked into the Izium Defensive Line after
1678, thus shifting Muscovy's border substantially southward.) The Sevsk
Military-Administrative Region (*Sevskii razriad*), when it separated from
the Belgorod Military-Administrative Region (*Belgorodskii razriad*) in
1665, had about 14,000 contributing households but grew to about 20,000
by 1678.[25]

The average payment per household remained at approximately one
chetverik of rye and one of oats (or a total of about 54 lbs. of grain) until
1667, when the Peace of Andrusovo ended the Thirteen Years' War. Over
the following three years, 25,000 new formation troops were mobilized
by the Belgorod and Sevsk regions to fight against Hetman Doroshenko,
representing nearly one-quarter of the Muscovite forces. In addition, after

Andrusovo, Muscovite garrisons remained in several Ukrainian cities, including Kiev. The new formation troops in those garrisons and in the field armies fighting Doroshenko could not be provisioned from the local market, which was unreliable, and local taxation and requisitioning proved partial and unsatisfactory solutions.[26] Consequently, the assessments of eighth-grain rose abruptly to an average of 81 pounds (three *chetveriki*) of each grain per household. By 1678, two years into the Russo-Turkish War, the Belgorod and Sevsk armies under Prince Romodanovskii had nearly 32,000 men in the field, and the grain collection was demanding on average some 325 pounds of grain per household (six *chetveriki* of each grain or 1.5 *chetverti* altogether).[27] In some provinces near the border and close to the fighting, such as Belgorod, household assessments rose to 216 pounds of each grain per household (1 *chetvert'* of each grain, or more than 400 lbs. altogether).[28]

The annual collection directives continued to assign the levied grain for immediate military use. In 1668–1669 the grain was explicitly earmarked for campaign and garrison supply in Ukraine, as well as for grain reserves and Don Cossack salaries. Concern for campaign armies likewise figured prominently in the directives for 1677–1678.[29] Nevertheless, it should not be imagined that the new grain supplies were always for the exclusive use of southern new formation troops. The process of grain distribution offers a clearer insight into the real workings of that system.[30] In addition to new formation supply, other uses continued to include emergency local supply, food shipments to the Don Cossacks and Russian troops on the Don, and shipments to Kiev and other Ukrainian garrisons after 1667 (*Kievskie otpusky*). The distribution and storage system used by the granaries clearly reflects the relative needs and importance of these alternative uses for the proceeds of eighth-grain collections. Fortresses on the frontier retained their emergency grain reserve, except in extraordinary circumstances, which clearly demonstrated the continued military importance of their garrisons to the region. Provincial granaries continued to be filled by local levies, grain purchased on the market, and some (usually minor) contributions from eighth-grain. The amounts to be found in provincial granaries from year to year varied greatly among cities, from a few bushels to quite large amounts. In 1670, for example, some towns each had 25 or more tons available in winter reserves; others had up to 130 tons on hand each. The Sevsk region cities had amassed 1,300 tons from a variety of sources at the same time.[31] Eight years later, the garrison granaries in the Belgorod and Sevsk regions alone held reserves of 3,322 tons of grain.[32]

The provincial granaries thus acted very much as they had since the 1640s and 1650s, as sources of emergency supply, seed loans, and supplementary grain for garrison populations in times of hardship. Payment to priests, convents, and monasteries, and gratuities for craftsmen still appeared in their accounts. Local military salaries were issued to garrison

Cossacks or musketeers as before.[33] The six or seven major depot granaries also served this older function in their own provinces although, relative to other functions, the volume of their disbursements in this regard was insignificant.[34]

It should come as no surprise that the granaries did not give up their original functions. Garrison defense still played an important military role for both the Belgorod and the Sevsk regions.[35] Of particular importance were the fortress towns along or beyond the frontier itself. The small farms of those provinces continued to be as vulnerable to agricultural and military disaster as Boboriko had been in its day. And the market still failed to provide these towns with ready reserves. Apart from the great trade routes that skirted the edges of the southern provinces, commercial trade in grain and grain products in the south operated in narrowly circumscribed areas and involved small volumes. The marketplace in Belgorod recorded merely 80 rubles' worth of grain sales in 1660. In Vol'nyi customs officials recorded a declining volume of grain sales, from 190 rubles' worth in 1660 to 45 rubles' worth in 1678. The combined worth of grain sold in four other towns only came to 100 rubles in 1678.[36] Musketeers and other military servitors played prominent roles in these smaller marketplaces. Relatively few customs officials served in many of these towns, which also suggests a generally low level of activity at their marketplaces.[37] Thus, between 1663 and 1683, it was emergency granary supplies that in the main supplied garrisons and that served as a necessary auxiliary to frontier defense.

The vast majority of eighth-grain, however, did not remain in garrison granaries; rather, some five towns acted as storage depots for the household grain payment, collected over the whole south, as they had during the 1663 levy. The annual collection instructions specified whether the grain should be taken to one of the depots or stored locally for the garrison. The contributors themselves arranged cartage if ordered to the depot towns, thus bypassing the local granary altogether. Cost of delivery was calculated into the assessments, so a household's grain payment diminished roughly in proportion to the distance traveled. Between 1665 and 1682 the depot towns were Belgorod, Voronezh, Korotoiak, Sevsk, and Briansk, and on one occasion each, Kozlov and Tambov.[38]

Grain stored in these depots went primarily for two purposes. With the institution of regular grain dues, the southern regions took over the shipment of grain to the Cossacks (486–648 tons or 4,500–6,000 *chetverti* annually) and sometimes also contributed to the provisioning of Russian troops on the Don.[39] The most significant share of grain disbursed from the depot granaries went to the Muscovite new formation troops as payments in kind. The proceeds from this collection were not typically used for replacing cash payments with grain or for paying year-round food allowances in kind. Whatever their original intentions,[40] granary officials did not try to issue regular grain payments to most new formation troops in the 1660s and 1670s. Exceptions were officers lacking personal lands (approximately 5 percent of the new formation regiments) and one Moscow-ranked musketeer regiment serving with the southern campaign regiments. More intermittently, individual officers and others eligible for food allowance (*kormovye den'gi*) also received payments in grain in lieu of cash.

The main focus of disbursement from these five granaries was food for active campaign duty, which is why the depot sites selected were usually border cities rather than peacetime regimental headquarters, farther from the front.[41] Grain salaries for members of the Belgorod and Sevsk armies on campaign or in distant garrisons were major expenditures from these granaries. Maintaining forward garrisons, as Muscovite armies moved south and west, required reliable sources of large quantities of grain. The Sevsk region regularly dispatched between 500 to 1,000 tons of grain westward to support the Muscovite troops in Kiev (the Kiev shipments or *Kievskie otpuski*) after 1667. From 1660–1669, 1673–1679, and again after 1695, the Don shipments to the Cossacks would be accompanied by an equal or greater amount of grain destined for the support of Russian troops on the lower Don.[42]

It should be noted here that, as with garrison supplies, military needs ran counter to the regional trade in grain. The southern market did occasionally act as a supplementary source of army supply but on an ad hoc rather than a regular basis.[43] Nor did there appear to be great confidence that the southern market could provide needed supplies; Belgorod army commanders were ordered to reinforce both the market and the collection system by purchasing for later use any leftover grain from cavalrymen returning from a short campaign.[44] Granary supplies provided what the market could not, which helps explain why Muscovy, unlike some of its European counterparts, did not use contractors to supply their armies. The supply system was intended to replace such impractical and unreliable arrangements.

Providing campaign supplies strained the newly organized granary system more than the other duties with which it was charged. The volume of grain in question was particularly large, having to meet a variety of army needs beyond salaries, such as fodder and supplementary supply. Moreover, the granaries had great difficulty anticipating the amounts of grain needed and pinpointing where and when to ship supplies. The granary system learned to contend with these problems by redistributing each year's grain among its five depots. Although the same depots were generally used from year to year, a single province's tax revenues could be allotted to different depots in successive years; thus the system benefited from experience and concentrated grain in different granaries, according to past demand and present military activity.

Once the campaigns in Ukraine against Hetman Doroshenko were over, for example, the distribution of the household grain tax throughout the southern provinces settled into a pattern that would remain characteristic of the system for several decades. In 1669 depot granaries in Belgorod received the largest share of collected grain, or 46.5 percent of the total assessment of 3,400 tons. Military salaries to Belgorod army troops made up the preponderance of the expenditures from this depot; much smaller sums went to maintain local craftsmen, clerks, and the clergy.[45] Grain concentrated in four other areas was used differently. The city of Voronezh on the Don was one such storage point. Grain sent there was primarily destined for shipment to the Cossacks and to Russian troops on the Don. In 1669 Voronezh received 22.5 percent of the Belgorod collection, in large part disbursed as Cossack salaries, which had doubled since the 1650s. Deliveries from outside the south were added to the Voronezh stocks to make up the Don shipment. Seven towns to the west of the city of Belgorod did not ship grain, storing 645 tons in their garrison granaries to supply southern troops' activities in Ukraine. In other years these towns had sent grain to the Sevsk depot, where it was transshipped to Kiev. Now supplied by its immediate region and areas to its north, the depot at Sevsk dispatched flotillas with up to 1,300 tons (12,000 *chetverti*) of grain to Kiev every spring. This grain was targeted for members of the Belgorod and Sevsk armies in Kiev's garrison. Finally, in 1669 eleven of the south's northernmost cities, all of them from 75 to 125 miles from the frontiers, retained the grain they collected. This amount (12% of the total assessed) was the system's uncommitted reserve and could make up shortfalls or extraordinary demand.[46]

Spurred by food shortages in the lower Don area and by a Don shipment (*Donskoi otpusk*) that fell short of expectations, the Razin rebellion (1667–1671) tested both the flexibilities and failings of the supply system developed during the Thirteen Years' War. During the rebellion the normally uncommitted reserves from the north were sent to Belgorod, where a poor harvest could not meet the needs of an unusually large massing of troops. Four of the cities that had sent grain to the Voronezh depot the previous year shifted their deliveries to Belgorod in 1669–1670. The seven western fortresses did likewise, rather than reserving their grain to supply future campaigns in Ukraine. Thus Belgorod received grain from twenty-three provinces that year. Nearby Kursk and Belgorod itself, muster points late in 1670 for the Belgorod army, were therefore able to supply troops departing for the southeast frontier. The Belgorod infantry regiments of about 4,500 men therefore received most of the 430 tons (4,000 *chetverti*) they needed for a short campaign close to the frontier. Soldiers brought from outside the south were not as well supplied. Poor harvests had resulted in a low eighth-grain collection,[47] although emergency grain collected for them from three provinces at the western end of the Belgorod defenses and the Sevsk region helped to make up the shortfall.

Because of the Razin rebellion, Don Cossack supplies were not sent in 1671. Seven of the cities near Voronezh used this additional grain to bolster local supplies for garrisons approached by Razin's forces from the southeast. A special collection in Tambov assisted in this effort and eased the strain on local supplies when reinforcements arrived.[48] Overall, the system functioned adequately but only with the support of ad hoc collections. During the following years, the grain distribution met changing demands in a similar fashion. In 1674, for example, the emphasis was on shipments down the Don. Fifteen cities sent grain not only to Voronezh but also to depots at Korotoiak for shipment southward. Five other towns held their grain for Ukrainian campaigns, none held reserves, and thirteen delivered it to Belgorod for regular salaries. Surpluses tended to concentrate in the west-southwest part of the region, where the demand was least heavy.[49]

Reflecting the needs and peculiarities of the southern provinces, the south's regional supply system differed both in its purpose and in its contributors from others operating in Muscovy. The system's threefold task—to provide emergency food for garrison servicemen, geopolitically valuable payments to the Don Cossacks, and campaign provisions for regimental servicemen—was unique, not surprisingly, because the south was one of the few places where garrison and campaign services coexisted.[50] Between 1663 and 1683, however, the south's new formation regiments grew significantly without a corresponding decline in its garrison forces; the resulting demand for grain contributions placed great pressure on the region's agriculture.

Given who contributed to eighth-grain collections, and other unusual features of southern service and its support, the special status granted the south's regional supply system seems more likely to have been the result of deliberate policy than bureaucratic and administrative convenience. To begin with, eighth-grain was not a peasant tax in the south, as both musketeers' grain and eighth-grain were elsewhere. According to introductory remarks written in collection registers, all local households with year-round access to arable land owed eighth-grain to the granary system. Comparison of these registers with service lists and other materials leads to the conclusion that contributors were usually members of the local garrison service (*gorodovaia sluzhba*) who held land. Thus hereditary servicemen in the garrisons and their relatives who owned land were the principal eighth-grain contributors in most provinces. Contributors also included some Ukrainian settlers enrolled in fortress garrisons, whose tax-exempt status on the land expired in 1665, landed Cossacks, and militarized peasant communities. Peasant households rarely appeared in the eighth-grain rolls and then only if they were not paying musketeers' grain. Musketeers and regimental Cossacks, if they were reimbursed in grain and cash and not in land, were technically exempt; so were most town residents (*posadskie liudi*) and occupants of postal and artillery suburbs (*iamshchiki, pushkarei*). The entire campaign branch of military service (*polkovaia sluzhba*) and its peasants appeared rarely in eighth-grain collection books. Estates with large serf populations probably paid musketeers' grain, which exempted them from this new contribution. In sum, therefore, southern hereditary servicemen without serf households (smallholders or *odnodvortsy*) dominated the grain contributors.[51] Contributions to eighth-grain thus retained the character of service dues, not taxes, as they had when garrison servicemen paid into granaries to provide their own reserves. Now, however, they were paying to support their neighbors while away on campaign, an unusual arrangement that had evolved from grain collections in the south prior to 1663 and one that was clearly adjusted to the peculiar population distribution of the southern regions.

The configuration of the south's grain collection system had important social and economic implications, even while the southern provinces remained apart, isolated from central Muscovy and its standards. Eighth-grain was collected by flat quantity per household, a kind of assessment not in general use in Muscovy until 1672 or 1678.[52] Such flat assessments were regressive in principle, making no distinction between wealth and poverty, although some provinces chose to permit redistributional and partial payments.[53] In central Muscovy, where flat assessment might have led to significant impoverishment of the poorest stratum, contributors to eighth-grain paid instead on the basis of cultivated land, a more progressive arrangement. The very different flat assessments on southern petty service households without peasant labor may have impoverished them relative to Muscovites in the central provinces but, given the homogeneity of most southern service economies, need not have increased southern stratification.

Grain dues in the south not only ignored differences in wealth but further undermined a variety of social distinctions already challenged by the creation of a modern army. The occasional inclusion of the traditionally taxable population (*tiaglye liudi*) in the dues-paying service lists failed to respect the principal Muscovite social distinction between taxpaying and service populations. By taxing landed members of the middle and lower service class equally, southern grain collections ignored the boundary between hereditary and contract service, as had the new formation infantry regiments in drawing men from mixed service origins. The eighth-grain collections instead created a different and fluid division among southern servicemen. In other parts of Russia, servicemen paying food support and other service dues for campaign troops often paid cash in lieu of service.[54]

Because southern dues payers remained in active garrison service, distinctions common elsewhere in Muscovy were replaced by a separation between garrison servicemen (gorodovaia sluzhba) and campaign servicemen (polkovaia sluzhba). However, supply and other payments helped to equalize the costs of garrison and regimental service,[55] and garrison servicemen might be reassigned to campaign duties, so the boundary between suppliers and supplied remained highly permeable.[56]

It is perhaps not surprising that the socially and economically distinctive features of this supply system were strictly confined to the Belgorod and Sevsk regions. Beginning in 1664, the Military Chancellery consolidated its demands for grain in the south and attempted to make them as equitable as possible, given southern conditions. Measurements used in collection were standardized in 1667–1668, when sample Muscovite chetverti were sent to a number of southern cities. The collection rolls were updated and revised with some frequency, using at times even military service rosters as sources. The collections themselves, however, were quite explicitly bounded by the Military Chancellery's authority, which was increasingly territorial and which derived from military administration of the southern army groups. Despite eighth-grain levies in other parts of Russia, the boundaries of this particular supply system encompassed only the Belgorod army cities, or the Belgorod and Sevsk army cities. The number of granaries involved in the system rose and fell with the number of cities associated with the army groups.[57] When the Sevsk army separated from Belgorod, for example, its administration briefly argued that eighth-grain should not be collected in the Sevsk cities. Similarly, the residents of one southern province who were not administratively part of the Military Chancellery disputed the requirement that they pay dues. Furthermore, southern granaries only accepted grain from southern collections;[58] other chancelleries' efforts to coordinate central Muscovite tax policy with southern military goals were quite limited.[59] The jurisdictional lines around the south's grain collections appear to have been remarkably rigid, confining the unusual collections entirely to this homogeneous but atypical region of Muscovy.

On the surface, at least, this regional isolation simply allowed a more severe exploitation of southern resources by the Military Chancellery. Moreover, with the institution of eighth-grain collections, other pressures were brought to bear on the south. The most dramatic of these was the persistent drain of men from southern farmlands and garrison service into the Belgorod campaign army. Between 1658 and 1667 the Belgorod Army Group lost some 10,000 men in the field. Regional musters transferred men from garrison service and initiated new campaign servicemen to fill the gaps and keep the regiments growing in 1658, 1666, 1669, 1675, 1679, and 1680; military conscription filled Belgorod's infantry regiments in

1653, 1660, 1668, and 1673. So many adult males were drawn from individual households that special orders were issued in 1660 and again in 1675 reminding reviewers and recruiters (*okladchiki, razborshchiki*) to leave at least one adult male to cultivate the land, if others from the same family had already been taken into military service. Such economic pressures on small farms led to the adoption of various stratagems, including the reorganization of landholdings, hiring (and hiding) of extra labor, and widespread shirking of service obligations.[60]

In at least one respect, this intensive use of southern resources was accompanied by the central government's effort to bring southern social and economic standards into line with those of central Muscovy, to the detriment of the south. As the Thirteen Years' War drew to a close, and the absolute need for military men declined somewhat, attempts were made to limit the flow of fugitive serfs from central Russia into service on the southern frontier. Searches increased, penalties for violations were enforced, and the enrollment of serfs and other inappropriate social groups into military service in the south was reduced.[61] This effort enforced central Russian social standards, but it also deprived the Belgorod and Sevsk regions of new servicemen and new labor.

Muscovy's effort to impose uniformity failed to take into account the dynamics of southern provincial life in the third quarter of the seventeenth century. After the Thirteen Years' War, for example, new formation cavalry regiments throughout Russia were purged of peasants, soldiers, and other socially incongruous elements who had been pulled into their ranks by the pressure of war. Peasants and others of low social status were assigned to the infantry or to other appropriate service categories, leaving the new formation cavalry as much as possible the preserve of hereditary servicemen. These purging efforts were not applied at all systematically by southern commanders, who still had pressing need of men. Men of various social origins continued to serve in the southern cavalry.[62]

Other policies reflected the standardization effort much less forthrightly. Restrictions against the purchase or acquisition of southern lands by the Moscow-ranked nobility, for example, persisted until the 1670s. In 1672 these prohibitions were briefly withdrawn for many southern provinces, only to be almost immediately restored. The restrictions did not entirely prevent the acquisition of land by the capital's elite, particularly in the south's northernmost provinces. In 1676 the prohibitions were again eliminated because so many men of Moscow rank already owned southern land and because their larger estates would produce more grain (an anticipation of the needs of the Russo-Turkish War). After the war ended in 1681, the restrictions were reinstated.[63] These policies were not the only example of ambivalence toward southern regional issues on the part of the center. Even the policy on fugitive serfs was applied variably and was relaxed in cases of extreme need for more servicemen.

Local conditions contributed to the inconsistencies of Moscow's policies in the south. First, as A. A. Novosel'skii argued more than sixty years
ago, the persistence of the service city in the south provided a considerable
base for local power. The wealthiest and most prestigious of southern servicemen exercised their influence through local military and administrative figures such as recruiters, reviewers, and even granary heads (razborshchiki, okladshchiki, zhitennye golovy). Town elites, though neither
wealthy nor prestigious by the capital's standards, thus held direct sway
over the lives of the lesser servicemen of their communities—in the appointment to an infantry or cavalry regiment, the assignment of salary,
and the like. The social cohesiveness of service cities, although eroding by
the 1660s and 1670s, still made itself felt, at times dramatically. Much
detailed research remains to be done, but what we already know suggests
that, at least in part, it was the coincidence of interests between the central state's military concerns and the landholding servicemen of these
cities that permitted the government successfully to prohibit Moscow-
based nobles from acquiring southern estates. Petitions from the lesser
servicemen, complaining that they were being displaced from the northernmost provinces of their region, as well as the interests of the local service elite, are certainly associated with the reinstatement of the prohibitions.[64]

Other issues potentially pitted petty servicemen against the provincial
elites. Under the pressures of the Thirteen Years' War and its aftermath,
for example, lowlier servicemen appealed to the center for protection
against the malfeasances of their local superiors: enrollment of infantrymen who might have been cavalrymen, cavalrymen appointed and salaries
established through friendship, patronage, bribery, and the like.[65] The ap-
peals were not always in vain; redress through direct central intervention
occasionally followed, serving the interests of the military and of lowlier
southern servicemen, as well as extending central authority in a very limited fashion.

The persistence of frontier conditions also limited the central government's effectiveness in the south. For example, given the pressing and persistent need for fighting men, even desertions and failures to appear for
service often went unpunished.[66] Not surprisingly, less urgent efforts to
centralize and standardize southern behavior were simply unrealistic. The
Military Chancellery's reluctance to enforce its demands on the southern
petty service population was also evident in grain collection. That is,
eighth-grain yielded considerably less grain than assessed. Payments were
adversely affected by bad weather, military alerts, and poor harvests. Belgorod province, for example, paid only 46 percent of its assessment in
1670. In the same year, arrears payments from other provinces close to the
defensive line were canceled, probably to encourage loyalty to the government, given that Stenka Razin's forces were not far away.[67] In short, the

grain actually received was frequently a distressingly low percentage of what was expected, and the returns were unpredictable from year to year. This should not obscure the continued improvement in rates of payment since the institution of regular collections in 1664. About 52 percent of assessments were paid between 1665 and 1670, which rose to some 60 percent between 1671 and 1676. In the final years of eighth-grain nearly 80 percent of assessments were paid annually.[68] On the face of it, this was indeed a respectable return for the seventeenth century—especially when the object of the collection was subject to drought, hail, and plagues of locusts.

These numbers, however, are misleading. First, they conceal significant regional variation in contributions. A particular area might have no grain to contribute because of pests or inclement weather. Towns south of the Belgorod Defensive Line (militarily and agriculturally the most vulnerable) were persistently remiss in their contributions; prior to 1672, northeastern provinces also often paid less than their share of the south's assessment.[69] Second, the payment rates, as calculated from arrears books, conceal tax exemptions. Thus the 205 tons in arrears owed by three southern border towns was canceled in 1669. In 1670, 1673, and 1681, again because of arrears' cancellations, actual collections were much smaller than expected.[70] Cancellations of this sort were insignificant by comparison with wholesale dismissal of arrears in 1670, when 8,184 tons of overdue grain disappeared from the rolls, and again in 1680, when all outstanding payments were dismissed "until ordered otherwise."[71] Thus eighth-grain, although a marginally dependable tax by comparison with its predecessors, fell substantially short of its assessments.

Shortfalls were readily accepted by local granary administrators, who only occasionally imposed sanctions for unexplained failure to pay. When enforcement was attempted, it began with special orders from Moscow to collect arrears.[72] When payment was not forthcoming, a local investigation was launched. Punishment should have followed, unless circumstances adequately explained why the grain had not been paid (in which case an exemption could be granted).[73] But, the threat of sanctions by local authorities was sometimes the only outcome. Households might remain under threat for some time with no further action taken. If the matter was pursued further, failure to pay led to flogging, imprisoning the debtors' dependents (wives, children, serfs), fines in money or grain, or in extreme cases the reclaiming and sale of lands and possessions.[74] But sanctions were enforced only on the rarest of occasions. In most cases, despite large accumulations of arrears, no attempt at enforcement was made at all. Pleas from regional headquarters in Belgorod or Sevsk and even from Moscow went unheeded; arrears remained on the books for years, perhaps even a decade. Little attention was granted to these lapses beyond perhaps a journey to the offending estate by the local granary head to request payment. More often, arrears were simply recorded in the account books. This applied not only to estates but also apparently to whole provinces; some towns were noted only as having "no report," "no record," or "no grain."[75]

When, however infrequently, sanctions were enforced, they seem to have been successful. The years 1670 and 1673 were harsh with widespread crop shortages, but troops nonetheless required provisions to face the Razin rebellion, fight on the Don, or engage in the persistent contest over Ukraine. In these and other cases, the military was used to collect taxes. In Belgorod province, for example, the presence of troops led to collection rates exceeding those of neighboring provinces in 1670 and even to payment of half the Belgorod arrears in 1673,[76] which suggests that some southerners may have had more labor (and therefore more grain) at their disposal than reflected in local records.[77] Why, then, were the central government and its local representatives so reluctant to apply the sanctions?

It should first be noted that objections to the grain dues were not hard to find. Some individuals or small groups objected in petitions, asking to be exempted from dues.[78] Others objected by simply refusing to pay them. And these objections came not from peasants but from servicemen, whose military functions remained in considerable demand. Occasionally, there were stronger reactions. In 1660–1661, when the governor of Borisov in the extreme south sent troops to pick up reserves owed the granary, his soldiers found another grain collection in progress, one run by local Cossacks and recent Ukrainian migrants. Open battle ensued, which the Cossacks won; a second government detachment was likewise defeated, and several soldiers were fatally wounded. No government grain was collected in Borisov that year.[79] In Belgorod in 1682 the serfs of the Metropolitan of Belgorod and Oboian also refused to pay their taxes. Although their revolt was eventually quelled by troops, investigations dragged on for months, and still no grain was forthcoming.[80] The central government took infrequent revolts such as these very seriously, even if they rarely escalated into outright rebellion against southern grain collections during the second half of the seventeenth century.

The open frontier to the south of the Belgorod and Sevsk regions was good cause for both Muscovite authorities and local officials not to pursue enforcement of grain contributions. The flight of settlers across the frontier toward the Don, where their labor, military prowess, and contributions were out of reach, remained a chronic problem in the south. Not just individuals but households, even whole villages, would abandon their lands and move southward with their belongings in tow. Despite some effort to limit access to territories beyond the frontier (by restricting travel with the Don River trade caravans), flight persisted evidently in quite large numbers, especially after 1660.[81] Some provincial military governors believed grain collections were a contributing factor in their residents' decisions to flee. For example, contributors in a Don River province owed 260 pounds of grain in 1671. The governor reported that the fields were deserted and people were running away; he refused to recoup the eighth-grain arrears.[82] In 1668 in Kursk the Military Chancellery blamed refusals to pay grain on the military governor, alleging that he had intentionally failed to initiate the collection at the proper time of the year.[83] Even when Moscow was willing to apply sanctions, local servicemen sometimes sided with their delinquent colleagues rather than enforcing Belgorod's or Moscow's demands. When the Metropolitan of Belgorod and Oboian's serfs rebelled against requests for more grain and their recent loss of status, infantrymen living nearby refused to help quell the rebellion.[84]

The character of personnel operating the granaries may have also contributed to the failings of the southern supply system. The Military Chancellery expended little on the southern granaries, running them "on the cheap."[85] Although granary officials maintained accounts, collected grain, enforced payments, built granaries, and arranged transport, these operations cost Moscow very little. Most granary functionaries simply added granary and collection responsibilities to their other duties. For example, the military governor of each town was responsible for his granaries, their contents, state of repair, and so on;[86] he and the province's "best people" selected local individuals (from among townsmen, military servitors, or very rarely peasants),[87] who were placed in charge of guarding the granary, accepting payments into it, and supervising disbursements from stock. These sworn deputies (tseloval'niki) were directed by a headman (zhitennyi golova), who with a clerk (pod'iachii) kept the accounts.[88] The actual collection process was conducted by these granary officials or by members of the local garrison. A clerk of the local administration (s"ezzhaia izba) might accompany them. The grain, when collected, was shipped at the payers' expense or by individual payers in their own carts, again sometimes with a garrison escort. Local residents contributed money and labor to the building and maintenance of granaries in their town. The usual checks on the system consisted of inventories when there was a change of granary personnel or military governors, the calling in of clerks and records to Belgorod or Moscow, and, once in a great while, the auditing of records by an auditor from outside the region.[89] In short, the grain collection system was staffed primarily by servitors whose sympathies were local, not by functionaries with direct allegiance to Moscow (unlike the more strictly enforced fugitive investigations effort). Enforcement of sanctions against delinquent contributors by local officials, both of whose participation was still required along the southern defensive line, was one area in which even the strong centralizing government of Aleksei Mikhailovich was unable or unwilling to proceed.

That inability to extend central authority through local officials in the south exacerbated the failings of the regional supply system created after 1663. The southern grain collections were, in the last analysis, not very reliable. A granary official, if he were uncertain how much grain would be forthcoming the following year, would be loath to expend that year's stock as it arrived. A cautious administrator would stockpile a healthy percentage of one year's grain to safeguard against next year's shortfalls. Evidently, such practices were quite common. While large stockpiles minimized the uncertainty of an unreliable tax, they reduced still further the amount of grain the Military Chancellery actually had at its disposal. In 1669–1670 the Belgorod region's reserves were between 3,200 and 3,700 tons; in 1675, more than 4,300 tons; in 1676, 6,000 tons; and in 1678, 4,200 tons. That is, throughout this period, the reserves equaled or exceeded the annual grain dues collection (see table 1 in the appendix).

Stockpiling was not the only insurance against unreliability, however. On occasions when grain dues failed, the regular collections were occasionally supplemented by ad hoc local or special collections.[90] This represented an understandable contradiction in Military Chancellery policy. In the mid-1660s there had been efforts to eliminate competing demands for grain, such as local requests for arable tenth from the same households that were now paying the regional collections. Despite the priority of regional over local dues, however, local dues were not eliminated entirely. Some Kursk residents were paying both arable tenth for local use and regional grain dues even in the 1680s. In moments of particular desperation, the Military Chancellery called on all provinces to contribute such local resources to its purposes. There were also occasionally calls for larger extraordinary collections, such as a campaign supply collection in 1677, when the Belgorod cities' collection was inadequate.[91]

Chief among the problems for the southern supply system was its inability to begin the transition to some kind of year-round provisioning, one step on the way to a truly modern standing army. Muscovy acknowledged that regular provisioning was desirable by quoting some salaries in terms of regular grain payments; in practice, however, it issued year-round provisions to less than 10 percent of the campaign forces, and these were sometimes paid in cash.[92] More realistically, the central government fed the growing new formation infantry rank and file only while it was in the field. Although the daily food allowances given to soldiers fell by half between 1660 and 1679, even the lesser amount provided more than enough grain.[93] As indicated in table 1 of the appendix, Muscovy could not have paid year-round grain allowances to the southern new formations in 1663, even if it renounced other obligations; the amount of eighth-grain received was only 70 percent of the amount required for grain salaries for the rank and file. Military, economic, and political pressures, coupled with the central government's inability to enforce its will on the south, made it difficult to improve upon this situation. The dependence on land as a principal source of supply and maintenance, which had been retained for new formation cavalry and even infantry, thus could not be expected to change (even had status and other considerations permitted it to do so). In any event, given the magnitude of tasks facing any supply effort in the bellicose 1670s, striving for such fundamental change was out of the question. No efforts were made to improve the level of military supply by expanding the categories of men eligible for either campaign or year-round support.[94] Almost all of the Muscovite army remained firmly wedded to land support during peacetime if not on campaign. These same shortcomings, however, permitted the southern region to fulfill its obligation to supply other groups. In particular, it continued to supply the Don Cossacks, its own frontier fortresses, and some of the new garrisons in Ukraine.

In the mid-1660s, in the context of serious inflation and a rapidly expanding army, a regional supply system developed in the southern provinces of Muscovy. Its primary purpose was to supply the new formation infantry from the Belgorod and Sevsk army groups while on campaign, although it retained other functions such as emergency garrison supply and the payment of Don Cossack salaries. Drawing grain from the small farms of southern garrison servicemen, the system had severe limitations. Rather than expanding the range of military supply, the system's inadequacies locked southerners into continued dependence on land. It should be remembered, however, that there were also very real accomplishments. The consolidation of this supply system took place under conditions of almost continuous military activity. Despite the relative poverty of the south, its troops bore a heavy share in the fighting. The south's regular supply to some of its forces was a crucial addition to the support small farms with limited labor resources could provide individual fighting men. The unusual pool of contributors from whom the system drew grain meanwhile helped establish new distinctions among southern servicemen, hinging less on issues of status than on the more flexible division between garrison and campaign service. The south's strategic geographic position and its peculiar political configuration introduced a degree of leniency in the central government's enforcement of policies there. Confined as the southern supply effort was, however, the impact and implications of that leniency (such as impoverishment and greater homogeneity) were, between 1663 and 1683, largely limited to the Belgorod and Sevsk Military-Administration regions.

4

THE
INCORPORATION
OF THE
SOUTH

The 1680s and 1690s

Tsar Fedor's reign began in 1676 with considerable drama. The victory of Hetman Ivan Samoilovich over his rival Peter Doroshenko signaled the return of Cossack and Ukrainian allegiance to Muscovy, an event Moscow probably regarded as a mixed blessing. Although the return of Ukraine represented an enormous gain in strategic, political, economic, and cultural terms, it also presaged war with Turkey over the fate of the lower Dnepr lands. In 1677 the hard-pressed south contributed some 32,000 campaign servicemen to the Russian army to help prevent the Turks from taking Ukraine.[1] Prince G. G. Romodanovskii, longtime old-style military commander, led a combined force of new and old formation troops and was ably supported by high-ranking new formation officers.[2] Their mission was to defend Kiev and other Ukrainian cities garrisoned by Muscovy, as well as the Ukrainian fortress capital of Chigirin. The first year's campaign was successful, but the Turks returned in 1678 to capture Chigirin after its fortifications were destroyed by the retreating Russians. Thereafter, despite the numerical inferiority of its forces, Russia surrendered little to the Ottoman Empire until the Peace of Bakhchisarai ended hostilities in 1681: Muscovy retained left-bank Ukraine but surrendered its influence in the lower Dnepr lands and agreed to pay an annual tribute to the Crimean khan.

Partly to meet the Turkish challenge to its new frontiers, Fedor's administration launched an ambitious program of bureaucratizing reforms in 1678–1682.[3] Some of the changes it introduced were administrative and financial, designed to allow Muscovy to pay and direct its armies more efficiently. Others were military, eliminating remaining differences between old and new formation troops and providing Muscovy with more men, infantry, and supplies. Many of the reforms advanced or acknowledged transformations already under way, but the changes were also intended to remedy problems from which the army unquestionably had suffered during the 1670s, such as desertions and failures to appear for service. Altogether, the reforms aimed to standardize and centralize the Muscovite administration, introducing similar rules and structures even in outlying regions, such as the southern military-administrative regions (*razriady*). In the south, more than elsewhere, the reforms met with mixed success. Military necessity, local conditions, and the existing organization of the military-administrative regions undercut the process of standardization as it applied to hereditary servicemen and led to complex, ultimately unproductive compromises.

Standardization of the social and economic conditions of hereditary military service was a particularly important element of the 1678–1682 reforms. The keystone of this effort was a decree of December 1678,[4] which defined the conditions of military service in the new and old formation campaign regiments (*polkovaia sluzhba*) for members of the entire hereditary service class (*sluzhilye liudi po otechestvu*) and which limited access to the elite, old-style regiments; to the new formation cavalry; and to the infantry, establishing minimum standards of wealth, lineage, and status. These definitions converted what had been a web of relative, flexible, and tacit understandings by the central service elite into a series of absolute, explicit, and inflexible rules. Subsequent reforms also curtailed mobility among the military services, thereby limiting social mobility as well. Finally, at least in principle, the reforms of 1678–1682 conflated the older styles of military service into the new formations, thereby finally completing the military reorganization initiated earlier in the century.[5]

Access to the elite heavy cavalry units (*sotni*) was firmly restricted by stipulations that were part of an ongoing process of rigidifying social categories. Among provincial servicemen, only those with twenty-four or more peasant households remained eligible for this elite, old-style service. Because this number of peasants was seen as guaranteeing adequate support for their owners, cash salaries to this group ceased. The honor of elite cavalry service was denied those who had in the past failed to appear for service.[6] The criteria governing promotion up the provincial ladder toward Moscow rank (from *gorodovoi* to *vybornyi* or *dvorovoi*) were narrowed, and every provincial serviceman was made aware that his children would serve in the new formations unless he, in his lifetime, attained Moscow rank.[7] Once the Moscow ranks were thus restricted, service in the capital was also partially reorganized. The long-overdue abolition of the system of precedence-ranking (*mestnichestvo*) in 1682 was accomplished in the name of military efficiency; the male children of court-ranked Muscovites entered military service as junior officers in the new formations.[8] The end of the *sotni* was in sight, with the wider consequence that access to the capital's elite was to become more difficult.

These changes to the elite old-style regiments had little effect upon the southern provinces, where there were few hereditary servicemen with the twenty-four households of peasants that might gain entrée into the old-style cavalry. Among the 10,000 heavy cavalrymen constituting the entirety of the Russian army's postreform, old-style troops, there were 200 or 300 from the Belgorod cities and perhaps three times that number from Sevsk. Only six men were named to the *sotni* from Tambov (a new military-administrative region briefly separating the Don River cities from the rest of the Belgorod region in 1680–1683).

Many of the southern old-style cavalrymen preserved their positions despite the new regulations. In a sample Sevsk province none of the cavalrymen actually had the requisite twenty-four dependent households, although all had some dependent labor.[9] There was no discernable military reason for such exceptions to be made. Whatever the reason for preserving these troops, it appears that the economic limitations on *sotni* recruitment in 1678 remained widely unenforced, at least in the south. Peter I established a lower economic threshold for entry to the old-style cavalry from the southern provinces when he first attempted to reorganize the army in 1696, but he was equally unsuccessful in enforcing it.[10]

The reforms of 1678 had more dramatic impact in the south at other levels of service. The institutional and social isolation of the southern provinces from central Russia before 1678 had protected their military organization and their servicemen's aspirations. From 1679 on, the new regulations introduced permanent distinctions between the new cavalry and infantry services, distinctions that had been largely ephemeral in the south. Three standards were enforced. First came a purge along social lines; the decree of December 1678 specified that cavalrymen and lancers mustered in 1679 and 1680 were to be men of hereditary service family only. Men of inappropriate social standing were to be rejected, even if they were wealthy or landholders.[11] Although this social standard was enunciated for all of Muscovy and had been enforced outside the south since the end of the Russo-Polish War in 1667, its enforcement in the southern provinces was another matter. There, the principal concern throughout the 1670s had lain rather in filling the ranks of the southern armies to fight the incessant struggles over Ukraine, and not a few cavalrymen with long service records were of Cossack or even peasant background.[12]

After 1678 entry into the new formation cavalry required not only hereditary rank but also wealth. Muscovite cavalrymen were now to be men who could support themselves from their property and who had served without shirking when called (a measure of material wealth as well as willingness). This requirement completed and clarified the links among cavalry service, hereditary status, and access to service landholding. Hereditary servicemen with land and some dependent labor were assigned to the new cavalry. In practice, however, many individuals were unable to support themselves from their land while on campaign, and cash payments were offered to those who had less than ten dependent households.[13] This economic standard for entry into the new cavalry was less rigid, as well as less demanding, than that applied to the old-style cavalry (*sotni*).

In the south, however, even this economic standard was not the final criterion in determining access to the new formation light cavalry (*reitary*). A third standard, applied by the central government to the south alone, used the service city organization of southern cavalry regiments as the ultimate basis for cavalry selection, rather than the social and economic criteria enunciated in the reform decree and enforced elsewhere in Muscovy. In the late 1670s both officers and men of a given southern regiment lived and held land in a particular province or group of provinces. For precisely this reason, landholding in the many southern provinces continued to be forbidden to any but local servicemen throughout the 1670s and into the 1680s.[14] In addition to stipulations of rank and wealth, therefore, the Military Chancellery also specified the total number of cavalrymen and lancers to be mustered from each southern military-administrative region (Belgorod, Sevsk, and Tambov). It also identified specific provinces from which each regiment was to be drawn. The entire new formation cavalry and lancer component of the Belgorod army (excluding Tambov in 1680–1681) was set at exactly 7,500 men in six cavalry units. Later plans for reincorporating Tambov into the Belgorod Military-Administrative Region in 1683 named seven regiments, each centered in a regimental town and each drawn from surrounding provinces.[15] This method of defining cavalry enlistment minimized the influence of local elites and limited the discretionary power of recruiters (*razborshchiki, okladchiki*). Unlike the social and economic criteria, these recruitment quotas were stringently observed; out of the eight or nine cavalry regiments that had existed in 1674–1678, exactly 7,500 cavalrymen remained in the Belgorod army of 1680. Other former cavalrymen were demoted to infantry or garrison service or fell within the jurisdiction of the new, short-lived Tambov army.[16]

In thus limiting the numbers of new formation cavalry, the central government successfully exercised its authority in the south. But the application of the service city standard, far from introducing Muscovite qualifications for cavalry service throughout the southern provinces, instead protected southern servicemen from central Russian norms and from the whims of local elites.[17] Establishing a quota of 7,500 cavalrymen for the Belgorod army ensured the presence of men who did not meet the government's social and economic criteria. In a muster of 1681, for example, only one-third of the lancers from Belgorod province had already purchased their own pistols; two-thirds had to rely on state-supplied firearms and therefore were not self-supporting.[18]

Some southern cavalrymen thus protected by the service city quotas of 1678 nevertheless soon lost their status and position. Their relative prosperity declined in the years after the reform. Given the small land grants and relative absence of labor typical of the south, it became increasingly difficult for them to serve under the conditions prevailing for cavalry regiments. The number of southern new formation cavalrymen (reitary) presenting themselves for duty declined, despite the government's attempts to maintain the forces at the size specified in 1678. In 1681 only 5,218 lancers and cavalrymen appeared at a Belgorod army muster; in 1683 there were the requisite 7,500 men, but they came from a much larger region (Tambov rejoined Belgorod that same year).[19] Almost as surely as any government norms might have, the reality of southern economic conditions limited southerners' ability to serve in the new cavalry units.

Two decades later, in 1696, Peter I's new army would limit entry to the light cavalry in ways similar to the 1678 reforms. Then as in 1678, cavalrymen were to be "prosperous, mounted, provided with weaponry and clothing." Unlike the earlier reforms, however, the Petrine reforms would stress economic over social criteria. As a consequence, groups of landed Cossacks would join Peter's cavalry regiments. By contrast, in 1679, such Cossacks were attached to the Belgorod military forces as members of separate Cossack regiments (based in Akhtyrka, Sumy, Khar'-kov, and Ostrogozhsk); they remained outside the ladder of social advancement and apart from the hereditary service class.[20] In this respect, the reforms of Fedor's reign retained some distinctive categories of service peculiar to the south and other borderlands, rather than imposing the categories described in the 1678 reform decree, which were more typical of Muscovy's central provinces.

The most visible impact of the 1678 military reform on the south was the expansion of the infantry. The general reform decree stipulated that hereditary servicemen were not to be forced into demeaning infantry service. If cavalrymen agreed to serve as new formation soldiers, their honor would be upheld, and they would have the option of rejoining the cavalry in the event of improved material conditions. In the south, however, this lenient approach was impractical if the reforms were to have their intended impact on troop distribution. Musters of southern servicemen resulted in the demotion to infantry service of many cavalrymen who claimed hereditary status. Military inspectors (razborshchiki) were explicitly instructed to demote the poorest cavalrymen to the foot regiments;[21] southern hereditary servicemen with little or no land or labor became soldiers. The slim hope of a return to the cavalry was held out to them, that is, until the manpower needs of a campaign against the Crimean khanate in 1687 had been met.[22]

These hereditary servitors were not alone in being forced into the new formation infantry units. Beginning in 1679 many Cossacks, artillerymen, some local administrators (including granary personnel), and their adult relatives were also assigned to infantry regiments. A year later, only 7,000 Cossacks remained in regimental service as cavalrymen, including those in separate Cossack garrisons south of the Belgorod line. The musketeers also felt the hand of reform, if rather differently. Their troops stationed in Ukrainian garrisons were diluted with levied serf militiamen (*datochnye liudi*) in 1679; the following year, the command structure of musketeer units was shifted from the older (*prikaz*) style of organization to the new formation hierarchy. Musketeer officers acquired new designations and responsibilities: the old heads (*golovy*) became colonels (*polkovniki*); their seconds in command, lieutenant colonels (*polupolkovniki*).[23] After their role in a rebellion in the capital in 1682, Moscow-ranked musketeer regiments were reduced in force by further reorganization: nine of twenty-eight troops were disbanded and became eligible for other branches of service. Regiments of provincial musketeers, on the other hand, were simply renamed and converted—lock, stock, and barrel—into infantry regiments.[24] The influx into the infantry of various categories of contract servicemen was supplemented by the recruitment of "wanderers" (*guliashchie liudi*) into the same regiments.[25] In this way, the number of military serving in units that did not fit the new formation army's categories was drastically reduced. Overall, emphasis on infantry service was reinforced, and decreasing attention was paid to status considerations in selecting those regiments. Cavalry troops, however, remained the preserve of a clearly defined hereditary group, with social standing the key to entry.

These less than thoroughgoing efforts at standardization, centralization, and redefinition of the southern army groups were immediately brought up short by a persistent southern problem: a limited pool of men to serve in the military. A decree of 1682 confirmed that fugitives who had joined the Belgorod and Sevsk army groups before 1674 would not be returned to their former residences; furthermore, they were to continue in their current service positions, regardless of social origin. Serf militiamen who had deserted were even promised land and infantry service in the south if they surrendered themselves.[26] The ambivalence of the central government over the competing demands on the southern frontier persisted.

Reforms in the south did not lead to quite such an abrupt mixing of social and occupational categories as it might appear. Less dramatic arrangements preserved the social and military norms made possible by the institutional isolation of the south during the preceding half century. For example, since the 1660s, southern infantry regiments had also been formed on the service city principle, and new infantrymen in 1679 joined the geographically closest unit.[27] Colonel Jacob Leslie's Belgorod infantry regiment, for example, drew the vast majority of its men from three neighboring provinces: Belgorod, Bolkhov, and Korocha. Limited efforts were made to maintain some social parity within individual regiments; infantrymen of hereditary service background served in one regiment, while former Cossacks and musketeers were assigned to others. In addition, the initiation process still protected the status of hereditary servicemen, although many infantrymen served uninitiated.[28] Even with these adjustments, the new standards were not easily accepted. Demoted cavalrymen, petitioning for elevation out of infantry regiments on the grounds of honorable former service, met with some success. The musketeers objected to their reorganization. And foreign officers who commanded the new units urgently requested reassignment to their old troops.[29]

Concessions and adjustments to local conditions notwithstanding, the impact of reform on the distribution of Russian forces was dramatic. From 1674 to 1678 there were less than 8,000 foot soldiers in the Belgorod army;[30] in 1681 the postreform army had 16,000 men in twelve infantry regiments. After the Russo-Turkish War (1677–1681) these regiments grew to 17,000 men.[31] Infantry reform had particularly dramatic results in the poorer Belgorod region, but the infantry grew in Sevsk, too; indeed, in Muscovy as a whole, it was the fastest growing part of the new formations during reform.[32] Considerable confusion resulted from the rapid changes. Some individuals, for example, discovered that even though they had inherited one set of obligations (dragoon service), recruiters imposed another (infantry service).[33]

The Petrine reforms instituting the new army of 1696 would share certain elements with the infantry reforms of 1678–1682, beyond limiting entry to the cavalry. Peter would draw 20,000 southern infantrymen from a group that also included landless and land-poor hereditary servicemen. Peter's intent was different, as we shall see, and his attempt to end the infantry's dependence on the land would founder on the inability of the remaining southern population to sustain their colleagues year-round.[34]

Virtually unmentioned in the 1678 reform decrees, but certainly affected by them, were garrison troops of the hereditary service. In 1678 few of these servicemen remained in active service outside the south.[35] By any reading of the reform decrees, retired, poor, or disabled servicemen should have dominated this entire category, but southern garrison duty continued to be an active military service. In the Belgorod region the garrisons numbered more than 35,000 men, even after the reforms. In the Sevsk region their numbers were to diminish considerably, but a few towns retained significant garrisons.[36]

The military redistribution of Tsar Fedor's time partially acknowledged a political and military reality. That better-trained but fewer Russians had held the Ottoman army at bay between 1677 and 1681 only reinforced an already familiar lesson. New formation troops, particularly the infantry, were by far the most effective elements in the Russian army. Older-style troops were of relatively little practical value, as well as being more susceptible to desertion.[37] Thus the reforms provided an acceptable framework for an army entirely composed of new formation regiments.

That framework, however, was neither fully elaborated nor implemented in the south during the pre-Petrine period. Accommodations to local standards and the unusual demands of a military staging area were partly to blame. In addition, some old-style cavalry and garrison servicemen remained active, incongruous remnants at opposite ends of the hereditary service spectrum.[38] Their elimination would be gradual, in ways still not completely understood. The reforms of 1678–1682 did not encourage replication of the central Muscovite social hierarchy in the southern provinces. Administrative centralization was not accompanied in the south by the kind of standardization envisioned by reformers, which required realignment of the relative positions of social status and military authority. Instead, with its many compromises and local adjustments, the reforms further blurred the south's already imprecise and overlapping social and military distinctions.

Furthermore, the concentration in the infantry of landless and land-poor men with little labor, regardless of their social status, raised new questions about their supply and sustenance. Muscovy did not believe it could reduce the size of its army, which limited its ability to invest in military training and supplies. The number of troops fielded by the Ottoman Empire, however providentially held at bay in recent years, surely acted as a goad to maintaining a large Russian force. It was the scale of operations rather than any innovative training and organization of Ottoman forces that made them so formidable.[39] Under the circumstances, the Muscovite reforms of 1678–1682 did not attempt to eliminate the dependency of its valuable infantry troops on land and agriculture in favor of other, more modern, more expensive year-round arrangements.[40] Landholding for southern infantrymen was not disavowed but rather extended by the reforms. As artillerymen in garrison service became eligible for infantry service in 1679, for example, about four-fifths of Artillery Chancellery employees were settled on land.[41] Land distribution to dragoons, musketeers, and infantrymen continued after the reforms and increased after 1685.[42] Like those before and after it, Fedor's government encouraged and exploited a variety of devices that had emerged in the south for stretching land and labor resources to their limits. Such devices helped provide for the new infantrymen during peacetime; the government also significantly expanded—but otherwise left virtually unchanged—its supplementary supply systems for the infantrymen in time of war.

The pressures to supply and pay the new distribution of troops generated by military reform motivated countrywide changes in fiscal and organizational structure. Significant advances toward a simplified direct tax were made in 1679, with the intent of increasing revenue and efficiency. Not the least of these was the consolidation of postal taxes, captives' ransom taxes, and musketeers' cash taxes. Under the consolidation, assessments were based on the new household census of 1678, itself the product of an effort to record landholding patterns countrywide.[43] Financial institutions were also somewhat rationalized and simplified in 1680 with the creation of the Great Treasury (Bol'shaia kazna) and the first Russian state budget.[44]

Efforts at consolidation and simplification were echoed in military administration. Nine military-administrative regions (razriady) were formed, most of which used the military-territorial principles already well established in the south. Building on existing administrative patterns, the central government encouraged similarities across all its regions, making the southern military-administrative regions less unusual in their organization and the southern provinces somewhat less isolated in their character and administration. On the other hand, the Military Chancellery now assumed control of many facets of life in the Belgorod, Sevsk, and Novgorod regions; its concentration of power remained unusual.[45] The chancellery also took direct charge of all military campaigns, which thus acquired a central, national focus. By contrast, other administrative bodies diminished in importance: the Musketeers' Chancellery retained control only of the Moscow-ranked musketeers and the Foreigners' Chancellery only of the capital's select (vybornye) troops.[46]

This battery of reforms was in progress as new expenses that had a particularly dramatic impact on southern servicemen appeared. During the final years of the Russo-Turkish War, not only were campaign armies mustered for battle, but construction on a new defensive abatis line began, with the goal of further protecting the southern provinces. Members of the southern campaign armies as well as garrison services helped to build the Izium fortified line. Campaign regiments under P. V. Sheremetev (the Younger) gathered at Userd, Poltava, and Valuiki. The threat of Tatar attack in 1678 mobilized the garrisons of Iablonov, Novyi Oskol, and Khar'kov. Even so, Tatar raids crossed the Russian defenses in 1680, and reserve units under Prince Khovanskii moved toward Belgorod from Kursk to repulse them.[47] Because many regiments active along the defensive lines and those serving in Ukraine were entitled to pay and supplies, supply pressures on the south sharply increased. The changes to financial and military administration already in place proved inadequate to meet the exigencies of renewed fighting in the south, particularly with regard to needy southern regiments. As a result, military events in 1678–1681 encouraged southerners to rely more than ever on the complex and varied alternatives that poorer servicemen in the region had developed to support themselves.

In the 1660s and 1670s, heightened demand for service in the campaign units and garrisons, coupled with the pressure on servitors to farm for themselves in the absence of serf labor, resulted in household consolidations. The average household size rose from 2–3 men in 1646 to 4–5 men in 1678.[48] Recruiters recognized this consolidation as a strategy for lowering the burdens of military service and developed norms to compensate. By the mid-1670s southerners were complaining that campaign service was taking one man per household and garrison service a second, leaving only one man behind to farm—often a minor or someone incapable of serving elsewhere. (Campaign service was also taking a household's fourth man, if there was one).[49] The result was that a number of active servicemen depended on the same small plot of land for support. The pressures were greatest on households that neither owned nor could hire dependent labor. A number of ways were devised to deal with these labor pressures. Those left "on the land" (na pashne) to farm for a campaign serviceman were usually relatives of the serviceman or his family, although others (prokormshchiki, also pod"emshchiki and podmoshchniki), who were often but not always outsiders, could be assigned to perform this role. Under such an arrangement, service obligations rested with the servitor, while his support rested with the prokormshchik. Another device was for the serviceman to divide his land, service duties, and other responsibilities in half (with a polovinchik), or even in thirds (with two tretchiki)—an arrangement most common among recruited servicemen.[50]

When these devices were formally acknowledged and even institutionalized by reform, the result was not to equalize southern service conditions with the center, as originally intended, but to introduce new kinds of compromises between the needs of the state and those of southern servitors. Migrants from Ukraine were assigned as polovinchiki and prokormshchiki by the state. Later in the century the state was to use prokormshchiki in labor brigades at considerable distance from their farms. Family members "on the land" who served in labor brigades were even granted the right to initiation (verstan'e). Along with issuing land to infantrymen who were not hereditary servicemen, these practices made ownership of service land and other forms of land tenure increasingly difficult to distinguish.

Compromises recognizing the arrangements servicemen devised to support themselves obviated the need for peacetime salaries and thus permitted Muscovy to maintain its army at a maximum size; they did not diminish the need for, or expectation of, campaign pay to infantrymen, which was met with some regularity. Nor did they resolve the problems posed by the relative poverty of the southern regions. The inability or unwillingness of the relatively weak governments following Tsar Aleksei Mikhailovich's death to enforce prohibitions against Moscow-ranked servitors' acquiring land in southern regions combined with the subdivision of existing provincial service plots to perpetuate, if not worsen, poverty in the south. Desertions and failures to appear at service musters continued on a significant scale, either in protest or for lack of resources.[51]

As a result, the military readiness of southern new formation regiments declined after the reforms. Lacking resources, southern servicemen were unable to muster annually into service, as men of their rank had formerly done; as a result, regiments were often mustered at half strength. After 1683 artillerymen served alternate years in garrisons close to home and on campaign. By 1687 only half the cavalry regiments of the Belgorod campaign army were called up annually, and only half the available soldiers were called to muster, especially late in the 1680s.[52]

Commanders, apparently aware of persistent economic hardships, began using southern campaign servicemen for less demanding purposes than field campaigns. The need to staff forward garrisons and left-bank Ukrainian cities was so acute by the late 1680s that, throughout the next decade, the poorer regiments of the Belgorod campaign army served there on three-year rotas. Musketeers and other recruited servicemen were also assigned to Ukrainian garrison duties.[53] The least prosperous campaign regiments were used for labor brigades, rather than for fighting.[54] Because many southern servicemen had in preceding decades announced their preference for garrison over campaign service,[55] despite its lower prestige, such changes were probably well received, insofar as they reduced a serviceman's obligations away from home.

The reforms of 1678–1682 and local devices for stretching land and labor resources had a profound impact on regional food supply, by exacerbating regional poverty and social misalignment. The military reforms greatly increased the overall demand for reliable deliveries to the army when it was in the field; the local devices made several servicemen dependent on individual plots of land, if they did not lead to subdivision. Such devices, however, also diminished the number of prereform grain contributors still able to produce substantial grain surpluses from their land, at exactly the time more grain was needed. These changed circumstances in both supply and demand were acknowledged by Regent Sophia's government after Fedor's death in 1682. By 1683 a new version of eighth-grain was in place, called "quarter-grain" (*poluosminyi khleb*) after its one-quarter-*chetvert'* assessment size. This collection used the structure and organization of eighth-grain but drew on somewhat different groups of contributors. In the late 1680s Russia's increasing aggressiveness vis-à-vis her southern neighbor, Crimea, required ever-larger field armies and, as a consequence, more food than even the new dues could supply. In 1686 an all-Russian on-demand grain levy (*zaprosnyi khleb*) provisioned the first Crimean campaign. Thereafter, on-demand levies gradually displaced regionally organized grain dues. These changes in food supply, like the other changes of military reform, introduced a measure of centralization, without a corresponding standardization of southern with central Muscovite norms.

QUARTER-GRAIN (*POLUOSMINYI KHLEB*)

The first reforms to the southern regional supply system were largely administrative. The continuing effort at countrywide coordination was evident here as in other reforms: between 1678 and 1682 records were collected regionally as before, but administrative procedures were standardized and the workings of the system more carefully monitored from Moscow. The governors of the southern provinces came under closer surveillance from the Military Chancellery as they collected grain and maintained granary accounts. The household census of 1678 gave a more up-to-date count of the southern population, added to the old eighth-grain rolls, and distributed the dues more evenly. Until then, for example, eleven provinces had had no accurate list of contributing households.[56] An effort, although ineffective, was also made to consolidate information about all southern grain collections.[57]

Rationalizing the entire Muscovite tax system had important implications for southerners, implications that went beyond the granary system. With the 1678 census, cash taxes shifted to household assessments (many southern grain dues had made this shift in the first half of the century). Outside the south most cash taxes were paid by peasant and urban households, as for example a revised musketeers' tax (also paid by some southern petty servicemen). Rationalization thus emphasized the resemblances between two groups making the same payments: servicemen in the southern provinces and peasants elsewhere in Russia.[58]

With respect to grain collections, the administrative changes did not generate supplies sufficient to meet the demands of new army regiments. The population contributing grain in the Belgorod region rose by 15 percent after 1683, while infantry regiments grew by 70 percent. In absolute terms, grain collections lost the ability to pay food support, even to half musters of troops.[59]

Adjustments to the existing grain collection system followed. After the Peace of Bakhchisarai in 1681, the slate was wiped clean; all arrears of grain for the preceding decade were canceled. The cancellations were offered not out of generosity or at the promptings of a rational bureaucratic spirit. They followed on the heels of two years of hard labor on the new Izium Defensive Line by garrison servicemen and a wave of urban rebellion—neither of which could be expected to promote agricultural productivity (and payment of arrears) or continued willing service.[60]

In 1683 the assessment and name of the grain collection changed together. The new rates were a half-*osmina* of each grain per household (a half-*osmina* was equal to two *chetveriki*, one-quarter *chetvert'*, or 72 lbs. of rye). The dues became known as "quarter-grain" (*poluosminyi khleb*), although orders and account books on occasion still mistakenly referred to them as eighth-grain. The new assessment represented a large drop in average payments per household. As in the case of the grain dues before it, however, both the contributing population and the amount assessed rose very gradually over the next decade and a half.[61]

Orders to collect quarter-grain (also called *novo-okladnyi* or "newly assessed grain") specified that all urban and rural residents of a province should contribute[62] "according to the great sovereign's decree, from the Belgorod army cities, from urban and rural, from all ranks of people . . . by household according to the new assessments." The grain collection was still called eighth-grain outside of the southern regions.[63] Collection records indicate that the new dues no longer drew upon the same population as before 1682. First of all, rather than being regional, as the original eighth-grain had been, quarter-grain collections were carried out across Russia. In the south new groups were asked to contribute to quarter-grain who had not contributed to its predecessor: "all ranks who do not pay musketeers' grain . . . so that collections take place from all cities and all ranks in Russia." Orders to bring in the collection explicitly mentioned peasants and cotters (*bobyli*) both in the south and elsewhere.[64] More surprisingly, campaign servicemen were assessed in large numbers: dragoons, infantrymen, cavalrymen, lancers, and even the occasional old-style cavalryman.[65] The lists of potential contributors, like the comprehensive lists of emergency granary suppliers before 1663, encompass the full panoply of provincial residents.[66] These lists were also used to solicit other dues: for building boats, carting grain, and feeding horses, as well as cash contributions for tools, saddles, and metal.[67]

The comprehensive collection instructions, however, were misleading. In practice, at least in the south, not every member of the groups mentioned actually was asked to contribute to quarter-grain. Who, then, did pay the new southern grain dues? Unlike the original eighth-grain, which was levied only on households with land (*za kotorye pashne est'*),[68] quarter-grain was levied on all households that did not pay musketeers' grain, whether their men were landless or landed, in active service or not.[69] Wealth figured into the new collections in another way, however. On the one hand, large landholdings, and the peasants on them, were more likely to be on expanded musketeers' grain rolls; they were not the target of the new quarter-grain collections. On the other, the new collection singled out households with little or no dependent labor. A document from Mtsensk province even labeled contributors as *odnodvortsy*, that is, servicemen without peasant labor.[70] The new grain assessments further compounded the burdens of those households supporting more than one servicemen. This was clearly a problem in Belgorod province, whose 3,000 servitors in both regimental and garrison service came from only 2,000 households.[71] Losing 144 pounds of grain (2.5 months' ration for an adult male) to quarter-grain, in addition to offering off-season support to servicemen who could not help with the summer's farming, could hardly have eased the burden. It is difficult to ascertain the impact of the collection on such households, since we still have little information about alternative sources of labor these households may have used.

When campaign servicemen, or their households, were asked to pay dues, the character of dues paying changed. In the past only local garrison duty was considered compatible with grain contributions.[72] The new assessments were not only regressive, they also challenged the established relationship between service dues and service itself. The character of the new demands did not pass without comment. Petitions from infantry households argued that contributing and carting grain in any given year should release the contributor from regimental service in Ukraine, an argument widely repeated elsewhere.[73]

The countrywide organization of quarter-grain highlighted regional anomalies, rather than obscuring them. Southern servicemen without dependent labor were paying dues while on active duty, when traditionally they had not. And peasants elsewhere in the country were also paying quarter-grain as a tax, which gave the dues lowlier social and legal connotations. The unorthodox attitude toward central Muscovy's social-military system embodied in the original eighth-grain dues was thus continued in quarter-grain payments. The joint emphasis on dues paying and service that had evolved in the south had no resonance nationally, and most southern servitors appeared to be part of a regionally homogeneous, anomalous, low-status group.

Quarter-grain was innovative in other ways. It extended the tax reform of 1679. The move to household assessments regardless of ability to pay[74] presaged the introduction of the "soul tax" under Peter I.[75] Southern collections overturned the traditional understanding of service dues, since they did not universally excuse servitors who paid dues from campaign service (they did do so occasionally).[76] Finally, the continuation of in-kind dues was evidently intended to continue campaign supply without relying on cash or markets and without extending it to year-round coverage or to new branches of the military. There are, however, no direct statements to that effect.

Quarter-grain innovations did not seriously affect remaining older collections. Musketeers' grain continued to be delivered to Moscow from southern provinces for a variety of military salaries. Revisions to the musketeer grain rolls in the 1680s added some new serf households, but the same provinces paid the tax as in years past.[77] Ironically, except in the south, the amount paid by each contributing household was lower for such serf households than for a service household paying quarter-grain.[78] Other grain payments, such as arable tenth, continued to be collected in a few southern cities.[79]

Uses of the grain from the quarter-grain collections gradually shifted to meet new military conditions. The stocking of depot granaries in the large volumes needed beyond Russia's borders had already become a feature of granary collection and distribution in the 1670s, but these volumes increased in the 1680s and 1690s. Voronezh and occasionally Korotoiak received large amounts of grain for shipment to the Don Cossacks and to the Russian armies moving south. In the Sevsk region, increasingly, grain was also accumulated for shipment from Briansk to Kiev and left-bank cities.[80] Only rarely was grain held in the towns, although Kursk and other fortresses occasionally received large quantities for particular purposes. Local uses for the grain, such as loans, became minimal, with provincial granary supplies totaling only 1,000 tons in 1684, an indication of the greater integration of the supply system.[81]

Belgorod and Sevsk were still major depots. In the mid-1680s, for example, sixteen cities sent grain to the regional center of Belgorod to pay Belgorod army officers and the local Moscow-ranked musketeers. These payments persisted, but they did not remain the major use of the grain, which often went to new formation troops departing the regions on active duty. In December 1687 and January 1688, for example, 640 cavalry and 1,806 infantry troops crossed the eastern boundaries of the Belgorod region carrying their provisions, including grain. They also carried a smaller amount of grain as payment for 1,500 Cossacks.[82] Some salaries were also paid through the southern granaries to men and commanders from outside the regions; 10,000 infantry under Peter Gordon's command received grain (originally from northern court lands) left in Voronezh after the Don Cossack payments had been dispatched.[83]

By the mid-1680s a number of improvements had been made in the southern grain collection system. Administrative reforms had made a noticeable difference in the payment rates and reliability of quarter-grain. Twenty-seven provinces in the northwest of the region paid, on average, nearly 90 percent of the grain they owed from 1683 through 1694.[84] Overall, as with eighth-grain in the late 1670s, an average 80 percent of regional assessments were collected. There were still exemptions and failures to pay; the Don River cities were excused arrears of 1,700 tons in 1694, as were cities within the path of locust swarms in 1689–1691. Otherwise, quarter-grain had fewer large overdue payments than its predecessors, and these arrears were less frequently dismissed.[85]

Some improvement may have resulted from the quarter-grain's reduced assessment per household and from the distribution of assessments over a larger group of contributors. There is no indication that southern agricultural productivity might have been responsible. Lamentable agricultural circumstances in the south were as commonplace before as after 1683, and some scholars have argued that southern agricultural productivity actually declined in the 1680s.[86] A look, however, at the kinds of sanctions imposed against those who failed to pay quarter-grain adds another dimension to our understanding of the improving collection rates. In general, quarter-grain was characterized by fairly severe penalties for failure to pay. Land confiscations, double payments, and fines were typical sanctions for non-payment in the last two decades of the century, which suggests a more successful exercise of the central government's authority. Both collections and local administrators were more stringently monitored from Moscow and the regional centers. A major regional audit occurred in 1686, which checked provincial against regional accounts, in the process encouraging officials to keep their collection levels high, and reports of expenditures current and up to the capital's standards.[87] More stringent and more centralized enforcement in grain collections after 1683 contributed to higher collection rates, in the process curbing the former laxity of local officials.

An additional impetus behind strict enforcement of collections during the last fifteen years of the century derived in part from changing priorities. Although reforms in grain collections were successful by comparison with other military changes, demand for grain continued to grow with Muscovite aspirations. Muscovite garrisons in left-bank Ukraine were reinforced by new salaried recruits (*pribornye soldaty*) from the north in the 1680s and 1690s, and they urgently needed food support. The limitations of a system whereby farms in a region provided grain only for servicemen from the same region were increasingly obvious. In 1686 and 1688 preparations for campaigns against the Crimean khanate added new urgency to needed improvements in supply: the two campaigns were to move through uninhabited territory. Conquests and forward garrisons further south (by the 1690s at the Dnepr narrows and on the lower Don) continued to expand the army's requirements. When the south had ceased to supply exclusively its own troops, southern grain assumed a much greater importance to Muscovite military efforts, perhaps surpassing the contribution of reluctant or relatively impoverished southern troops.

As demand swelled, annual quarter-grain collections were increasingly replaced by new, larger but less frequent collections, which did not entirely halt periodic use of quarter-grain or similar levies in kind. In the 1690s a regional collection of the quarter-grain type, called "collected grain" (*sbornyi khleb*), was used to pay Belgorod army officers; in the Don cities an unnamed collection was still gathered and shipped downriver to supply men on the Don.[88] And former recipients who were not part of new formation regiments on campaign continued to receive southern grain; the Belgorod musketeers, for example, were paid from ongoing arable tenth collections.[89]

ON-DEMAND GRAIN (*ZAPROSNYI KHLEB*)

The gradual abandonment of regular regional grain collections during the 1680s was the logical outcome of other military reforms and goals. Because Russian armies had grown larger, and in part because southern regiments had declined in military readiness, field campaigns of the period contained proportionately fewer southern troops. Regular southern grain collections by themselves were scarcely capable of feeding these large armies. Additional collections, in excess of normal musketeers', regional quarter-grain, or even court land collections,[90] appeared and for practical reasons superseded all others. These increasingly took the form of on-demand grain collections (*zaprosnyi khleb*), multiregional or countrywide levies intended to supply a particular garrison or campaign. The new on-demand levies abandoned the older principle that southern collections supply southern troops only, making little allowance for local uses, musketeer salaries, or seed loans. On-demand collections approximated, more closely than earlier collections, a national supply system in their organization, but no effort was made to extend that supply system to year-round payments, to all troops, or for more than one campaign at a time.

On-demand grain collections were not a new phenomenon. Earlier levies in 1657 and 1663 had helped supply southern troops during the Thirteen Years' War; a third in 1677 had gone to Kiev and its Muscovite garrison. In the absence of a regular collection in 1682, some southern provinces paid 36 pounds (1 *chetverik*) per household to support the Cossacks and the musketeers on the lower Don. But the special grain levies of the 1680s and 1690s differed from those before them; a number of them (in 1686, 1688, 1695, and 1697–1700) were much larger and necessarily more varied in the regions they drew from and in their modes of collection. However diverse their contributors, recipients of on-demand grain collections were almost exclusively infantrymen of forward garrisons and field regiments. After 1686, these levies became nearly annual. Table 2 of the appendix lists the dates and amounts of such collections for the south.

All fifteen of the collections identified in table 2 of the appendix relied heavily on southern contributions. Half of these levies were paid by the Belgorod and Sevsk regional populations alone, and their contributions to the other, larger collections were often substantial. But grain was not all the south provided in connection with on-demand collections. Southern granaries were used as depots for southbound grain from central Muscovy. Granary personnel from nearby towns became the deputies and record keepers for massive transactions. Transportation also became a peculiarly southern contribution. Southerners put grain in their own carts and moved it to transshipment points. In 1687 some southern servicemen were excused from serving in the first Crimean campaign, not for contributing grain but for transporting it. Again, in 1694, the men of up to nineteen southern towns provided grain, but men from thirty more provinces carted it, 576 pounds (2 *chetverti*) per cartload, across the south to the Don River ports. Southerners also built and loaded boats and barges along the Don and Dnepr.[91] Although some labor came from more northerly provinces, the south was distinguished by the size of its transport contributions, which were often in addition to the usual demands[92] and which, in both 1687 and 1695, were so large they were formally recognized as a substitute for service itself.

A further characteristic of the large on-demand grain collections was the remarkably diverse sources from which they drew grain. The first of the large collections took place in 1686 before the first Crimean campaign. As regional center, Sevsk received musketeers' grain, quarter-grain, and collections still referred to as eighth-grain. Some grain was purchased on southern and western markets, all postal grain reserves were mobilized, and the dragoon community on the Komaritskii court lands sent grain to both Sevsk and Kursk. Grain was also sent to the ports of Smolensk, Briansk, Khotmyzhsk, and Akhtyrka from all over the country; of these, only Akhtyrka received any southern grain. Moscow and Novogorod accepted grain for salary distribution. The collection prior to the 1689 campaign against Crimea drew on an extra musketeers' grain levy. To amass from these diverse sources the large amounts of grain needed for Peter's Azov campaign in 1695, diverse tactics were again required. There were several collections that year: one for the lower Don garrisons, another for the Kiev garrisons, and a third for the troops bound for Azov.[93]

The contributors to on-demand collections varied as widely from region to region as the economic geography. In some years collections were paid only by the traditional taxpaying population (*tiaglye liudi*): the peasantry and urban residents. In other years Belgorod's and Sevsk's garrison and campaign servicemen were assessed as they were for quarter-grain and similar collections. In such cases, peasant households that paid musketeers' grain and those that paid quarter-grain (whether servicemen or not) again appeared together on the same grain collection lists. The joint assessments finally united on a single tax roll almost all the contributors who, since 1678–1682 in particular, had been paying similar contributions for similar purposes from different jurisdictions or regions. Even more starkly than quarter-grain collections, the new assessments emphasized the unusual status and economic position of the southern petty serviceman: part servitor, part taxpayer.

There may well have been some method to the seeming confusion of changing assessments. For one thing, varying who was to be assessed from collection to collection allowed contributors to recuperate between levies. Many contributors were also paying other annual grain contributions, and some were consistently unable to do both.[94] The changes were also key to the maximizing collections based on the geographic distribution of taxpaying populations. Any levy outside the south necessarily drew heavily on the peasantry, who dominated the Muscovite population as a whole. By the end of the century this was also true of the northern part of the Sevsk region, where peasants significantly outnumbered the rest of the population. On the other hand, in the Belgorod region, where the peasants were still few in number, servicemen made substantial contributions to on-demand collections. Varying the taxpayers assessed, quite simply, drew the maximum amount from contributors overall.

But there were problems inherent in the on-demand grain collections. At the simplest level, the changing assessments caused some bureaucratic confusion. By the late 1690s the collections had been so frequently alternated that even the Muscovite scribes occasionally mislabeled them.[95] More important, large grain collections often disregarded or even undermined the administrative and physical apparatus and the economic coherence of the old regional collections. In 1686, as V. M. Vazhinskii has pointed out, the collection basins arguably coincided with regional market basins and regional organization. Later collection basins simply defied common sense: in 1696 and 1698 the Sevsk cities delivered grain to the Don River port of Voronezh, while Riazan' and Tambov cities sent their grain south to Korotoiak and Ostrogozhsk.[96] Levies that abandoned existing networks required major new investments of bureaucratic (and sometimes financial) support. Supervisors had to be appointed, granaries built, and boat-building or carting organized; these activities were major undertakings sponsored by the central administration with varying success.[97]

The uses to which the collected grain was put highlight Moscow's interest in a single facet of military supply: the provision of food to troops beyond Russian borders. Thus, for example, 3,844 tons (26,694 *chetverti*) of the on-demand collection in 1686 were issued by the depot town of Sevsk to the garrisons of two Ukrainian fortresses, to newly recruited field soldiers in Ukraine, and to the Kursk and Sevsk musketeers. The amount of grain collected that same year for shipment to Crimea-bound troops was explicitly calculated to feed more than 40,000 infantrymen for two months; the men were issued one month's food on departure. In the end, however, the army that left for Crimea in 1687 mustered more than 49,000 infantrymen.[98] As before, cavalry in this campaign were instructed to feed themselves from cash salaries and their own grain, and there was no discussion of postcampaign arrangements.[99] The major grain collections for 1689 and 1695 also designated grain for infantrymen on campaign, issuing some salary grain on departure and shipping still more forward to depot granaries along the army's path, at Novobogoroditsa and elsewhere.[100] Only occasionally did the extra grain left at collection points after these shipments go to local uses, and then only a relatively small quantity.[101]

Several explanations suggest themselves for Muscovy's continued emphasis on supply beyond its borders. At times, special circumstances arose: 10,000 infantrymen, sent down the Don under Peter Gordon's command, were issued their cash food allowance (*kormovye den'gi*) ahead of time; they spent it all before reaching Voronezh (not, one gathers, on food) and had to be issued fresh supplies in kind from the Don port's granaries.[102] In addition, market supplies had undeniably improved, but they were still unreliable sources to provision large armies, especially those beyond the Muscovite borders. As landholders with larger estates and with more peasants moved into the northernmost provinces of the Belgorod and, particularly, Sevsk regions, food became more readily available on markets there. Near the southern border, however, agriculture was still dominated by small landholder-servicemen, and large-scale purchases remained problematic.[103] In Belgorod in 1683 officers' cash allowances for food were pegged to the market price of 0.28 rubles (9 *altyn*, 2 *den'gi*) per *chetvert'* (288 lbs.). However, the government had recently devalued the currency to enlarge the cash supply, and the allowances no longer had the intended purchasing power. The allowances were paid half in cash and half in furs. Notwithstanding the risks of relying on the market to supply troops beyond Russia's borders, devices like market equivalency were taken increasingly seriously in depot towns; the Sevsk granary accepted cash based on the market price of 0.27 rubles (9 *altyn*) per *chetvert'*, instead of in-kind collections from the Komaritskii district dragoons that same year. By the 1695 collection, accepting money instead of grain seems to have been quite commonplace. Contractors and purchased grain supplied an increasing percentage of on-demand grain collections. As evidence of Moscow's growing reliance on the market, grain trade through Ukraine was halted in 1688 to provide more grain for the troops.[104] Food allowances were often quoted in cash, but grain was requested in kind when the prices were high.[105] And prices were evidently monitored during large collections.[106] It is worth adding that the monthly food allowance per soldier, which declined from 1 ruble in 1668 to 0.30 rubles (10 *altyn*) in 1688 and 0.26 rubles (8.5 *altyn*) in 1689, was still capable of purchasing 1 *chetvert'* (288 lbs.) of grain at normal prices. A new concentration of resources and organization was being mobilized to deal with the problem of feeding the army.[107]

At first, on-demand collections supplied only the new requirements of the reformed army, while regional collections continued to fulfill their previous obligations. Gradually, however, the regional collections became little more than adjuncts to the larger levies. By 1695, in view of the south's regular contributions of grain and labor to on-demand collections, regional collections of quarter-grain were suspended, never to resume. Don Cossack payments and similar obligations were returned to the local level.[108] The central government's drive for administrative centralization and standardization in the military reforms of the 1680s, which brought an end to regionally organized supply, cannot be seen as successful in the south. Efforts at standardization are visible in national recruitment standards, national grain collections, and the like. But neither the economic circumstances of southern life nor the ongoing need for southern grain and servicemen permitted draconian enforcement. Continued violation of service standards, the peculiarities of southern labor arrangements, and the atypical use of southern service personnel all bore eloquent testimony to the ambivalence and failures of late-seventeenth-century attempts to draw the southern provinces fully into the social and political sphere of the Muscovite center.

Despite its declining importance, regional supply was not forgotten altogether. In the first of his efforts to create a true standing army, Peter launched another series of financial and military reforms, which began in the southern regions in 1696. Peter wished to pay his troops full cash and grain salaries, as his predecessors had never done; to that end, he instituted reforms that quite astonishingly re-created the south's previous collection system, except that the taxes were paid by individuals, not by households. These reforms foundered on other demands being made on the same taxpayers, difficulties in forming the new regiments, and the imminence of Tatar attack. In 1698 Peter abruptly returned the southern armies to their former numbers, in the face of Turkish approach. The troops' food was provided by those appointed to farm for them, by their relatives, and presumably by the occasional campaign levy. This effort was, if anything, less successful than similar devices used in the 1680s. Over the next years, labor drafts and cash payments increasingly replaced taxation in kind. Peter's late-seventeenth-century reforms in southern Russia were thus the last in a series of grain collection schemes attempted in the south during the preceding sixty or more years.[109]

Until the eighteenth century Muscovy would only partially succeed in feeding its armies. By the 1680s infantry regiments on campaigns beyond Russia's southern and western borders could be provided with food rations similar in quantity to those of western European armies,[110] but given the low productivity of Russian agriculture and the priorities of Muscovite leaders, military grain supply extended no further. Other concerns, such as the continued payment of Don Cossack grain salaries and regular allowances to army officers, were more important and relatively less expensive. Wartime supply for cavalry units and peacetime supply to the entire army were apparently not seriously considered before 1696. Even then, as the Petrine state moved toward the creation of Russia's first national institution devoted to year-round military provisioning, the limitations imposed by agricultural and economic conditions were evident. Peter I's first efforts still assumed a land-based, self-supporting cavalry; the days of reliance on commercial resources to supplement military collections in kind remained far distant.[111] Nevertheless, the military supply system that evolved over the second half of the seventeenth century brought major improvements in the quality and quantity of food available to an expanding army. These improvements had a major impact not only on the character and capabilities of the Muscovite army but on the status and solvency of the petty southern servicemen whose contributions helped make them possible.

PART
II

5

SUPPLY TO THE CAMPAIGN FORCES

Southern grain collection evolved during the second half of the seventeenth century from local emergency supply into a regional and then a national system. As Moscow exerted intermittent pressure to integrate the southern regions according to a more uniform, centralized format, the system of collection and distribution grew in volume of grain collected and in specific uses for which the grain was distributed, responding to a number of regional demands, capabilities, and demographic limitations. The southern grain collections thus became an important, if somewhat unusual, companion to the local implementation of national military and administrative change during the latter part of the seventeenth century.

Much about the effects of these combined reforms on the southern population remains to be examined, despite a number of very useful studies. The goal of the second part of this book is to contribute to such an examination by focusing on the military and socioeconomic impact of the reforms as these affected grain supply to the troops. This chapter analyzes the effectiveness of grain supply to the campaign army after 1663. Chapter 6 examines, particularly after 1679, the effects of increasing economic pressure on the south's still numerous defensive forces, while chapter 7 assesses the cumulative impact of these military changes on the southern servicemen's social and economic standing.

A number of military historians have touched upon the successes and failures of the postreform Muscovite army in campaigns of the late seventeenth century. Their studies, however, have generally concentrated on the number and organization of forces and on the progress of individual campaigns, with some attention given to the quality of leadership, command, training, and the technological resources of the army.[1] Such studies seem almost to have overlooked the impact of logistics, despite its immediate importance to the Muscovite army, as to other European armies. In two of the largest military campaigns of the period, the 200,000-man armies led by Prince V. V. Golitsyn in 1687 and 1689 against Russia's old enemy, the Crimean khanate, ignominiously returned to Russian territory, the first time even before battle was joined. Whatever else could be said about the organization and prosecution of those campaigns, the logistics of provisioning was the immediate problem: Golitsyn turned back in the first campaign after Tatars burned the steppe grass, depriving his army of fodder, and in the second when his army ran out of food and water.[2]

Despite the silence of both commanders and bureaucrats on the subject of provisioning in the late seventeenth century,[3] the impact of the organizational changes described in the preceding chapters was considerable. A regional supply system, based on the southern army groups and the cities that supported them from the 1660s on, provisioned Russia's expansion into Ukraine and its maneuvers against Stenka Razin's rebellion; on the other hand, the system's limitations exacerbated military problems such as desertion. Later in the century, despite other organizational and technical problems, periodic national collections would sustain much larger campaign armies.

The multitude of institutions involved in providing for the military at any point after midcentury and the absence of any single central organ of military supply complicate examination of logistics for the late-seventeenth-century army. The material that follows looks at logistics by analyzing two particular cases. The first involves supply to Russian garrisons of about 5,000 men at Kiev and other Ukrainian towns after the Peace of Andrusovo in 1667, at the outset of regional supply in the south. These garrisons competed for provisioning with Muscovite field armies, engaged against the Cossack forces of Hetman Peter Doroshenko in 1668 and 1669 to establish Muscovite influence in Ukraine. The competition stretched available supply sources to the limit, and Kiev was forced to rely on regional and national grain collections, on the one hand, and cash payments and local market supplies, on the other. The inadequacies and unpredictability of this combination severely limited Muscovy's abilities to garrison and defend its new acquisitions.

The second case involves supply to the 200,000-man Russian field army during Prince V. V. Golitsyn's first campaign against Crimea in 1687, undertaken as part of Russian commitments to the Holy League (the alliance of Austria, Poland, and Russia against the Ottoman Empire). By this time a less rigidly regional supply system helped to provide for a massive campaign force, permitting Muscovy to fulfill its treaty obligations to its allies, but the system's limitations compromised the success of the campaign itself.

Both militarily and symbolically, the Russian presence in Kiev after 1667 was a vital one. The Thirteen Years' War had been exceedingly costly for Muscovy; as a result of long and difficult campaigns, it had lost much of its best old-style cavalry. In response, the state marshaled its newer forces and put them into the field in ever greater numbers, but that process entailed increasing expenditures and considerable administrative acumen to sustain. The Peace of Andrusovo allowed Muscovy to continue garrisoning Kiev and other cities of left-bank Ukraine (occupied by Russian forces during the war years); the garrisons represented Muscovy's expectation of gaining permanent possession of the territory. The Russian occupiers, however, cooperated uneasily with the Cossack hetmanate, which, despite its divided leadership, made immediate military and political claims to local sovereignty. Consequently, Moscow's investment in maintaining and defending its garrison outposts was considerable. After 1654, for example, the upper town at Kiev was fortified by the Russians; they would progressively add to the formal fortifications over the next decades with the construction of earthworks around the lower town in the 1670s and then with new stone fortifications, completed in 1682. By that time more than sixty mounted guns defended the walls; powder and shot for the magazine were provided or purchased by the Muscovite commander.[4]

A substantial military presence was also an important part of Moscow's investment. Even before the Peace of Andrusovo was concluded, Kiev was garrisoned by 4,500 Muscovite infantrymen and musketeers and frequently even a cavalry regiment. It quickly became apparent that the troops in Kiev and left-bank cities could not rely on local supplies, whether purchased, collected as a tax, or simply requisitioned. Therefore, grain was sent from Russia down the Desna River from ports such as Briansk in the Sevsk region. At the same time, because Muscovy was trying to supply and pay the field armies of the Thirteen Years' War, the garrisons in Ukraine received only a limited share of the incoming grain. Thus through the winter of 1666 and only shortly after southern regional supply had been organized, the Kievan garrison's foot soldiers received 18–24 pounds of grain monthly (only half their usual rations) from the city's magazines, supplemented by the expensive grain that could be purchased on the city's market.[5]

The provisioning of Ukrainian garrisons faced fundamentally the same problems immediately after the peace as before. Food allowances in kind were owed infantrymen of the garrison as on-duty pay, but there were Muscovite field armies nearby that also required provisions. In addition to food supplied in kind from Muscovy, Kievan infantrymen were forced to

rely on cash salaries and market supply. Barring any grain brought by cavalrymen from their own estates, these were the only alternatives. The successes and failures of this cobbled-together provisioning would prove crucial to maintaining the garrisons' valuable new formation contingent at
strength.

After 1666 the official size of the Kievan garrison fluctuated considerably, from about 3,000 men to more than 5,000. A usual contingent could
be expected to contain several regiments (*prikazy*) of musketeers, two new
formation infantry or dragoon troops, and a new-style cavalry regiment.
Among other Ukrainian cities garrisoned by the Muscovites, Pereiaslav
and Nezhin also had relatively large troop contingents.[6] Of the troops assigned to Kiev, one musketeer troop (*prikaz*) was permanently resident
there, but most of the remainder were rotated through the garrison as part
of their campaign service responsibilities, ostensibly for periods of six
months to one year. The troops themselves came from a variety of locations in Muscovy. The Tula and Smolensk regions sent musketeers, for
example, as did the southern army groups, although there were explicit
instructions that the cavalrymen should not be members of the Belgorod
army, presumably on the grounds of their relative inability to supply
themselves.[7]

While on duty, these men should have been paid exactly as if they were
on campaign. In 1668–1674 cavalry and lancer regiments received 2 to 6
rubles per man per year, while infantrymen of the rank and file were paid
from 0.37 to 0.50 rubles (10 to 13 *altyn*) per month and about 40 pounds of
rye (1/4 *chetvert'*). In the absence of allowances in kind, musketeers and
infantrymen received cash: 2 rubles per year, or 1 ruble every six months.
Lower rates applied to men who held land. These were often of the Belgorod and Sevsk armies, who were more likely to own land than musketeers or infantrymen from other regions. Officers' pay at this time averaged
nearly 4 rubles per year, with about 80 pounds (1/2 *chetvert'*) of grain and
36 pounds (1 *pood*) of salt per month as food allowance.[8] These food allowances were often paid in advance; troops received grain and cash as they
prepared to leave for Kiev from the western Muscovite frontier fortress
towns such as Sevsk and Putivl'. In 1668, for example, troops departing for
Kievan garrison duty were issued two months' pay (including 1/4 *chetvert'*
of hard tack and 1/4 *chetvert'* of oats per man).[9]

Maintaining the size of Ukrainian garrisons proved exceedingly difficult. Desertion along the road to Kiev became very common—and still
more common after troops reached their destination.[10] Fortresses were
critically undermanned; in 1678 General Peter Gordon declared that the
garrison of Kiev was only one-sixth the size needed to defend the city in
the event of siege.[11] As a result, men in Ukrainian garrisons found their
tours of duty extended; one group of musketeers in Nezhin claimed to

have been there for fourteen straight years. It is hardly surprising that garrison service in Kiev came to be seen, and indeed was often used, as a punishment.[12] But Muscovite commanders pointed to poverty—in particular, the absence of food, fodder, horses, and even powder and shot—to explain the high rates of desertion and absenteeism in their garrisons. Ironically, troops were occasionally urged to proceed on to Kiev from the Russian frontier with the promise that the garrison magazines there would provide food and salaries.[13]

Regular provisioning of Kiev began in 1668 with the Kiev shipments (*Kievskie otpusky*)—on average, 1,080 tons (10,000 *chetverti*) of grain dispatched each year by riverboat from southwestern river ports, although the actual amounts sent varied considerably. The first year, 1,296 tons (12,000 *chetverti*) of grain were sent; in other years, the amounts fell as low as 540 tons (5,000 *chetverti*), but the Kievan garrison was significant enough that some annual shipments were made regardless of other, more immediate demands. Grain in the late 1660s came partly from the new southern regional granary system supplied by eighth-grain. In 1668, for example, the Sevsk region split its eighth-grain collection between the town of Briansk, where grain was sent downriver to Kiev, and the town of Sevsk, where salaries and food allowances were issued for troops departing for Kiev overland. Meanwhile, in some southern provinces, household extractions of grain doubled to meet these and field regiments' needs.[14]

But this was not the only source of rye, oats, and other provisions to Kiev. Part of the Kiev shipments regularly came from provinces farther to the north and east of Briansk, near the Tula Defensive Line. Here peasants and townsmen bore a substantial share of the burden of collecting military supplies, preparing, bagging, and carting the grain all the way to Briansk for dispatch to Kiev. These same northerly provinces also helped in the construction of barges and riverboats to carry the Kiev shipment downstream. Grain contributions and barge building were often required in alternate years; some 75–100 households shared in the expense and labor of building each boat, either at Briansk itself or at some town upstream of it. Such boats could also be contracted or purchased at a cost of about 7 rubles each, or some 0.17 rubles (2 *altyn*, 3 *den'gi*) per household. One hundred fifty boats were typically needed for an annual shipment. The flotilla also required rowers and a military escort, which was drawn from garrison troops.[15] On arrival downriver, the grain had then to be carted to Kiev's magazines or on to other garrisons; the cartage to Nezhin, for example, took an additional ten days.[16]

The Kiev shipments were intermittently bolstered by shipments from other parts of Muscovy. In 1669, with Muscovite campaign forces in the field and Muscovite garrisons in Ukraine, the region around Smolensk contributed about 1,080 tons (10,000 *chetverti*) of its own regional grain collection, as well as iron, gunpowder, shot, salt, and money, to support the men of the Smolensk region fighting in Ukraine; contributions were also forthcoming from the Novogorod region, the Chancellery of Foreign Affairs (*Posol'skii prikaz*),[17] and, in other years, the territories around Galich and Vladimir.[18] Such supplemental provisioning was ordered as needed; these collections were not regular annual events. Still other collections supplemented supplies to the Kievan garrison.

An average Kiev shipment amounted to 1,080 tons (10,000 deposit *chetverti*) of grain, enough to maintain a garrison of 4,000 infantry if a minimal 486 pounds (3 issuing *chetverti*) were distributed to each soldier and no more. This was rarely necessary because Kiev had other resources. For example, the tsar's representatives in Ukraine had the right to impose certain local collections in grain and cash on Ukrainian residents. Labor, horses, and carts were also sometimes requisitioned. These latter contributions were valued at a minimum of 30 rubles a year (enough to purchase 240 monthly rations of grain). These supplementary sources of food, however, were neither predictable nor always reliable. Local collections would fall short, or the Cossacks of the hetmanate would collect grain first for their own purposes. In any case, requisitioning from local supplies incurred responsibilities; it was assumed that the Muscovite commander would eventually reimburse the suppliers. Such arrangements led to numerous disagreements between occupiers and the Kievan population.[19]

It is clear, however, that the Kievan garrison was not expected to live solely from granary reserves, and food supplies did arrive in other ways from Muscovite towns. Military men leaving Putivl' or Sevsk were often paid for as much as two months in cash and kind; furthermore, in emergencies, food could be carted overland to Kiev and left bank towns from the western frontier.[20] These resources, too, were ad hoc, irregular, and unreliable.

Regular provisioning of the garrison was also supplemented by grain purchased on the local market. Kiev was a fairly lively center of trade in food preparation, among its other activities. Mills surrounded the city, and merchants appeared not only from nearby Sevsk and Putivl' but also from cities on both the left and right banks or in the Sevsk region.[21] Prices and market supply were no more stable in Kiev than in Muscovy proper. Nevertheless, cash salaries were perforce a major part of provisioning for Kievan garrison troops; even monthly food allowances were quoted and often paid in cash. Although lead and saltpeter for ammunition were purchased locally in the late 1660s, the problems of relying on market supply were made abundantly clear in 1668, when neither commodity was available on the Kiev market.[22]

In any case, Kiev's granaries and supplies did not serve only its own garrison any more than southern town granaries did theirs. Kiev's reserves also held supplies for nearby garrisons and field forces as needed.[23] Particularly during the Russo-Turkish War, with large numbers of Muscovite troops campaigning near Chigirin and elsewhere, Kiev acted as a magazine for local collections and as a transshipment point for grain sent from Muscovy to the field armies.[24]

The abilities and shortcomings of this rather unpredictable supply system are illustrated by the events of 1668 and 1669, years of extraordinary upswings in demand. In addition to Kievan and other garrisons, some 10,000 new formation troops from the Sevsk region and 15,000 similar troops from the Belgorod region were active in Ukraine against Hetman Doroshenko, who reunited the right- and left-bank Ukraine but who, until 1676, sided with Ottoman Turkey rather than with Muscovy. Russian infantrymen sent to Ukraine expected to receive salaries and grain allowances from regional collections as they departed Muscovy proper, but they also anticipated provisioning from downstream granaries once they were in the field. Supply difficulties were threefold. First, the depot granary system, supplied at this juncture by eighth-grain, was required to produce exceptionally large quantities of grain quite rapidly. Second, the resulting grain had to be moved quickly from Muscovy to its destination and to distribution points along the border or inside Ukraine before desertion from the ranks became widespread. As a final complication, the eastern provinces of the Sevsk region, also under threat of attack, needed whatever supplies and men were available in the vicinity; garrison troops from many towns were on special alert along the border.

The supply situation in Ukrainian towns was particularly pressing. In view of the number of forces of all political allegiances living off Ukraine over the previous decade, market supplies to Kiev were scanty in the winter of 1667–1668. Because food shipments from Muscovy had been small in 1667, shortages quickly appeared in Kiev and other garrison towns. Kievan shortages were exacerbated by the presence of nearly a thousand cavalrymen, who constituted the mounted contingent of the city's garrison. Prices were so high by January 1668 that the now-impoverished cavalrymen sold their horses to pay for food; they salvaged their pride by refusing to take on the duties of the lowly infantry. Under most circumstances, cavalrymen had no right to allowances in kind, and the granaries even now steadfastly refused to issue them grain. Market shortfalls had forced the Kievan infantrymen into greater reliance on the granaries, and there was only a two-month supply left for the foot soldiers. Even this margin assumed a salary paid half in grain and half in cash; otherwise, the margin would have been less than one month. In addition, other Russian garrisons in Ukraine required supplies and horses. The officers of one garrison had already been paid from the Kiev granaries; further allowances were refused them in view of the gravity of the situation. Some garrisons, cut off by weather, distance, and hostile forces from other sources of supply, resorted to early harvesting and local collections, only to find that the Cossack troops of the hetmanate had already done the same. Another garrison was besieged.

Extraordinary measures were in order. One commander even paid his troops out of his own pocket to avoid flight.[25] Requisitioning was put into effect around Nezhin.[26] Garrison commanders were chiefly concerned that their manpower not be depleted by desertions. The crisis eased in early spring of 1668, as shipments of food from Briansk began arriving and men on duty were issued back salaries and current allowances. Local markets improved into summer, and garrisons could again rely on them for food.[27]

With the approach of summer, reinforcements rotated into Ukrainian fortresses to take up garrison responsibilities posed a new complication. Depot granaries in southern border towns were nearly stripped of their resources earlier that spring in mustering, paying, and dispatching campaign troops from the Belgorod and Sevsk regions.[28] Seven more of the regions' campaign regiments were due to rotate into Kiev; however, given local conditions and national fiscal pressures, these men were already owed up to eight or nine months' back salary. Even the officers of Colonel Eric Luk's infantry troop, usually among the most regularly paid, reported having received no food allowances for the preceding four months.[29] The seven regiments preparing to leave Muscovy should have collected cash salaries, arrears, and grain allotments for their trip and for the next few months at their departure point, Kamennoe, but because other forces had already been in that fortress for some months, food was scarce and expensive. Other towns in the Sevsk region were of little help. Briansk, which had just dispatched a Kiev shipment of 1,296 tons (12,000 *chetverti*), was preparing for siege and was undersupplied, even with ammunition for its own defense.[30] Money sent from Putivl' was inadequate to pay off the cash debt owed the troops; short of food and itself under threat of siege, Putivl' could send no grain.[31]

The only immediately available grain in the southern regions was in the Sevsk granaries, where part of the eighth-grain collection remained, diverted from its usual destination of Belgorod. There is no record that any grain was requested or received from outside the two southern regions, which were thus held to their obligation to support their own campaign troops. The amount of grain left in Sevsk was insufficient to pay reinforcements departing for Briansk and also to resupply the city itself. A supplemental grain collection was therefore organized late in the season on the Komaritskii militarized district, with its 4,500 resident dragoon households. The dragoons, who were already part of an understaffed Sevsk garrison helping to rebuild the town's fortifications, collectively contributed almost 1,300 tons (12,000 *chetverti*) of rye and oats and carted them to Sevsk.

Once the grain was collected, the absence of transportation proved a further hindrance. Briansk's need for provisions was judged to be more immediate, and all available carts moved grain northward from Sevsk to Briansk, where it was used to pay the garrison's musketeers. Finally, Sevsk postal carts (*iamskie podvody*) and a local requisition of horses began moving grain from Sevsk to the troops still waiting to leave for Kiev. By the time it arrived, however, those men had begun to desert.[32]

While food itself became abundant in the months that followed, the bottleneck in supply caused by lack of transportation did not ease. The movement of ammunition, grain, and salt to the army during the summer was slowed by shortages of carts. A meager eleven carts were borrowed from distant Kursk to move grain out of Sevsk, and these made multiple trips. A further request for carts from Komaritskii district went (understandably) unfilled.[33] As a result, troops returning from garrison duty in Kiev were awarded back pay only as they crossed the border at Sevsk into Muscovy proper.[34] At the same time, the indignant citizens of Kiev demanded the return of their own confiscated and borrowed carts.[35]

Despite these annoyances, food did not again become a pressing issue to Kievan and other garrisons until the winter of 1668–1669. Part of the problem then lay in the 4,500 new troops who rotated into the Ukrainian fortresses early in 1669. Kiev and other garrisons had not yet received the expected shipments of grain or money from Briansk when the reinforcements arrived, and the new arrivals had already consumed the salaries and allowances paid them for the trip.[36] Because two garrisons had already sought help from Kiev's larger granaries, the commander worried about depleting the city's meager supplies. The situation was compounded by the local commander's inability to purchase or collect local resources. Grain requisitioning by the Cossacks meant that Ukrainians were at best reluctant to allow a second Russian levy or even cash purchases.[37] As a result, the first shipment from Briansk was more than half depleted as soon as it arrived; even the cash provided for salaries was inadequate. Kiev resorted to half salaries for May and had no reserves for June. Desertions began, and the musketeers scheduled for permanent settlement in Nezhin refused the assignment, understandably skeptical of promises of regular grain supply.[38]

Further supplies from Briansk, due in Kiev on 31 May, were delayed, compounding the problem. Musketeers of the Briansk town garrison were to escort the shipment toward Kiev, but they had no provisions; all supplies in that river port's granaries had already been loaded on boats or sent downriver. While the shipment waited, the musketeers were provided with loans from Sevsk, cash, and promises that they would find grain at their destination.[39] Despite pleas to send an early, if incomplete, shipment, the forty-eight barges from Briansk appeared in Kiev only in early July, with a meager 540 tons (5,000 *chetverti*) aboard. By that time, however, resources mobilized from further north were also arriving, and the relative ease of summer provisioning and purchasing had begun.[40] Furthermore, although administrators in regional centers were particular about supplying only their own region's troops, granary employees in Ukraine were less finicky about using food once it had arrived at its destination. In the interval, shortfalls were exacerbated by continuing problems with overland transportation; carts had again to be requisitioned from the Komaritskii district.[41]

The efforts to provision Kievan garrisons in 1668 and 1669 show a supply system stretched to its absolute limit. Partial provisioning for 2,000 to 4,000 infantrymen would not appear to be an insurmountable task.[42] The garrison's needs were relatively small, predictable, and consistent. Muscovy's intermittent successes and failures in providing for them were in part a question of priorities. Provisioning the Kievan garrison was less vital than feeding the army in the field. Kiev, it was rightly seen, had other resources at its disposal. Despite the regularity of the demand, Muscovite efforts to provision the city were seasonal and reactive. In both 1668 and 1669 the early months of the year held the greatest demand for food; this is hardly surprising because the lowest availability of grain was and is just before a new harvest (in this case, before July). Nevertheless, troops were each year forced into dependence on nongranary sources during the spring months. Although it was predictable that other food sources would be cut off by military action, the garrison was unable to build up stocks of minimum food allowances in its granaries.

It should be noted that the failures or delays in supply just described were, at times, more the result of distributional problems than of poor harvests. Of course there were instances to the contrary. In 1670, for example, the Military Chancellery declared itself flatly unable to pay departing southern servicemen because the grain collected and stored in the Belgorod and Sevsk regions was inadequate.[43] Even in such circumstances, when the south lacked grain, its servicemen were rarely offered grain from other regions. In 1668 and 1669, however, it was the organization of transport that proved the principal problem. Because a single cart normally carried only 450–550 pounds (about 3 issuing *chetverti*), sources like the postal system could not supply enough carts to move large amounts of grain. The usual means for enlisting the necessary number of carts, carters, and horses in the south was to require that grain suppliers themselves do the hauling, but distances and the garrisons' location beyond Muscovite borders made this inappropriate. Temporary borrowing, ad hoc collections, and the long-suffering militarized Komaritskii district provided inadequate and overtaxed substitutes. Complaints and petitions from both Ukrainians and Muscovites confirm the persistence of the transportation problem.[44] By the late 1670s a more efficient system would be in place, which organized food and other resource supply on a national, rather than a rigidly regional, basis.[45] Even so, rather rugged supply conditions persisted in Ukrainian garrison cities, which remained below the field army in supply priority. Over the long run the stretching of Muscovite supply to its limit no doubt helped the Russian field units sustain a more significant military presence than would otherwise have been possible. More immediately, however, it also led inevitably to desertions and refusals to serve in key garrisons in Ukraine.

Providing for field campaigns was quite a different—and a monumental—task for Muscovy, as it was for most contemporary European states. First, as the size of campaign armies increased in the seventeenth century, the problems associated with supply took on new dimensions. Neither the number of troops nor the speed and path of their movements could be anticipated for the convenience of supply officers, despite the efforts of numerous European armies to do just that.[46] Nor was the declaration of war itself necessarily predictable. By the late seventeenth century Muscovite field supply required grain, transportation, arms, and timely mustering for 40,000 to 60,000 men in relatively unpredictable locations at unpredictable intervals. Such an undertaking was significantly more complex than provisioning a garrison of 4,000 men in a set location annually (Kiev)—and none the easier for its greater priority.

Such problems as these confronted the Russian army wherever it fought. Different, highly site-specific supply problems also confronted Russian and other European armies in the seventeenth century. Muscovy did not expect to provide its forces with all supplies from behind the lines. Campaign armies still relied heavily on local sales and foraging, in addition to food and other provisions they brought with them or found in magazines along the route. The possibility of using such resources on any given occasion clearly depended upon specific local conditions. Muscovite commanders recognized the dependence of their armies on food and fodder obtained en route, and the risks associated with it. Like other seventeenth-century European officers, Prince G. G. Romodanovskii in 1674 was concerned about how he could lead his troops through a territory that had been "campaigned over." P. V. Sheremetev paid some of his men from his own resources to keep his troops mobilized.[47] Efforts to increase the amount of grain and fodder for sale en route were taken seriously; limited controls on grain trade were occasionally imposed in areas through which troop concentrations would pass.[48] Nevertheless, field supply remained enormously important.

One of the largest seventeenth-century Muscovite efforts to mobilize supply for a campaign was undertaken in 1686–1687, as an enormous Russian army, under Prince V. V. Golitsyn's command, prepared to attack Crimea. By the end of April 1686 Russia had committed itself not only to an alliance with the Habsburgs and the Poles but also to hostilities against the Crimean khan. Preparations for war formally began five months later.[49] The following spring, in mid-May 1687, some 112,000 Russian troops crossed Russia's southern frontier, headed for a rendezvous with Cossack forces. Potentially, the Muscovite government owed cash payments or food allowances to at least one-half its forces; others relied indirectly on the state for firearms, ammunition, or other matériel.[50]

Providing for the campaign was unprecedented both in numbers and in scope. In contrast to a previous occasion when Golitsyn had commanded about 100,000 men, this force included a larger proportion of soldiers who required state support.[51] The need to provide for these unusually large numbers of infantrymen was a major concern in 1686, and that concern was institutionally reflected. More important, the 1687 campaign marked the first time that Muscovy, using a modern field army, had launched a direct attack on Crimea, the Ottoman client state to the south. Previous military encounters, largely defensive actions against Tatar raiders, had used tactics that limited the size of the pursuing armies and the theater of combat; these encounters were of little help in planning for 1687. Previous confrontations between Muscovite campaign forces and regular Ottoman troops—whether on the lower Don or in the war over right-bank Ukraine—had allowed Muscovy to rely for its provisioning on established river transport and forward magazines.[52]

The Crimean campaign of 1687 imposed a very different set of conditions, both logistically and militarily. Reaching the isthmus at Perekop required that the army march across some 300–400 miles of all but uninhabited steppe land. This eliminated a number of established Russian supply procedures. The absence of garrison towns south of the frontier meant forward magazines were impossible to deploy. When the army moved south and east of the Dnepr rapids, as it would be forced to do for much of the way, it would be out of reach of easy river transport. Finally, the empty steppe offered fodder but little food along the way. The campaign had thus to rely on untried supply methods. The planners of the 1687 campaign seem to have been aware of the manifest military advantages accruing to Muscovy's army once it reached Perekop; indeed, the skirmishing light Tatar cavalry seemed incapable of offering serious resistance to the modern Muscovite forces. But the Russians do not seem to have anticipated the probable difficulties of feeding their troops along the way; I have found no materials discussing plans for alternative methods of supply, adjustments of troop movement and size, and the like.

This first national effort to coordinate troop supplies for a major campaign was initiated by the Military Chancellery[53] and relied heavily on southern contributions and on precedents set in earlier grain collections. Chief among the concerns of its planners were (1) how to amass an adequate volume of various supplies and (2) how to provide adequate means for their transportation. These concerns were broached largely as internal administrative questions, with little discussion of what might happen beyond the frontier.

There are indications that by 1686 various parts of the supply system had been under pressure to reform and centralize already for some time. In 1680, for example, a massive inventory of the army's weaponry took place in the context of the ongoing war with Turkey. Weaponry was standardized so that each lancer was required to produce a lance and pistols, each cavalryman (reitar) a carbine and pistols, and each infantryman a musket or harquebus and poleax; this equipment, if not provided by the servitor, was to be issued by or purchased from the state. Some additional equipment was also provided; after 1680 the Belgorod region's infantrymen were issued both pouches and cartridges, which had never before been the case.[54] The simultaneous introduction of quarter-grain was not only intended to extend and improve on the size and reliability of the grain collection at the army's disposal. It also had the express purpose of ensuring that grain levies drew on all cities and all ranks in Russia, making the southern frontier an integral part of national efforts. A system for collecting carts and escort troops for distant shipments had been in place since the late 1670s.

Centrally organized supply for the Crimean campaign faced some unique logistical problems. For a force of 112,000 men, daily food requirements were in themselves formidable. At the rate of 2.2 pounds of bread daily (a Europe-wide estimate of food needs to which Muscovy adhered), a three- or four-month campaign required between 218 and 245 pounds (about 1 issuing chetvert') of grain per person or 12,000 to 15,000 tons (112,000–140,000 chetverti) of grain all told. The more than 20,000 men[55] accompanying the army as baggage slaves, workers, drummers, trumpeters, and carters had also to be fed and the transportation of arms and ammunition to be arranged.[56] Furthermore, men of higher rank would expect more than a minimum ration. Altogether, this might bring the totals to half again as much grain, that is, 18,000–23,000 tons. Although the army could carry some of this grain as it marched, a substantial proportion would have to be shipped separately. Any rations carried or shipped in the form of grain or flour would also need to be prepared en route; only hard tack and biscuit required no preparation. Providing fodder for the army's horses represented yet another task; more than half the army was mounted, and there were cart horses and second mounts to be considered. Over 18 pounds of various dry fodders and at least 50 pounds of green forage were required daily for each horse.

As noted above, the Muscovite government did not hold itself directly responsible for providing for all these needs. All cavalrymen collected their own provisions, whether they received cash support or not. Some of their food and other supplies were shipped ahead, along with state provisions. In any case, the field army moving across the steppe included the carts and provisions of those who supplied themselves, as well as those supplied by the state; the army had to be prepared accordingly, or it would be unable to mobilize.

Amassing, organizing, and shipping the appropriate volumes were only part of the task. Although they were little discussed, decisions about the quantity of materials and the organization of their transport depended on the method chosen for staging their delivery. In terms of the effort and cost expended, for example, the simplest way to feed an army was to permit it to draw on the local economy for fodder and food. The ability of an area to support the passage of an army in turn depended on the time of year and on the density of cultivation and settlement of the territory through which the army passed. Two hundred years after this Crimean campaign, Kanerin, the Russian army commissary, would argue that an army could live entirely off the land if the population exceeded 90 people per square mile; in practice, much lower densities of 20 or 25 people per square mile might have been adequate right at harvest time.[57] These numbers assume a high rate of extraction and no technical difficulties. Furthermore, such collecting and foraging methods were by no means optimal; they were time-consuming and hindered the progress of the army.

In any case, Prince Golitsyn's army would have to pass through relatively unpopulated land. Thus while the prospects for fodder (from steppe grass) were good, prepared foods or even grain (except for what individual farmers of the frontier area carted to the army for sale) would be almost unavailable in adequate volumes south of the Russian frontier. In 1687 the obvious decision was taken to rely heavily on provisioning from inside Muscovy. But carrying food for the entire army was also impractical. A baggage train of 80,000–100,000 carts would have been necessary to carry the quantity of grain the army needed for three or four months—an unwieldy procession eight to ten carts wide and almost one hundred miles long.[58] Instead, some grain and other supplies were disbursed at the border; Muscovite troops habitually carried one or two months' food with them.[59] A second amount was carted forward, and the remainder was shipped ahead down the Desna and Vorskla Rivers toward the Dnepr rapids.

The staging area for the massive accumulation was, naturally, the southern provinces. Grain and some fodder were collected and stored at frontier depots or at southern river ports. Carts and river barges were constructed, loaded, and dispatched from the south. Items like arms and ammunition were sent south to be collected in the cities where the army would muster. Those responsible for their own provisioning added to the confusion by sending their own supplies to the same points. The effort would prove so large as to excuse many southern residents from active participation in the campaign.

The complexity and intensity of organization involved were truly impressive. Groundwork began even before any official declaration of hostilities. Late in 1865 and early in 1686, inspections were begun to determine what resources were genuinely available in the south and elsewhere. Five clerks (*pod'iachie*) were sent out from Moscow by the Military Chancellery primarily to audit southern grain supplies. Only half of the 4,289 tons

(39,350 *chetverti*) of grain purportedly stored in forty-eight southern cities proved actually to be there, and it was quickly concentrated either in Belgorod or in Voronezh and Korotoiak for shipment to the Don Cossacks.[60] Selective repair of granary buildings followed in the summer.[61] The grain trade to the southwest was halted in June. And these were only the preliminaries.

On 10 August 1686 a decree ordered an on-demand levy of grain from 73 to 146 pounds (1/3–2/3 *chetvert'*) per peasant household, which was assessed on the service and heritable lands of those who were not campaigning at that time. This grain was sent to seven points, with about 40 percent going to Smolensk and Briansk for shipment downriver to advance depots; the remainder either went to the western end of the Belgorod defenses for disbursement to the main forces that would muster at Akhtyrka, Sumy, and Khotmyzhsk before crossing the frontier, or to Novgorod and Moscow, where other troops were stationed. The on-demand grain collection produced 13,100 tons (91,600 *chetverti*) of grain from almost half the peasant households in Muscovy. This special collection was paid, bagged, and carted overland to the appropriate destinations by February.[62] Meanwhile, other grain collections, such as quarter-grain and musketeers' grain, took place as usual. A variety of local collections supplemented the larger ones. In Kursk province some 900 service landholders paid arable tenth, while 1,814 service households contributed to quarter-grain.[63] With some purchased grain, secondary collections yielded another 9,260 tons (64,310 *chetverti*), which were carted to the same destinations. All told, nearly 22,283 tons (156,000 *chetverti*) were prepared for the campaign.[64] Meanwhile, cavalrymen, who had no right to food allowances from the state, were each ordered to send 650 pounds (3 *chetverti*) of their own grain to Krasnyi Kut and other forward points southwest of the Belgorod line over the winter; their army commanders then made arrangements for the receipt and storage of these private stores, which would become part of the baggage train.[65]

While regular collections proceeded as usual, the on-demand grain collection required the allocation of special administrative powers. In Briansk, *stol'nik* (a court rank) F. G. Davydov oversaw various grain transactions taking place there, while Radion Nepliuev, the Sevsk commander, dealt with day-to-day matters such as selecting heads for the new granaries from among local townsmen and state peasants.[66] Much of the procedure was borrowed from the annual dues experience. Musketeers and other recruited servicemen were dispatched around each province to announce the tax. As grain was collected, it was shipped to its particular receiving point, bagged and carted by each estate separately; the receiving points were open night and day to reduce congestion. Receipts were then returned to the military commander of the town where the servitor lived; the commander in turn checked that all local residents had contributed as ordered. In one distant fortress, the military commander complained that his lone scribe could not keep up with the work.[67]

Many of the problems and difficulties with the collection[68] appear to have been resolved by strict enforcement; the penalties for nonpayment were severe, and the grain gradually accumulated at the depot points. More than 98 percent of the expected amount actually appeared.[69] The collection of food in kind was thus more successful than the collection of cash for wages. The food amassed should have been adequate to provide for the entire Muscovite army. Even though some grain would be used for fodder, and the distribution of the rest would vary according to rank, it is clear that Muscovy was more than capable of collecting food for its troops.[70] The effort relied on successful central chancellery supervision of local officials, who in turn activated an established machinery of grain collection. Notably, in this collection at least, southerners carted, collected, and shipped grain intended for use by troops from all over Russia; they were exempted from campaign service, thus creating a kind of national division of labor, as opposed to the rigidly regional system in force prior to 1678.

Distribution of the collected grain to the troops began immediately. By early March, Sevsk alone had dispensed 2,290 tons (21,000 *chetverti*) as salaries for specialists, for the Sevsk and Kursk musketeers, and for the Kievan garrison forces, few of whom would ever join the campaign.[71] The Briansk musketeers were also paid, as were 10,000 men from campaign regiments.[72]

Arms and ammunition were also prepared for the campaign. Artillery divisions held several hundred guns, supplied from Russian and foreign sources; the Belgorod and Sevsk armies each had in excess of 45 field artillery pieces. Ideally, in addition to these and individual weapons, regiments of 1,000 men were to have had 11 guns, smaller regiments 6 to 8 guns, and the select (*vybornye*) regiments 20 guns each, with gunpowder and shot sufficient for 100 to 150 firings per gun.[73] The army leaving the southern borders in 1687 appears to have been underarmed by these standards. Small regiments had to be content with 3 or 4 artillery pieces.[74] New guns from Moscow were supplemented by the repair of older guns and firearms stored for the troops in southern cities and by the collection and manufacture of ammunition. By early 1687 Sevsk held 9 large guns, 230 regimental guns, and 7,000 firearms, with ammunition to match.[75]

In addition, at fortress headquarters individual regiments prepared most of their own weaponry and shipped it to the muster points. For example, of 406 infantrymen belonging to three regiments from Briansk province, only 154 men were in possession of firearms at the military review; the remaining 252 (62%) had to be supplied from regimental stores. In this case, by the time the troops reached Sumy, Briansk and other towns had deposited more than 1,500 muskets there for their use.[76] To prepare firearms and ammunition, skilled men and matériel were drawn from cities and treasuries all over the south and beyond. Regimental commanders demanded artillerymen, drummers, even trumpeters; local manufacture and repair of wartime necessities required blacksmiths and carpenters.[77] Efforts were also made to provide the troops with doctors, apothecaries, and medicine.[78]

The distribution of arms was like that of grain supplies. After repair and manufacture, weapons and ammunition were shipped from local centers, from Moscow, or from a military center such as Belgorod or Sevsk to a forward point under guard. Individual arms and ammunition were available for collection at the departure point (in the case of Briansk regiments, Sumy), while supplies and heavy matériel went on to the forward point (from Sumy to Krasnyi Kut). At each distribution point regimental supplies were kept quite distinct from those belonging to an army group or to the command regiment. Thus guns and matériel left at Sumy by various regiments were later dispatched back to their different points of origin.[79]

For grain, as for food, arms, and ammunition, however, transportation to and beyond collection points was as complex as the collections themselves. Transportation required the repair or construction of riverboats to carry goods and their escorts down the Vorskla River and toward the Dnepr rapids. Furthermore, carts and carters had to be provided to move goods overland to troop muster points and forward storage areas and to make up the army's baggage train. Finally, artillery carriages and carts required horses to pull them, and the horses needed fodder.

As with the Kievan garrison in 1668–1669, the problems of transportation proved crucial, imposing a particular strain on the south in view of the new, less regional, organization of supply. There were, for example, 660 riverboats built at three river ports for the 1687 campaign. One hundred of these were built along the Vorskla River; the remaining 560 were built near either Briansk or Smolensk. To provide the labor, the equipment, and most of the materials to build a single boat took the combined resources of nearly 100 households. The state contributed (low) salaries for the workers and any iron needed in construction. On the Vorskla River, Belgorod service households were contributors, while in the Sevsk region, peasants and even townspeople built boats at Briansk.[80]

The reluctance of both servicemen and peasants to work on the docks (rather than in the army or their own fields) and the absence of skilled carpenters and blacksmiths considerably slowed the effort. The goal was to complete boat construction by early fall, but Briansk quickly fell behind schedule: less than half the blacksmiths appeared on time, supplies were tardy in arriving, and one-third the workers never came at all. Twelve hereditary garrison servicemen tried to locate absent laborers in nearby provinces, and other servicemen were posted at the docks to ensure that the work stayed on schedule as much as possible.[81] Still, by 20 September fewer than half the boats were built, and some of those completed were less than riverworthy because of knotholes, green planking, or because they were not long enough.[82] In the end, to keep to schedule, the available boats were simply overloaded.[83]

The laden riverboats did not proceed immediately downriver to Kiev that fall, as originally intended. The Military Chancellery, anticipating an early start for the campaign, had wanted advance supplies to winter near the army muster points. As it happened, however, not only were the boats completed late, but their escorts also arrived late and without essential supplies. The launches in Briansk were postponed until spring and high water.[84] The first thirty-two boats left Briansk on 24 April; another sixty-four followed on 26 and 27 April, and the remaining twenty-nine left two days later. Because the last were the most heavily laden to make up for the shortage of boats, they were also at greatest risk from bad weather, and their captain halted them before he had even left the province. It would be well into May before they reached their destination.[85] About half the food supplies that the state provided to the campaign (two months' worth) moved on these 125 boats.

Supplies not traveling by water had to follow the army. Immediate provisions would leave the frontiers with the regiments, and the baggage train would then be replenished from advance shipments. To that end, an immense assembling of carts, carters, and other supplies began in February 1687. The south provided nearly half the 20,000 carts that accompanied the army. A cart, a carter, and all attendant paraphernalia were drawn from every five service households; regimental servicemen were exempted from active duty for the purpose.[86] Finally, the southern postal service (iama) lost most of its carts to the campaign.

In each military-administrative region horses were retrieved from the households where they had been maintained since their last campaign. Old animals were sold and new ones purchased, often at much more than the anticipated cost. In the south between two and four wagon loads of hay were also collected from each southern service household to feed local animals. A staggering 24,000 wagon loads of hay were collected in the Sevsk region and another 43,000 in the Belgorod region,[87] but this hay was winter food, used on the spot to feed up the animals before the campaign and before fresh grass was available. Little if any of it was intended to follow the army.[88] Although fodder remained a concern for the duration of the campaign, relatively little followed the armies across the frontier, nor are there indications of large fodder shipments forward. Instead, like most European armies, Muscovite troops gathered a few days' supply of raw fodder at a time, which they then carried with them.[89]

These complex arrangements yielded some important successes. The collections produced a volume of grain more than adequate to feed the infantry for three or four months of campaigning and additional grain to pay overdue salaries, escorts, and the like. Guns and ammunition were amassed to arm the troops and provide field artillery. The means to transport all these supplies were also provided: carts, horses, and boats. A national organization used its capacities for overseeing, enforcing, and coordinating regional grain collection systems to advantage.

Nevertheless, glaring problems in the supply system remained. For one, despite the mass of provisions accumulated, the army was still forced to depend on local foraging and self-provisioning. Infantrymen directly supplied, in the end, constituted just over 43 percent of the forces. The Muscovite army continued to rely heavily on cavalrymen's ability to organize and pay for their own food and supplies. As in Kiev twelve years earlier, the possibility that the cavalry would run out of food was very real.[90]

A second significant problem lay in coordinating the supply apparatus and the army proper in time for the launch of the campaign. The main forces met at Akhtyrka, Sumy, Krasnyi Kut, and Khotmyzhsk near the southwest end of the Belgorod defenses; there were smaller musters elsewhere.[91] The men were to assemble early to allow for a long campaign season, and troops began arriving in late January. The collection of supplies, in this instance, seems to have proceeded more smoothly than that of men. Nearly 400 servicemen from a nearby Sevsk regional province alone failed to put in an appearance on time.[92] Even after substantial delays, some 17 percent of the troops failed to appear. Reviewing those of his troops who were present, the Sumy regimental commander ordered them to remuster in mid-April[93] and sent them home before they could use up their supplies. It would be 1 May, not 1 March, before regiments crossed the Merlo River to begin the journey south. Under the circumstances, the delayed departure of supply boats from Briansk to Kiev and toward the Dnepr rapids was of little consequence.

Most important, once assembled, the army and its supplies were a nearly unmanageable mass. Once the forces began moving across the frontier, they marched for four weeks to the south-southwest toward the Samara River, where they met Hetman Samoilovich's troop of 50,000 at one of the last points accessible by river before the Dnepr rapids. The massive army led by Prince Golitsyn proceeded slowly across the steppe. It was organized with an advance guard of ten regiments, followed by a long rectangle made up of an estimated one hundred regiments and the supply train. In that long rectangle, the main infantry forces surrounded a moving barricade of 14,000 horse-drawn carts that were arranged in ten rows and flanked on the sides by 6,000 more carts in seventeen parallel rows. The front and flanks of this oblong—2.3 miles across and 1.2 miles long—were protected by cavalry, with the artillery bringing up the rear. This formation may have been safe, but in order to retain its shape the army was forced to move at a snail's pace. Furthermore, the wagon barricade was dispersed and reformed after every fourth or fifth day of march to allow a day for gathering fodder.[94] Wood and water were sought nearly daily. The Russians apparently did not stop for bread making but distributed hardtack and grain for individual preparation. Most contemporary armies (with more conventional organization and a much smaller baggage train) covered about twelve miles a day.[95] Assuming the appropriate number of gathering days, Golitsyn could by this standard have covered at most 280 miles in the first weeks of the campaign; he actually covered about two-thirds of that.[96] Allowing for the size and organization of his forces, the pace seems not unreasonable.

This brief review serves to call in question the entire enterprise of sending troops against Crimea. Even maintaining the faster pace, the army would have needed more than two and one-half months of any summer campaign to reach Perekop at the isthmus of Crimea and return. In addition, any such venture required the availability of at least some food, water, and wood along the route. A better-stocked baggage train was not an option because it would also have had to be a still larger one. Apparently, the Muscovites did not weigh the advantages of sending a smaller force, whose supply requirements might have been less of an encumbrance.

After meeting the Hetman's forces on 30 May, the march continued for nearly three more weeks until the senior Russian officers decided to turn back. The immediate reason was obvious. The Tatars had burned the grass of the open steppe; to cross that territory, the army would have had to invest enormous effort searching for fodder for its more than 100,000 horses. Within days of reaching the burnt-over steppe, the decision was reached to return immediately without seriously engaging the enemy even once. As the army recrossed the southern frontier, its regiments began dispersing, and its arms and provisions were returned to granaries and depots.[97]

By 1687 Muscovy could, by exerting extraordinary organizational effort, successfully gather more than enough food for that part of the 112,000-man army it chose to supply. Russian campaigns against the Crimea, however, posed unusual problems in the disbursement of supply to a large army. Elsewhere in Europe, similar disbursement problems would be resolved partly by reliance on local agriculture and partly by a series of provision magazines, at regular and quite short intervals when campaigning on or near home territory. Neither option was available for the Muscovites proceeding across scantly populated and hostile steppes against Crimea. The shipment of food to Kiev suggests that Golitsyn intended to use river supply in the limited and piecemeal fashion his route permitted. The construction of the fortress of Novobogoroditsa on the Samara River, an afterthought of the 1687 campaign, did extend the forward reach of Muscovite supply lines in 1689; the second campaign may have moved more rapidly across the steppe as a result, but the main problem remained unresolved. The campaign led by Prince Golitsyn in 1687 did perhaps contribute to

Moscow's international standing, allowing Russia to fulfill its treaty obligations to the Holy League and drawing the Ottoman army away from the Habsburg borderlands. Nevertheless, in both this and the campaign of 1689, Moscow was prevented from extending a military presence on the lower Dnepr; in both cases, the failings of Muscovy's supply system forced its armies to turn back. Supply and, more particularly, disbursement thus posed significant limitations to the Muscovite army's southern movement; these limitations would persist into the first third of the eighteenth century.[98] The effort to provide the food and transportation required by the army in these and other campaigns, however, had a different, if equally dramatic, impact on the character of Muscovy's southern defenses.

CHAPTER

6

THE RUSSIAN
DEFENSIVE FORCES

By the last third of the seventeenth century, the principal purpose of the southern supply system had become support of military action beyond the Russian frontiers in furtherance of Russia's aggressive southern expansion. But, perhaps even more than other European states of the time,[1] Russia made major investments of effort, manpower, and cash in defensive warfare. Over the last third of the century, garrison forces not only shared resources with but directly supplied the campaign troops, becoming the primary contributors to the grain provisioning system described in the previous chapters, as well as contributing other supplies. These responsibilities should not be viewed lightly. As recent monographs have made abundantly clear, the combined pressures of taxation, inadequate labor, and small landholdings subjected garrison servicemen to increasing economic degradation; by 1722 many had been reduced to the status of state peasants, although they were certainly not the only group so treated.[2]

What follows is an attempt to analyze the impact of army reform and, particularly, of the grain provisioning system on the military contributions of southern garrison service in the latter part of the seventeenth century. As one of the bureaucratic empires advancing southward into unclaimed steppe lands,[3] did Russia abandon its initial defensive strategy late in the century? More specific, did Muscovy come to rely exclusively on its campaign army, relegating its garrison defenders to the role of taxpayer serfs who supplied and paid for—but did not fight in—campaigns? Finally, in that context, who were the town servicemen, and what became of them as the century wore on?

As a brief survey of the evidence makes clear, Russia did not abandon the defense of its southern borders to the campaign army. On the contrary, it invested heavily in defense after 1650 in two obvious ways. The first and most visible of those investments was the physical fortification of the south already described. Defensive lines ringed the southern regions—strings of fortified towns connected by dense forest, felled trees, palisades, and earthworks that were intended to prevent the penetration of Tatar cavalry into newly populated territories. Such a line existed through Tula as early as the fifteenth century; it was strengthened and reorganized by Ivan IV, the better to protect the provinces around Moscow. By 1600 other defensive outposts were added further south, including the fortress towns of Voronezh, Elets, Belgorod, Kursk, and (Staryi) Oskol; the population moved deeper into the south in the decades that followed. After the Tatar incursions of the early 1630s, construction began on the Belgorod fortified line; when completed in 1653, it stretched some five hundred miles across the south of European Russia and cut off three of the four principal tracks used by Tatar raiders as they moved north.[4]

The building of such barriers was not restricted to the first half of the seventeenth century. Although the older lines were sometimes allowed to fall into disrepair, new defenses were added in the area of Tambov, and the fortifications were linked to another abatis line through the town of Simbirsk. In 1679–1681, the 300-mile Izium Defensive Line moved the frontier some 100 miles southward, enclosing 12,000 square miles of Slobodskaia Ukraina. More than 30,000 military servicemen and their commanders built and defended the new line during the last years of the Russo-Turkish War; there could hardly be a more eloquent testimony to Moscow's continued concern with defense. The maintenance and repair of old lines and the addition of new segments near Izium continued through the 1680s and into the 1690s, drawing heavily on local resources and diverting them from other military activity. Still further south, between the Dnepr and Donets Rivers, the Ukrainian Defensive Line would be completed only in the 1730s.[5]

Whatever their date of construction, these fortified lines remained an adaptation of an older-style defensive system. They were intended specifically as protection against Tatar cavalry raids, not against attack by a regular army. The fortress towns along the lines might be most properly described as havens during such raids; they were not designed for prolonged siege. Although their layered defenses architecturally resembled western European fortresses, they were wooden stockades or earthen walls. Nor did the fortifications exhibit the crownworks, redoubts, and other characteristics of the latest European designs that would have suggested they were intended to withstand siege fire (such a design would of course have been pointless, given the material of their construction). This was a matter of deliberate intent rather than ignorance or omission. Western European military engineers helped design the Belgorod line, and elsewhere on Russia's western frontier there were stone fortresses of different and much more expensive design, which were intended to withstand a different kind of warfare.[6]

These defenses clearly accomplished their purpose of defending populated Russian lands from raids and incursions from the south and east. After 1653 the Tatars rarely penetrated southern defenses; when they succeeded in breaking through the line, raiders did not travel far into populated territory. The single major exception occurred in 1659, when the Russian army was defeated at Konotop by the combined forces of the hostile Ukrainian Hetman Vygovskii and his Tatar allies. This permitted Tatar forces to circumvent the western end of Russia's fortifications by moving north through Ukraine and to raid the provinces of Orel, Mtsensk, and even the western end of Voronezh province.[7] Thereafter, however, the northern and western provinces of the Belgorod and Sevsk regions were untouched by Tatar raids, while Ukrainian lands to the west remained vulnerable.[8]

Tatar incursions, whether independent or at the behest of the Ottoman Empire, did not cease once the defensive lines were in place. Provinces along the Belgorod line were often attacked, and their fortresses and the line itself had to be manned to turn back raids. Voronezh province, for example, was attacked by Tatars in 1658 while most of its defenders were attending the initial muster of the Belgorod army in Belgorod. Periods of especially frequent hostilities along the line were 1673–1676 and 1679–1682, when Tatar attacks were strategic components of larger conflicts. Usman', on the northeastern section of the Belgorod line, suffered at least 150 small raids over those eight years. This area and the Don River towns remained vulnerable to Tatar and Kalmyk attack late into the century. Further west, once the Izium line was finished, the focus of Tatar skirmishes moved southward—to the towns of the new line and to fortresses further south; the new defenses rendered a number of fortresses on the Belgorod line less vital for protection against direct raids. Thus southern fortifications represented a successful defensive strategy; the haven they afforded against devastating raids from the south and east contrasted positively with the unprotected conditions in southern Poland. It has been suggested that the protection afforded by these fortifications explains in part the concurrent Ukrainian migration into Muscovite territory.[9]

The persistence in the south of garrison or town service forces was a second manifestation of defensive military thinking. Like the fortified lines, these forces were the product of military conditions prior to the introduction of new formation troops. Many Muscovite fortress cities had long had resident garrisons as a matter of self-protection; in the absence of military threat, they became local guards and police forces in many parts of Russia. Only on the frontiers did town service retain a distinct, military identity and significance. Siberian fortresses, in particular, maintained large garrisons; indeed, because the region fielded no campaign service troops, all servicemen there were involved in town defense.[10] Even before the building of the Belgorod defenses, a frontier garrison service manned the fortress towns in the south; an effective steppe patrol was already in operation by the late sixteenth century. The commitment of manpower to a garrison service persisted throughout the seventeenth century after the Belgorod lines were built and the Belgorod campaign army was in place; a kind of garrison militia persisted in this region even after the reign of Peter I.[11] The southern garrisons might thus be broadly described as an old-style service that survived the army reform. An examination of the size and function of the southern garrison service in the late seventeenth century must necessarily precede any analysis of its relationship to southern supply and military reform.

The undoubted successes of the southern defensive lines did not lead to the disappearance of the garrison service. Most southern towns did not demilitarize, as some have argued, when the frontier moved south.[12] Although, with the construction of the Belgorod line, Tula-area garrisons diminished in size and changed in character over the next three decades, a parallel process did not take place in provinces further south.[13] As table 4 of the appendix indicates, cities all over the Belgorod region maintained large garrisons in the 1660s and 1670s. Even late in the 1680s, when Muscovy was moving aggressively southward against Crimea, 45,000 southerners were primarily involved in garrison service; in 1695 the Petrine government still maintained between 23,500 and 25,000 servicemen in thirty-eight garrisons.

This persistent commitment to the southern defensive forces is particularly striking, given the formidable manpower demands of the campaign army units on the southern population (see table 3 of the appendix). The campaign forces grew nearly threefold in the latter part of the century, thus outpacing population growth. The Belgorod region's first campaign army, fielded in 1658, had 19,252 members. Its regiments declined to just over 15,000 men in the late 1660s, in part because the Sevsk region separated from Belgorod, and Sevsk's new field army necessarily included some former Belgorod servicemen. Moreover, during the war over Ukraine, which lasted until 1667, some 10,000 men of the Belgorod army were killed, died of disease, or were taken prisoner. The ranks of the Belgorod campaign army were quickly replenished, however; there were 19,452 men in Belgorod's new formation regiments by 1674, and 23,000 by 1679. Another 4,000 men belonged to Ukrainian regiments, based in cities south of the Belgorod line. Despite a brief drop in size at the creation of the Tambov region, the Belgorod region's armies numbered 27,000 men by 1687. Meanwhile, the independent Sevsk army had some 16,000 men in the mid-1670s, and nearly doubled during the period of the reforms, before dropping back to 16,600 men in the mid-1680s. Nevertheless, through all these increases, the commitment to garrison forces remained.

According to records of military inspections in 1669, 1673, 1675, 1679–1680, and 1685, the total number of town servicemen did not fluctuate a great deal, even during major campaigns.[14] Aside from short-term shifts away from garrisons and into the field regiments, throughout the turbulent decades before Peter I, southern servitors were still being assigned in large numbers (if diminishing proportions) to serve in local garrisons rather than in the campaign armies.

The size and location of the individual garrisons further demonstrate that Moscow steadfastly committed resources and labor to the urban defense network of the southern provinces. Each town in the Military Chancellery's jurisdiction filed annual military estimates (*smety*) over the last half of the seventeenth century. The compilers created a formal record of the military resources on hand for a province's defense, providing a description of the town's fortress, the number and character of administrative personnel and military commanders, the fighting forces available for defense, their arms, the grain, salt, gunpowder, shot, and artillery stored for defense and emergency distribution, and the extent of intertown communication. Only rarely, however, did the annual estimates record the number of campaign servicemen residing in the province.[15] The ten sets of books drawn upon here date from 1668 to 1695 and offer a rich run of material for the years of the military reforms, 1678–1682; they provide a finely detailed view of military preparedness on the frontier during the last quarter of the seventeenth century, a period for which the Russian army has not been intensively studied.[16] Not all the estimates deal with the same group of towns—in part because a significant number of them were founded south of the frontier during the period covered by these records. Furthermore, the Tambov military region was created, and some cities briefly separated from, and then returned to, Belgorod's sway. Those books that were compiled on site offer a more detailed look at the towns than the composite versions assembled in the capital. The estimates, moreover, vary in accuracy because not all southern cities were equally careful in all categories of their reports. The relatively large number of books extant over three decades nonetheless depict the broad outlines of change in the garrison service in the last years of the seventeenth century.

Garrison size closely reflected military need throughout the period. The distribution of garrison servicemen followed a fairly consistent pattern between 1667 and 1695. Generally, garrisons in the best-protected towns decreased in size. Once towns were secure behind the Belgorod and, later, the Izium defenses, twenty-two towns with fairly large garrisons began losing numbers in 1671; less than half of them ever regained their early size. Epifan', for example, was staffed by 865 men in 1668, but by 1670–1671 its garrison had dropped to 160–230 men; it would drop still lower in the 1680s. Equally abruptly, the garrison of Mtsensk, which numbered 1,653 men in 1668, dropped to less than one half that number by 1670–1671 and remained there for the remainder of the century. If most interior garrisons diminished in size as they outlived their need to deal with Tatar raids, not all interior garrisons experienced this change. Towns like Dankov, Elets, and Efremov recorded their largest garrisons in the 1680s (see table 4 of the appendix); these garrisons were concerned with regional rather than provincial defense.

However significant the decline in interior garrisons, there was no corresponding decline in the total number of southern garrison servicemen over the same period. Between 1675 and 1685, for example, the size of southern garrisons decreased by only 10 to 12 percent, despite enlistment drives and reforms in other areas of military service.[17] This relatively constant level of regional operations, however, conceals shifts in the allocation of garrison forces within the region. Garrisons directly on the frontiers grew, while interior garrisons declined in size. Between 1677 and 1678 the southern regions mustered the largest number of town servicemen ever, nearly 47,000 in seventy-three cities. The garrisons that helped to account for that growth, and that reached their peak size in the late 1670s, were concentrated in two areas—first, on or near the southwestern corner of the Belgorod line and the southern edge of the Sevsk region, facing Ukraine and Crimea; and second, along the eastern frontier, facing the Nogai track and the Kalmyk forces. This distribution made strategic sense. Russia was in the midst of war with Turkey into the late 1670s; the presence of Turkish armies and their Tatar client allies in the southwest required defense of the southwestern frontier by garrisons as well as by the campaign forces. The beginning of construction on the Izium line after 1678 also required the continued presence of laborers and defenders; with the campaign forces engaged against Turkey, the Kalmyk frontier was vulnerable.

Even after the military reforms of 1678 were well under way, the size and location of garrison forces remained a flexible instrument of military policy. The focus of garrison troops shifted after the 1681 peace with Turkey and Crimea and the virtual completion of the Izium Defensive Line. The garrisons of eleven Sevsk towns grew substantially between 1678 and 1682. In the Belgorod region the largest garrisons were once again along the Kalmyk frontier, with a particular concentration on the southeast corner of the Belgorod line. The number of men in some newly protected towns dropped quite abruptly: Bogodukhov, Chuguev, and Khar'kov, for example. New garrisons appeared beyond both the eastern and southern frontiers. The annual military estimates are less complete for the last decade studied, 1685–1695. Nonetheless, it is clear that garrisons continued to grow in newly settled areas and that there was renewed growth in some of the old interior town garrisons.

The process of selection for garrison duty allowed for the implementation of military goals with considerable room for local discretion. At musters from the 1650s well into the 1680s, men were selected for campaign service on the basis of relatively clear guidelines. Even before the reforms of 1678–1682, the informal rules that governed the actions of a military inspector (*razborshchik*) as he divided men among the various branches of the campaign army had to do with a serviceman's prosperity, his available land and labor, and his social status or rank. These apparently applied to all men eligible for new formation service, from peasants to hereditary servicemen. The 1678 reform formalized these rules.

The guidelines for assigning men to garrison service at a muster were less clear, both before and after reform. Musters, and those other occasions at which men of military age were separated into the various services, frequently took place prior to major campaigns, and filling the infantry regiments was their particular goal. The number of men who went into garrison service was defined only relative to the number called to campaign service. Thus in the 1660s inspectors were choosing one campaign serviceman and one garrison serviceman from a family with three adult males; the third was left to farm. Given the military requirements of the late 1660s and early 1670s, the chief concern in muster instructions was to leave behind a sufficient number of men to support the campaign armies; garrison service was barely mentioned. Indeed, on some occasions, all men newly joining the military from a particular province were recruited either into campaign service or left on the land, and none joined town service. In a similar vein, when the province of Kozlov required more infantrymen in 1673, inspectors were ordered to take them from the households of garrison servicemen, depriving these families of labor but not decreasing the number of defenders.[18]

Complaints quickly surfaced that too many men were being sent to the campaign forces. Concern over leaving too few tillers on the land to support campaigners has been mentioned earlier. In another vein, some military commanders complained of a shortage of men in frontier fortresses, even though men were still being sent to serve in them. The criteria by which servicemen were selected for garrison duty remain unclear, although poverty or physical disability were sometimes in themselves sufficient cause. Indeed, only solitary men (men without families or other labor) were automatically sent to serve in garrisons.[19] By 1675 recruitment instructions, although only somewhat more precise, grouped solitary men into fours, euphemistically called "a service family." One of the four would serve in a garrison, one in the campaign forces, and two would farm.[20] This change was, in part, a response to the problem of having too many campaign servicemen dependent on a single farmer, but it also resulted in better support for garrison servicemen.

Criteria for choosing town servicemen were as informal after the 1678–1682 reforms as before. Garrison service was not mentioned in the reform decree of 1678, which laid down economic norms for all campaign ranks; this is not surprising because most of Russia had no such active servicemen. Special instructions for southern military inspectors, however, were no more forthcoming. By implication, only those who did not fulfill the qualifications for campaign service were assigned to garrison service.

Like other instructions in 1678, this was not entirely new. Generally speaking, where it persisted, town service was for those unable to meet the arduous physical demands or the greater cost of campaigning. In the south, as in parts of Russia where town service was less active, regimental servitors could be retired to a garrison because of poverty or otherwise at the discretion of the local inspector.[21] The Komaritskii dragoons, for example, were selected for regimental service, only to be retired from it when they were found unable to support its economic demands. Among hereditary servicemen, it might seem self-evident that garrison servicemen were poor, because they routinely received lower entitlements than their regimental service colleagues. Indeed, according to a recent study, hereditary servicemen in Kozlov province were considerably more likely to be economically distressed if they served in the garrison than if they were in campaign regiments.[22]

It is important to recognize, however, that men of the southern garrisons did not at any point become a separate economic or military stratum from campaign servicemen. First, differences in wealth between garrison and campaign servitors selected at a particular inspection might be quite small, given the unusual (and growing) economic homogeneity of the southern service population. Second, because garrison service was often performed locally, it provided more time to search out and farm the land to which a serviceman was entitled. Thus hereditary servicemen in the Kozlov garrison, on average, tilled more of the land to which they were entitled than their regimental brethren; economic distress thus might be remedied. Involvement in local trade may sometimes have served a similar recuperative function for the household economies of recruited servicemen. Assignment to garrison service might be changed to campaign service with improving economic circumstances, and garrison defense was therefore not permanent, nor did it become hereditary. Campaign and garrison servitors could be drawn from the same families; the southern service population was also exceedingly mobile, moving southward to new lands and duties. Less than half the family names on the 1670–1671 military service roll from a district of Kursk province were still there in 1685–1686. Among those who remained in the district, the family names of garrison servicemen in 1670 were not often the same as the garrison servicemen of 1685.[23]

Instead, men moved between garrison and campaign service because of changing military circumstances, family economic conditions, and personal preference. Individuals could be moved back and forth several times if their services were needed.[24] Garrison duty was also seen as less difficult than campaigning, and not a few servicemen preferred it, regardless of their economic and social status.[25] One regimental officer accused local officials of taking bribes to make garrison assignments in defiance of norms; other servicemen were accused of underreporting their labor resources to avoid having family members recruited or transferred into the campaign forces. An initial appointment to garrison service in the south might also be to gain military experience. Such conditions, which ensured that garrison service did not become a separate economic and military stratum, appear to have held well into the 1680s.[26]

Physical incapacity could mean seemingly irreversible assignment to garrison service. On his judgment, an inspector anywhere in Muscovy could retire a regimental serviceman because he was aged, crippled, or even mentally deficient; some of these individuals were retired into garrison service.[27] This phenomenon made garrison service somewhat impervious to change, because such men did not usually resume field service; however, only some 5 percent of southern town garrison servicemen were retired regimental servicemen (see table 4 of the appendix).

In short, there was little to prevent the dividing line between garrison and regimental service from being extremely responsive to local discretion and needs into the 1680s. Evidently, local commanders were also able occasionally to reinforce their garrisons with regimental contract servitors.[28] Such flexibility supports the contention that the distribution of garrison servicemen in the south was not accidental; the location of large garrisons suggests that at least one powerful reason for their existence was still defense against raiding Tatars and Kalmyks.

The status, composition, and duties of the garrison servicemen confirm the same view that is suggested by recruitment. Garrisons were active military forces. Their servicemen did not, perhaps, need to be as well trained or prosperous as campaign servicemen, but their duties included important military responsibilities. Before 1678 the garrisons were composed of hereditary servitors, Cossacks, Ukrainian settlers who dominated the fortress towns south of the Belgorod line, and members of some recruited services, including musketeers and artillerymen. Townspeople and craftsmen occasionally appeared as members of the garrisons, while the relatives and dependents of military men were listed as auxiliaries if they were judged worthy of service.[29] On the whole, former members of the new formation regiments were not so named in garrison lists; a hereditary serviceman was thus referred to by status (*syn boiarskii*), rather than by the branch of the military in which he may have served (*reitar*). Large settlements of militarized peasants were an exception; the Komaritskii dragoons, for example, were listed as such in the Sevsk garrison.[30]

Before 1678 hereditary servicemen were the largest single component of garrison service, constituting about 40 percent of the garrisons in 1670 and 1671; they were particularly numerous in the interior towns. Ukrainian settlers were the next single largest group, constituting about 30 percent of all southern garrisons between 1670 and 1678 and concentrated in the areas south of the Belgorod Defensive Line. Recruited servicemen, primarily musketeers, made up between 12 and 18 percent of garrison servitors.[31]

The complexion of the garrisons changed with the reforms of 1678–1682. By 1682 the dominance of the middle service class in the southern garrisons was confirmed. Nearly half (up to 48%) of garrison servicemen were hereditary servicemen. The number of Ukrainian settlers in garrison service diminished both relatively and absolutely, as their towns became more protected, and Ukrainian campaign regiments were formed. At the same time, recruited servicemen became less common in the garrisons. The number of musketeers dropped when, as a result of the reform, their provincial regiments (*prikazy*) were explicitly recruited into the campaign army; they were replaced by landed dragoons.[32]

Petty hereditary servicemen could be notoriously ineffective field troops, but the concentration of these self-sufficient servicemen in the garrisons does not represent the abandonment of southern fortresses to the least useful troops. Cavalrymen were still needed on the frontier, just as they had been earlier in the century. Indeed, the reforms of 1678–1682 marked a slight increase in the proportion of military men in the garrisons. Increasingly in the 1680s, townspeople and others without military occupations ceased to be cited among garrison forces, although they were a growing proportion of the population. The absence of such individuals distinguished southern garrisons sharply from less threatened towns further north, where nonmilitary men dominated the garrisons. Iaroslavl', for example, listed only 60 military men out of 4,295 and Rostov only about 20 out of 765.[33] The Sevsk region's patterns followed Belgorod's—those of an active military population.

The military responsibilities of town servicemen did not vary widely. The primary distinction in daily duties was between mounted servitors (often hereditary servicemen) and infantrymen of the garrison. For example, the town of Valuiki, south of the Belgorod line, retained the special frontier service that had existed in the south since 1571.[34] Seventy mounted steppe patrolmen (*stanichniki*) left the fortress at Valuiki at six-day intervals from late spring through early fall. Their tour of the steppe was extensive: "to Sviatogorsk Monastery, to the Maiatsk River, then to Kalitva and the Burkukha River, and back to the settlement at Two-Creeks (*Dvurechnaia sloboda*)," watching for signs of Tatar approach. The garrison's other military duties were closer to home and characteristic of other towns on or south of the line. Mounted servicemen patrolled between outlying towers or small fortresses and into the distant districts. Cavalrymen in shifts of six relayed any messages or goods locally; sometimes they provided escort and protection to officially sanctioned groups traveling toward the lower Don. Beyond the frontier they also stood guard over work on distant and exposed fields or carried news of imminent attack to outlying villages so that residents could move themselves, livestock, and belongings toward fortified towns or forests.[35] Closer to Valuiki, fifty mounted musketeers and Cossacks patrolled the towers of the fortress. Another ten went to nearby Novyi Oskol on treasury matters; still others escorted couriers or official emissaries. Infantry musketeers and artillerymen stood guard near the river crossing and patrolled the town towers inside, as well as guarding the powder magazine and the granary. Forty of them served as couriers to Moscow. Ukrainian mounted servitors also patrolled the gates in rotas of ten and elsewhere in the fortress in shifts of twenty.

The recruited servicemen of Valuiki filled some specialized functions. *Vorotniki* guarded fortress gates; *zatinshchiki* and *pushkarei* were artillerymen who dealt respectively with light- and heavy-caliber mounted guns.[36] When Tatar raids took place, all these servicemen were responsible for the defense of the town; generally only small raids or unusual circumstances prompted them to emerge from the fortress to try to halt Tatar progress. All garrison members in Valuiki could be asked to guard dispatches sent to the Kalmyks. When described in 1671, this garrison numbered about five hundred men; a much smaller number from the same community, 184 men, served as campaign cavalrymen.[37]

The garrison of Korotoiak on the southeastern corner of the Belgorod line had similar duties. A slightly different distribution of tasks there emphasizes that garrison responsibilities were rarely attached to a specific rank from town to town. In Korotoiak hereditary servicemen were named to more jobs than in Valuiki, even though the garrison did not contain enough provincial servicemen (*deti boiarskie*) to fill them completely, even for one complete rotation.[38] The musketeer, Cossack, and steppe patrol contingents were sufficient to provide at least three rotations for their assigned posts. Twenty-one Ukrainians, thirty-three townsmen, and individual off-duty servicemen were left to fill those posts not assigned to a specific military rank. Relatives, children, and other dependents of the garrison's official members filled in for missing servicemen. In addition, the city reported twenty-two other individuals whose occupations were of military importance, such as skilled craftsmen. Sixteen artillerymen were presumably in charge of the fortress' fifteen guns and its artillery supplies.[39] Like Valuiki, Korotoiak was an exposed frontier fortress, and it supported a relatively small campaign service contingent—less than two hundred men.[40]

Besides these regular military duties, there were intermittent responsibilities that sometimes pulled town-based servicemen from their garrisons. Warnings of imminent Tatar attack led to general alerts, and town walls were manned more densely—often by garrison servitors from other towns. Musketeers and hereditary servicemen escorted criers with news, orders, and calls to arms around the province.[41] The musketeers, in particular, might be called upon to act as a police force in the event of rebellion or to track down serfs or judicial fugitives.[42]

Other towns on and beyond the fortified lines may have assigned tasks somewhat differently or spaced the rotations at different intervals, but the military duties of their garrisons were similar, as was the frequent under-manning of individual garrisons.[43] Prior to 1680 more than forty of the Belgorod region's sixty-six towns, as well as some of the southernmost fortresses in the Sevsk region, lay on or outside the defensive lines and required heavy staffing of the kind described above. Even a partial listing of alerts against Tatar raids suggests that garrison defense remained an important component of military activity.

Garrison duties in the interior towns, by comparison with those on the frontier, were numerous but less strenuous. Some towns, like Belgorod itself, were administrative centers for military affairs; others were the headquarters for a campaign regiment. In these cases, members of the garrison served as sworn deputies at the customs house or tavern; artillery-men and other recruited servicemen guarded the ammunition cellars, granaries, and storehouses; and musketeers guarded the prison. Escorts continued to be needed, but inside the fortifications their military caliber was less important. The town of Kursk used retired servicemen for these purposes even in the 1640s.[44] Towns maintained rotating guards at their gates and along their walls. In Sevsk this meant a guard of sixty dragoons and musketeers, which changed daily.[45] Military responsibilities in pro-tected southern garrisons were thus not much different from those of garrisons elsewhere in the interior of Muscovy.[46]

Although the primary responsibility of garrison servicemen from towns within the Belgorod line was to their own fortresses, some assignments took them away from their provinces. For example, the cultivation of ara-ble tenth beyond the frontier required extra men not only for farming but also for protection. Musketeers, Cossacks, gunners, and even gate guards (vorotniki) were sent from far into the interior to perform these tasks.[47] Defense against the Tatars, likewise, did not always require that service-men remain in their own towns. When border garrisons were understaffed, interior garrisons were used. Alerts in the 1660s brought other regional garrison servicemen southward to the border fortresses. In exceptional cir-cumstances, campaign troops served with the garrisons.[48] Anticipated Tatar attacks during the construction of the Izium wall placed nearby gar-risons on alert, even while town servicemen from further north were ac-tively engaged in building. On such occasions, half the garrison of a pro-tected town left, while the other half acted as a local defense reserve.[49] Garrison servicemen could be drawn directly into campaign units. The dragoons of one southern fortress were charged with tracking down desert-ers from infantry regiments in the 1670s; if they failed to apprehend them, they themselves acted as replacements.[50] Garrison servicemen, at least of the middle service class, also attended military musters for inspection and assessment.

In addition to particular fortresses that found themselves undermanned, there were not always enough men to meet the requirements of garrison service that drew on many towns at once. In the 1660s, for example, successive commanders complained that they had great difficulty in maintaining the fifty-man guard at the Tor salt flats and in garrisoning its isolated southern outposts; this was in part a function of Ukrainians' reluctance to serve under the Russian commanders there, when safer towns, and towns with Ukrainian leadership, were nearby. Flight from guard duty was reported from other points along the frontier. Elsewhere, particularly in the late 1670s, commanders complained that frontier fortresses were undermanned because too many men had transferred to the campaign regiments.[51]

In addition to their military responsibilities, southern garrisons helped provide for the campaign forces. These duties, which included the grain payments described in preceding chapters, had often started as labor, cash, or in-kind contributions intended to ensure the survival of an individual garrison. As with grain contributions, however, these additional dues had evolved into major contributions toward the support of regional goals or, specifically, of the Belgorod and Sevsk campaign forces.[52] These responsibilities, like their military duties, often did not reflect status distinctions; that is, they only occasionally distinguished among servicemen, or between servicemen and the peasantry. As already mentioned, these regionally organized service dues were similar to taxes paid by peasants and townsmen elsewhere in Russia.

Unlike grain contributions, intermittent labor dues often had visible benefits for all regional residents; the construction and repair of the defensive lines were a case in point.[53] Garrison servicemen also built granaries and warehouses and constructed new outlying defenses alone.[54] When the Izium Defensive Line was built, many Belgorod-region provinces sent every sixth garrison serviceman south for a month or longer in the summer. Some internal garrisons were stripped of personnel, with as many as half of their members leaving for Novyi Oskol, the muster point for construction and protection of the new wall. Workers from the garrisons received a small cash stipend, but they contributed their own muskets and pickaxes; in the interval, their farms were deprived of their labor.[55] Major construction on the Izium line, like that on the Belgorod wall before it, enlisted the labor of both garrison and campaign servicemen. One-sixth of some campaign army regiments were sent to the Izium line, despite the ongoing Russo-Turkish War. In all, some 30,000 men were involved over several years.[56]

After the 1660s, regular dues of all kinds became an onerous addition to long if occasional absences from farming and local military duties. Annual commitments were often related to campaign army matters, which included of course increasingly heavy payments to the granary system. Arable tenth remained in force in some areas; the fields at Bogoroditsa, for example, were farmed by shifts of garrison servicemen from towns that were nearby only in relative terms. Four shifts of fifty-six recruited servicemen each came from Efremov, Chern', and nine other towns. Some towns sent hereditary as well as recruited servicemen to work the fields. Gathering work parties proved difficult, and the work was labor-intensive; a plot of 540 acres (200 *desiatiny*) beyond the frontier could require an average of more than one hundred people monthly to plow, harvest, and stand guard.[57] In addition, garrison servicemen paid countrywide cash taxes, such as captives' ransom.

A growing annual investment of time and labor for garrison servicemen lay in transporting grain between destinations within the southern regions. Grain contributors, as a part of their payment, sometimes carted their payments one hundred miles or more to depot granaries and other points. Extra carts were occasionally required to move accumulated grain. In the Belgorod region, carts, horses, and escorts for them were drawn from garrisons without respect to service status; garrisons in the Sevsk region were frequently spared such duties, which were assigned directly to the Komaritskii dragoons.[58] Garrison servicemen were also responsible for building boats for annual shipment of grain to the Don Cossacks and to Russian troops on the lower Don or near Kiev; in the absence of peasant labor or acceptable cash substitutes, servicemen often contributed materials and worked on the docks themselves. The annual requirements for boats on the Don varied from fifty new boats (for an embassy) to six hundred barges to carry Cossack and Russian military salaries in the late 1670s. Because old boats could not easily be returned upriver, the gathering of labor, materials, iron parts, and the selection of loaders, escorts, and rowers were annual events.[59] After 1667 the Sevsk region also built boats to send regular supplies to Kiev and from there to other Ukrainian garrisons; its labor load was slightly lighter because it drew on its own provinces and on lands to its northeast, which were more heavily settled with peasants.[60] In both Sevsk and Belgorod, boat-building was a high priority; other responsibilities were canceled in its favor.[61]

The sum total of these demands on garrison servicemen was very considerable. For example, in 1674 the garrison of Verkhososensk, east of Belgorod on its defensive line, maintained long-distance patrols along and to the south of the line, as well as a fairly dense guard on the town walls. These town servicemen supported themselves from land or, in its absence, from trade or salaries. Despite a bad harvest that year, 384 garrison households in Verkhososensk contributed rye grain, milled it, and then bagged 83 tons (575 *chetverti*) of rye flour; they then carted it themselves to Korotoiak, about sixty miles away, and paid for at least one big barge to transport it down the Don. In that particular year, the shipment's 232-man military escort was not drawn from their number, and equipment and iron for the construction came from nearby garrisons to the north. (In the preceding year, however, about ninety Verkhososensk town servicemen had gone to Korotoiak to work on the docks.) Garrison households also repaired local fortifications, paid local dues, maintained army horses, and paid some countrywide taxes.[62] Despite significant local military responsibilities, southern town servicemen thus necessarily devoted a substantial proportion of their labor and resources to efforts other than local defense and their own support.

In one important respect, the reforms of 1678–1682 marked an important change in the lives of the south's garrison servicemen and in the organization of Russian defenses. Most significant, the distinctions between garrison servicemen and the least prosperous campaign servicemen began to disappear. The military dues assessed on garrison servicemen after 1678 were also assessed on poor campaign service households. As in the case of grain collections, contributions from the two groups quickly overlapped; in the postreform Belgorod region the households of campaign and garrison servicemen shared in many of the taxes and dues that had been garrison responsibilities alone prior to 1678.[63] The new, larger group also took on new tasks. The major campaigns at the end of the century drew on this combined population for grain through quarter-grain and on-demand levies, for cash contributions to purchase iron, gunpowder, fuses, lead, and other supplies, and increasingly for horses, fodder, and carts to move regimental supplies to distant destinations beyond the borders of Muscovy. Three cartloads of hay were collected per household in Belgorod cities for the Crimean campaign of 1687, for example.[64]

The conflation of functions performed by the south's poorer campaign servicemen and its garrison servicemen was to some extent also reflected in their military duties. The campaign servicemen rotated into Russian garrisons beyond the borders; these garrisons constituted another part of Russian defensive military activity, and the demand for men to staff them was rising. In the second half of the century a particular need for distant garrison defense lay in Ukraine, quite near the southern regions. From 1654 on, Russian military commanders and varying numbers of troops were stationed in Ukrainian towns. The Muscovite presence in Kiev, Pereiaslav, Nezhin, and Chernigov was contested from 1659 into the 1660s. Usman' and Bratslav on the right bank were lost by 1665, although the towns of Poltava, Gadiach, Mirgorod, and Lubny acquired Russian commanders. Later, Russian troops were also stationed at other defensible points: at Baturin, briefly at Chigirin, on the Don River, and still later on the Samara River. (Like the Siberian outposts, Astrakhan', at the mouth of the Volga, was different in that it had a resident garrison.)

Ukrainian garrisons had long included southern campaign servicemen. After the reforms, however, Ukrainian fortresses apparently were garrisoned by those same campaign servicemen who had recently begun to contribute to military dues. The occasional southern garrison serviceman thus joined them, acting as an alternate campaign servitor and salaried accord-ingly.[65] The garrisons of protected southern provinces were less frequently called to join in regional defense against the Tatars; instead, with members of the campaign army, they moved into a different kind of garrison defense. Indeed, by 1695 a significant proportion of southern garrison servicemen from the largest inland garrisons did temporary duty at Novobogoroditsa, the advance fortress on the Samara River.

This partial conflation of garrison and campaign service in the Belgorod and Sevsk regions, it should be repeated, did not represent an abandon-ment of the older southern defensive effort during the final quarter of the seventeenth century but a redistribution of garrison servicemen's duties. Active defense of the fortified line remained the primary mission for garri-sons on the border. One southern frontier garrison was alerted to possible attack by Cossacks, Tatars, Kalmyks, and others on some 170 occasions between 1680–1691.[66] Garrison service appointments still remained a real possibility at southern military inspections.[67] Nor were military authori-ties altogether convinced that garrisons north of the defenses were invio-late. Kursk, for example, was ordered to repair its central fortifications in preparation for the Crimean campaign of 1687, presumably in case Tatar counterattack penetrated or circumvented defenses further south.[68] The frontier moved ever southward, and new outlying posts were established in frontier provinces; the patrols leaving Putivl' included new territory in the mid-1680s, and construction on defenses south of Izium continued even in the 1690s.[69]

While defensive duties persisted, the situation of most southern garri-son troops was otherwise changing. Reliable protection against Tatar raids meant that garrison servicemen could safely farm their own lands when not on duty and that trade became more reliable. Correspondingly, mili-tary estimates (smety) cataloguing the distribution of supplies show less and less grain being stored in provincial granaries for local use. Unmilled rye, more useful to a settled population than to men on campaign, fell to as little as 15 percent of the annual collections by the 1680s. More important, however, the number of cities reporting any grain stockpiles at all de-clined. For example, 32 (54%) of Belgorod's 59 regional cities reported grain reserves in 1677; by the 1690s only a few cities had reserves, but they were large concentrations destined to support campaign regiments. The process was particularly visible in Sevsk, where 70 percent or more of the region's grain reserves between 1677–1682 were to be found in a single town (not always the same one). These supplies were clearly not intended for the use of the garrison service.[70]

How could defensive responsibilities be sustained, given the garrison service's growing contributions in grain, carts, boats, and other items to campaign support? The reforms of 1678 to 1682 did somewhat redistribute the burden of dues and, more important, shifted the burden of defense.

Military estimates from late in the century show that, as new demands were made on town servicemen, southern defenses were reinforced by artillery. Table 5 of the appendix lists the number of heavy mounted guns and fixed cannon reported by each southern town and the quantity of shot available for that artillery over time. Fortresses were careful to distinguish between guns stored in their armories for local campaign regiments and those available for their own defense; towns often had additional light artillery, portable firearms, and spare parts, but these are not counted in table 5.[71] Nonetheless, by 1686 garrisons had more armaments available than ever before.[72] In the postreform period the artillery was concentrated along the frontier and defensive lines. That is, the location of these artillery resources matched defense needs and paralleled the location of large garrisons. Some of these fortresses were also among the best provided with shot and powder, although several inland towns with large troop concentrations were also well supplied (Izium, Belgorod, and Iablonov, for example, may have been regional transshipment points for other garrisons.) It should be noted in passing that even the towns best supplied with ammunition fell short of Artillery Chancellery standards.[73] Throughout the last three decades of the seventeenth century, about one-quarter of the southern fortresses had 100 or more shot per artillery piece, while only three to five fortresses (less than 10%) had relatively abundant ammunition (more than 150 shot per piece).[74] Despite the financial investment in the artillery itself, in other words, very few cities would be capable of using their guns for any prolonged period. Given the south's wooden fortifications and its lightly armed Tatar adversaries, this seems of less significance than the new artillery capability of the Russian defenses.[75]

The weight of new obligations after 1678–1682 diminished some of the attractions of garrison service. Infantrymen from near Kozlov, for example, petitioned against their transfer to dragoon town service in 1684. But not all garrison servicemen were poor men, involuntarily enrolled in town defense. By 1690 the garrison at Kozlov had become mildly more prosperous than it had been before the reforms: 70 percent of its members had horses and over 80 percent of them had their own firearms.[76] If garrison servicemen perhaps found their original military duties lightened by better armaments, the campaign servicemen of this group also had compensations for their new duties. On one or two occasions, for example, they found themselves released from military duties so they could pay their dues; on these occasions, their value as duespayers outweighed their value as military servicemen.[77]

What remained unusual about this new group of southern servicemen, part garrison and part campaign servitors, was the duality of their contributions: active military service coupled with dues payments. The servicemen's tax contributions have received the lion's share of attention in the literature on southern Russia;[78] it is easy to see why. Other parts of Russia were making similar contributions to the support of the same campaigns by the 1680s; in this respect, the south was becoming part of a national effort to support massive field armies. In its countrywide efforts, however, the central government juxtaposed the dues-paying functions of this combined body of southern servicemen directly with the taxpaying functions of traditional taxpayers, a process nearly complete by 1693. In Sevsk the growing numbers of peasants and townsmen had already made it possible for some of the garrisons' dues-paying responsibilities to be shifted from garrisons to traditional taxpayers. The boats constructed for shipping supplies to Ukraine were built at the rate of one per 65 to 100 peasant and town households, while servicemen supervised and did escort duty. Carters were drawn from one in seven Sevsk peasant households for the Crimean campaign of 1687, while in the Belgorod region carts, horses, carters, and supplies came from every fourth household of peasants, townspeople, and servicemen. These collections served the same purpose and often went to the same distribution point.[79] These comparisons notwithstanding, petty southern servicemen of both the town and regimental service continued to fulfill significant military functions.

Town defense remained an important component of southern Russia's military reforms throughout the seventeenth century. The assignment of servicemen to garrisons closely reflected local military conditions into the 1680s and 1690s. After the military reforms of 1678–1682, however, the Russian state made other demands on garrison servitors, insisting on labor and grain contributions, in particular. These greater demands were offset by heavier reliance on artillery and by sharing the garrison servicemen's new responsibilities with households of campaign servicemen. Together, the two groups gave garrison service a new meaning—one that combined military service in garrisons with the payment of dues to support the campaign regiments. The apparent shift in emphasis from active military duty to supply and other responsibilities was part of a larger change in the status and role of the south's campaign and garrison servicemen.

7

THE COLLAPSE
OF SOUTHERN
STATUS

The Odnodvortsy

Military reforms and economic changes precipitated fundamental redefinitions in the traditional notions of status throughout the southern provinces. The destruction of old status categories and the attempt to create new ones were by no means restricted to the south; however, the impact of such reordering was particularly visible there because it failed to implant new social categories acceptable elsewhere in Muscovy. Instead, it reinforced anomalous, regionally specific understandings of the factors traditionally defining status, such as landholding, service, taxpaying, and family, often at the request of southerners themselves. This did not preclude the existence of social groups there whose status was clearly recognizable in central Muscovite terms, such as large landholders, serfs, and townspeople. By the late seventeenth century, however, the Belgorod and Sevsk regions also contained more than 100,000 petty service families whose conditions had few parallels outside the south. In discussing the collapse of status for southern servicemen in the latter half of the seventeenth century and their fate during the Petrine reforms, this chapter will focus in particular on the group that came to be known as "smallholders" (*odnodvortsy*).

Seventeenth-century Muscovite society was organized around four major social orders: "Ecclesiastical, service, commercial and agricultural"[1]—the church, the army, townspeople, and the peasantry. Although these broad categories existed in law, they were infrequently the basis of social identification, which for most purposes was based on narrower distinctions. Thus service was an order that included, at its upper levels, all hereditary servicemen from the highest Moscow ranks to the poorest cavalrymen in the provinces (such as the hereditary servicemen or *deti boiarskie* of the southern frontier); within this group, clan, service, and wealth helped define an intricate hierarchy. Members of the recruited services, such as musketeers, were of much lowlier social origins; they commonly viewed themselves, and were treated, as a group separate from the hereditary services.[2] These narrower distinctions were not rigidly defined in law or in practice; given appropriate circumstances, individuals could change the narrow categories to which they belonged and even cross the boundaries between the larger categories.[3]

This description of a fragmented but orderly society better fits Muscovy in the early seventeenth century than in later decades. During the latter part of the century, in particular, the boundaries between the orders hardened, making movement between them more difficult. The well-known limitations on the Russian peasantry and town residents, laid down in the Law Code of 1649, expressed only part of that transformation. At the same time, the narrower distinctions were also being changed. Military reform at midcentury and again in 1678–1682 necessarily realigned the service hierarchy to include the new formation troops. The abolition of the precedence system (*mestnichestvo*) in 1682 is only one of the better-known results. A process of formal definition, recategorization, and rigidification was under way; it would continue into the eighteenth century, by which time social realities would have so changed that Russians would need new terms to describe them. "Estate" (*soslovie*),[4] "state" (*shtat*), "condition" (*sostoianie*), and "occupation" (*zvanie*) were among those they tried.[5]

This simplified description of the changes in Russian social categorization over two centuries is misleading in a number of ways. It might be construed as implying that the more rigid categories of the eighteenth century were simply an ossified version of the seventeenth-century social orders; that, for example, Muscovite servicemen turned into the eighteenth-century service elite (the nobility or *dvorianstvo*). Nothing so simple occurred; rather, social categories were redefined, often in dramatic ways. Recruited servicemen, in particular, did not all continue in the army. Musketeers, in particular, were forced out of service altogether, officially to become townspeople, members of the urban commercial category.[6]

The category of smallholders (*odnodvortsy*) was one of the more peculiar consequences of the redefinition process. It was delineated legally by a series of fiscal and military changes between 1710 and 1724, when the smallholders included more than 600,000 Muscovite servitors and their dependents, most of whom lived in the Belgorod and Sevsk regions. As a result of the early eighteenth-century changes, smallholders joined the ranks of the state peasantry, a designation they shared with Siberian hunters and other populations who ill accorded with the rest of the fiscal and military structure of the Petrine state.[7] In many ways, these smallholders

were a kind of intermediate group, between an enserfed peasantry and the
nobility (*dvorianstvo*) of the eighteenth century. The *odnodvortsy* paid
taxes like peasants but simultaneously held military obligations and property rights that were more consonant with noble status. In the eighteenth
century many of them vociferously proclaimed their right to the nobility;
there were others, by contrast, who had every right to the status of nobility
and who voluntarily joined the ranks of the smallholders.[8]

These smallholders have aroused extraordinarily intense historical interest and debate. The interest derives, in part, from a single issue: Were
smallholders an identifiable social group in the seventeenth century,
whose status was radically demoted from serviceman to peasant? And if
so, how did they come to be demoted? A variety of causes have been ad-
duced for the altered condition of smallholders, including the military-
fiscal needs of the state, the peasantlike economic circumstances of these
former servicemen, and the long-standing peculiarities of local service.[9]
However valid each of these factors independently, they collectively indicate the collapse of central Muscovite social definitions in the south, a
process that helped to isolate this group even before Peter I came to power.
When the Petrine government officially designated the category *odnodvor-*
tsy for the group, it did not change the character of smallholder duties and
responsibilities so much as the social label attached to it. The mistaken
belief that this eighteenth-century category derived from an identifiable
seventeenth-century social group probably lies in the existence of the term
odnodvortsy prior to the Petrine period. Nevertheless, the rapidly shifting
terminology of military service and remuneration that occurred in the second half of the seventeenth century as a result of military and fiscal reform
makes it difficult to trace the origins of the eighteenth-century group.

In the 1630s and 1640s the first *odnodvortsy* were a fairly large subset
of southern hereditary servicemen[10] who held small service lands (*pomes-*
t'ia) that they worked by themselves without serfs. Within the south they
were thus distinguished from fellow hereditary servicemen by their relative poverty. Their small landholdings supported garrison service in local
fortresses rather than distant campaigning, a purpose for which the landholdings were quite adequate. While this kind of service differentiated
them from most central Muscovite hereditary servicemen, it was not uncommon on frontiers outside the south. Similarly, given southern frontier
conditions, Cossacks, steppe patrolmen (*stanichniki*), and others whose
family origins would not have passed muster in the central provinces enrolled in southern hereditary service, although again this was not unusual
along other frontiers. In the 1620s Cossacks also dominated the garrison
of Tiumen' on Russia's other great frontier, Siberia.[11] Indeed, precisely because of these frontier conditions, the assumed congruence among status,
family, landholding, and prosperity that underlay Muscovite hereditary

service fit the seventeenth-century *odnodvortsy* quite neatly. Their suspect family origins, small estates, and relative poverty placed them on the lowest rungs of the status hierarchy. The term *odnodvortsy*, however, was apparently not truly a status category but a description; it was used by the bureaucracy rather than by southern hereditary servicemen themselves.

The eighteenth-century smallholder was quite a different creature. He shared with his seventeenth-century namesake the right to hold service land, the right to acquire other lands, and to own serfs. In these ways, the smallholders of the eighteenth century resembled the hereditary service elite of the 1600s as well as the nobility of the 1700s; in other ways, the differences between the two groups of men were quite startling. A seventeenth-century smallholder shared a lifelong responsibility for southern garrison service with salaried members of the lower service class, such as musketeers. The eighteenth-century smallholder served for a fixed term (fifteen years) in one of up to twenty smallholder regiments of frontier militia. The early seventeenth-century *odnodvorets*, as a hereditary serviceman, paid few taxes; instead, he contributed military dues, like the grain contributions that went to emergency supply and to his own and his garrison's support. Service, however, was his primary obligation. By contrast, after 1710 all smallholder households, and later each adult male in them, shared the tax burden (*tiaglo*) with town residents and unfree peasants, as well as supported the militia regiments. The taxpaying requirement generally took precedence over service in the frontier militia, even though militiamen on active duty were released from some of their normal tax payments. While the obligation to pay taxes also placed the smallholders on the far side of a traditional social gulf dividing taxpayers from the service elite, their landholding rights and service obligations distinguished smallholders from the peasantry.[12]

But who, exactly, became a smallholder in the eighteenth century? Although the two groups called smallholders in the seventeenth and eighteenth centuries shared overlapping membership, they were by no means identical; indeed, eighteenth-century smallholders cannot be defined by any of the characteristics of traditional seventeenth-century social identification, as a single example will make clear. In Kozlov province, nearly 25,000 servicemen and their dependents fell into the smallholder category early in the eighteenth century. The men of this group had no military service in common; they included 10,500 family members of garrison servicemen, as well as more than 6,000 members of campaign service families from the new formations. They ran the gamut of military service possibilities in late-seventeenth-century Muscovy (except for the old-style cavalry units), from officers through cavalrymen to rank-and-file infantrymen. The Kozlov smallholders had no common social attributes; they included not only hereditary servicemen and recruited servitors but also several thousand ex-peasants who had been militarized and who appear in this list as new formation dragoons. Finally, landholding patterns provide no obvious clue to what bound them together; both those with a right to personal lands (hereditary servicemen) and those who had no such right (musketeers, artillerymen, and dragoons) were called smallholders.[13] Many were also landless because the province of Kozlov at this epoch recorded far fewer land grants than required to support its servicemen.[14]

The absence of clear identifying features among these smallholders is neither anomalous nor apocryphal; it is instead a startlingly clear example of the ways in which underpinnings of social status had changed in the south during the preceding century. By the 1690s southerners no longer conformed to older understandings of landholding rights, the importance of family background, prosperity, and the relationship between military service and taxation. Without conformity in these particulars, a social hierarchy that rested upon shared attributes among members of each stratum simply collapsed. In 1685 what was a hereditary serviceman, if not a cavalryman with enough service land and serfs to support himself and a family with a similar service record? This definition, drawn from the reform decree of 1678, was precise and adjusted to new military conditions, but it was not at odds with the older, vaguer definitions of hereditary service. But how does a southern hereditary serviceman whose status had been confirmed by initiation (*verstan'e*) fit in if he also served in the infantry and held less land than many musketeers? Or how about a militarized peasant on the frontier who was now a soldier with service land to his name? The following section briefly reviews the disintegration in the south of the four traditional components of social status—landholding rights, family status, wealth, and the relationship between military service and taxation—that served as a prelude to the emergence of new and more consistent ways of ordering social groups in the southern population.

One of the key developments in the breakdown of the seventeenth century's social congruencies involved the changing conditions of southern landholding.[15] During the second half of the seventeenth century, the acquisition of service land ceased to be the nearly exclusive perquisite of hereditary military service it once had been. Early in the century southern military commanders had generally followed established methods for distributing service land, a process that began with the ceremony of initiation. The award of entitlements during initiation permitted the seeking out and formal claiming of a particular plot of land. For southern servicemen without the lineage to back up their claims, initiation with the award of service land validated entry into the service hierarchy, although a few individuals, steppe patrolmen and some Cossacks, for example, received service land, while generally remaining outside the system.[16] Meanwhile, members of the lower service class were often salaried rather than supplied with land.[17] If they received land, it was likely a parcel (*nadel*) of land that was the collective property of, for example, all musketeers serving in

Belgorod province.[18] In short, the ways in which southern land was distributed during the period of colonization generally maintained the established relationship between status and service, on the one hand, and remuneration (cash, *nadel*, or *pomest'e*), on the other. Those groups to which this did not apply were usually clearly identified and were marginal to the service hierarchy.

Later in the century, however, the traditional distinctions of landholding became incongruous with the demands of the new army. The crucial issue was demonstrably the state's inability to offer year-round salaries or supplies to new formation servicemen; instead, when they lacked other resources, such troops were quickly settled on land. As long as the new cavalry was perceived as the preserve of hereditary servicemen, a cavalryman's acquisition of service land was a new but acceptable variant on established landholding arrangements. Because most soldiers did not have the antecedents to claim hereditary service and thus service lands, however, such grants to infantrymen were problematic. Nonetheless, in the mid-1650s, even before the creation of the Belgorod Army Group, southern infantrymen received *pomest'ia* and were enjoined "to hold [their] land in service tenure, plow it, and name peasants [to it]."[19] The arrangement might have been part of the government's efforts to attract servicemen to the frontier, and hereditary servitors to new formation service, but infantrymen qua infantrymen still had no claim to service land. Nor could individual members of this group of soldiers legitimately stake out such a right on the basis of their own lineage; several of them were militarized peasants. Nevertheless, they became "soldier-service landholders" (*soldaty-pomeshchiki*).

This label, which notably did not lay claim to hereditary service status, embodied an important distinction between these infantrymen and hereditary servicemen. Infantrymen were not initiated (*verstannye*) unless they could demonstrate that they had the lineage appropriate to their claimed hereditary status. Indeed, no effort was made to accommodate even more traditional hereditary servicemen among the ranks of the initiated;[20] because such uninitiated individuals were not yet on record as hereditary servicemen, they could be absorbed into infantry service without so flagrantly violating status norms.

The situation that produced soldier-service landholders and uninitiated hereditary servicemen persisted into the 1660s and 1670s, gradually encompassing more men. By 1675 nearly one half the men in Kozlov province with claims to hereditary service stature served without benefit of initiation and could not have claimed service land in the established fashion.[21] Meanwhile, active members of the new formation forces who often had no claim to hereditary status were receiving service land by other means. For example, soldiers in Korotoiak province in 1675 received individual service land grants.[22] Former peasants living on Belgorod province's court lands who had been militarized in the 1640s were returned to serf-dom in the 1670s. Those who had served in the campaign army in the intervening three decades demanded that their freedom be granted on the grounds of military service. Indeed, perhaps in part because their number included cavalrymen, they requested initiation (i.e., hereditary status) as well as freedom. There is nothing in subsequent documents to suggest that their status claims were granted; nevertheless, by 1681 these former serfs had received personal grants of land in different villages as free servitors.[23] This odd landholding system continued to be protected from purchase and takeover by large landholders from outside the region.[24]

As the acquisition of service land through nontraditional means and by unconventional social groups became increasingly common, uninitiated hereditary servicemen, some active campaign servicemen, and, by the late 1680s, even recruited serviceman (especially those transferred to new for-mation duty during the 1678–1682 reforms) might hold service land. Con-fusingly, some of these small service landholders practiced collective agri-culture and occasionally received grants as a group; these group holdings, however, depended upon the individuals involved, rather than upon their common service function, and their lands were formally referred to as *pomest'ia*.[25]

Contractually recruited servicemen remained somewhat apart. In the 1660s and 1670s they continued to receive collectively held land parcels (*nadely*) close to the fortress town where they served.[26] Even after the 1678–1682 reforms, this distinctive form of remuneration remained for re-cruited servicemen who had not been forced into the new formations but who still served as musketeers, artillerymen, and the like, that is, re-cruited servicemen by the early seventeenth-century definition. Consider-able differences in land tenure remained between service land and these parcel holdings (*nadely*). In the late 1690s many recruited servicemen who had not been shifted to the new formations and from there to service land by military reform were formally redefined as urban residents, who then abandoned cultivation as a means of support.[27]

By the 1690s unconventional usages meant that service landholding in the south was no longer an attribute predicated upon membership in an elite family or hereditary military service. Instead, *pomest'e* was related broadly to service in the southern frontier's new formation regiments; what apparently distinguished service land from other forms of land remu-neration in that region was that it was issued in the name of an individual (rather than a group), a usage that foreshadowed the more personal conno-tations of the later term for hereditary lands, *imenie*.[28] Although these holdings were deliberately protected by the central government, the tacit redefinition of *pomest'e* was not generally accepted outside the confines of the south. Given their origin and purpose, new formation service land grants came from the Military Chancellery (*Razriad*), which exercised extraordinary powers in the southern regions. The Service Land Chancellery, the usual grantor, also issued the oldest and largest southern grants; that the chancellery held fast to the established understanding of service land served to isolate the unconventional service grants, institutionally as well as territorially. Thus a decree of 1685, which declared that official land cadastres and other documents were adequate substitutes in the southern provinces for more formal titles to *pomest'ia*, referred to them as "Belgorod army men's lands".[29] At the same time, the Service Land Chancellery, rather than validating claims under the decree, made southern lands increasingly inaccessible to southern smallholders.[30]

In any event, when V. M. Vazhinskii notes that about 25 percent of southern service land was held by smallholders in the Sevsk and Belgorod regions in the 1620s or even the 1640s, he refers to hereditary servicemen. The smallholders who held nearly 83 percent of southern lands in the late 1690s, however, were certainly not all hereditary servicemen. The appellation "smallholder," in other words, retained its association with service landholding, but the social implication, namely, that such land was held by a member of the service elite, had been lost.[31]

The changes in southern service land tenure have been accurately associated with a decline in the average size of estates. Southern hereditary servicemen had always received land entitlements that were somewhat smaller than elsewhere in Muscovy for similar levels of service, as befitted the relative newness of their towns. It is possible that the entitlements offered southerners declined still further in size toward the end of the century. More important, the acreage claimed and then cultivated by service landholders definitely dropped. A hypothetical serviceman from the Belgorod region might be entitled to the relatively large grant of, say, 608 acres (150 *chetverti*). In the 1630s he would have claimed 40 percent of his entitlement (about 243 acres of land). By the 1670s he would typically have claimed only 10 or 20 percent of his entitlement (about 100 acres). After 1678, even in the relatively prosperous Sevsk region, servicemen characteristically claimed and cultivated only 10–20 percent of the service land to which they were entitled. This shrinkage has been attributed variously to labor shortages, intense military demands, and pressure from large estate owners moving southward.[32] The cumulative impact was particularly visible in the most recently settled provinces. Even in the 1690s the older towns of the south had some reasonably large estates, presumably because southerners had been awarded lands there earlier in the century and, in some cases, because outsiders had moved into these provinces. Nearly 15 percent of estates in the provinces of Kursk and Belgorod (each founded in 1596) were over 400 acres in the 1690s. Newer towns like Usman' or Khar'kov, where most land was awarded and claimed later in the century, frequently had no holdings at all of that size.[33]

Under the circumstances, service landholding (and hereditary service) no longer conveyed economic advantage, as formerly assumed. Lands held by southern hereditary servitors and their social inferiors were becoming closer in size. In Kozlov in 1675 a serviceman, if initiated, might own on average 20 to 60 more acres than he would otherwise. Occasionally, the uninitiated even held larger grants than their initiated colleagues. At the same time, musketeers and other recruited servicemen generally continued to receive full-sized parcels, some of which nearly equalled the small service estates in size. It was not uncommon for recruited Cossacks, for example, to receive 80 to 100 acres of land.[34] As a group, those members of the lower service class with land remained somewhat less prosperous than the service landholders, but the gap was narrowing. By the 1690s nearly 60 percent of all southern service lands were less than 122 acres; 11 percent of such grants were as small as musketeer plots (less than 41 acres).[35]

The diminishing size of landholdings for southern servicemen presumed a gradual loss of prosperity. In a society where economic conditions were broadly related to land acreage under cultivation, petty servicemen were by definition less than wealthy. Even for small holdings, the availability of adult male laborers was also an important determinant of prosperity. Unfortunately, it is extraordinarily difficult to document the availability of labor for these small southern farms. Generally speaking, petty southern servicemen had little serf labor at their disposal and still less as the century went on. Nor were other forms of labor readily available. Heavy recruitment norms and periodic attempts to search out fugitive serfs further depleted the available male labor force. Little is specifically known about the overall frequency and effectiveness of such devices as hiring laborers (*batraki*) and dividing or sharing land and its military responsibilities (among *prokormshchiki, polovinshchiki,* and the like). It seems unlikely that southern servicemen drew upon a significant labor pool. Furthermore, the region's economy did not provide numerous alternatives to unproductive agriculture. The burden of military dues and some taxes also drew heavily on the cash, surplus grain, and the manpower of small farms.[36]

This entire process could be interpreted as the movement of southern service economies toward something resembling peasant economies. Given servitors' general loss of prosperity, there were indeed increasing economic similarities between the peasantry, on the one hand, and southern smallholders (regardless of social origin and landholding) on the other.[37] But what concerned servicemen in the southern provinces was not this change so much as the elimination of economic differences between different groups of southern servicemen. Understandings about service status were being violated; the higher status services ought to have been more prosperous; in particular, hereditary servicemen should have been wealthier than recruited servitors. Thus hereditary servicemen complained that they were dishonored by receiving grants equal in size to those of musketeers (they also argued that recruited men should receive land parcels only as tradition dictated). In the late 1660s and 1670s recruited servicemen objected to household assessments of dues and taxes, arguing that their responsibilities should be less than those levied on wealthier hereditary servicemen with larger lands.[38] This erosion of traditional social distinctions (based upon land tenure and wealth) between different service categories had its roots in the creation of a new formation army that could be neither supported nor supplied by the state. At the same time, the experience of serving in those new formations, or alongside them in the garrison services, helped to alter the categories themselves.

Traditionally, military service itself conveyed status, and different kinds of service represented different levels of status. The existence of distinctions among military duties was an important part of the social equation for servicemen. But it proved difficult to transfer even the broadest of the old-style service distinctions to the new-style campaign forces. For the few southerners who remained in the old-style cavalry, such questions did not arise; the old congruencies of landholding, military responsibilities, and wealth survived. But for new formation servicemen, service ceased to reinforce a major element of social status. Southern cavalry and lancer units were not as exclusive as in other parts of Russia but were considered socially superior among new formation units. Men of all ranks enrolled in the infantry, so men of southern hereditary service families often served in the same kinds of regiments as recruited men and former peasants.[39] For these individuals, important social distinctions were clearly registered at ceremonies of initiation and mustering or by appointment to an infantry regiment composed of hereditary servicemen. But the military activities of the infantrymen did not reflect those distinctions, although theoretically that could be changed by reappointment to a cavalry unit.

Garrison duty on the frontier, which had always offered fewer opportunities for advancement than campaign duty, similarly entailed few military responsibilities that were exclusive to a particular social group. Mounted garrison servicemen tended to be of the hereditary classes. The duties of skilled artillerymen or blacksmiths remained distinct, but these conveyed low, not high, status. Fortress service on the southern frontier offered no haven against the erosion of distinctions between hereditary and recruited servicemen taking place in the southern new formation forces. The reforms of December 1678 continued the erosion. Barring the few thousand men who remained in the cavalry, most southerners became infantry soldiers or garrison defenders. Although they were relegated to the infantry with little regard for their social sensibilities, hereditary servicemen in the south had, until 1686, the right to be reappointed to cavalry units, if their economic circumstances warranted it.

The treatment of family and clan as a component in social status reflected the declining emphasis on distinctions between hereditary and recruited service for all but the most elite of southern servicemen. Social position in general certainly continued to concern southern servicemen in the latter part of the seventeenth century, but increasingly that concern was not recorded in the manner officially recognized. From early on in the seventeenth century, of course, southern military men of all qualities and conditions often lacked the family histories requisite to their positions. But hereditary servicemen at musters and initiations quite routinely (if mendaciously) cited family histories of service. As the century wore on, initiation continued to act as a symbolic differentiator, setting apart the hereditary serviceman even when he served in a lowly infantry regiment. But subtle alterations took place in the ceremony itself. Initiation records late in the century frequently note only that a servitor's father and brothers are in the military, often without even mentioning their names. Far from documenting distant connections to Moscow's great clans, some of these ceremonial lists are inadequate even to reconstruct immediate family units. Furthermore, an unusually large number of hereditary servicemen remained uninitiated.[40]

This should not suggest that all social strata of the southern population gradually became indistinguishable. At the upper end of the hierarchy, the few wealthiest and best connected of the southern service elite continued to have access to the capital and perhaps to its great clans. And the line dividing the southern service population as a whole from its social inferiors was constantly emphasized. For example, southern servicemen were expressly forbidden for reasons of economic distress to enroll themselves as serfs as early as 1671–1672. Furthermore, if it was discovered that southern servitors had been serfs, their former masters were frequently prevented from reclaiming them. Fugitive serfs who had been enrolled in southern service for eight years by 1675 could not to be returned.[41] However erratically enforced, the existence of these policies (and the intermittent protection of southern landholding against outsiders) protected the status of southern petty servicemen as a group when changing conditions threatened them; as already discussed, this protection originated in central Muscovy's military goals and in southern demands and conditions.

Notably, no similar protections differentiated between recruited servicemen and members of the hereditary service class within the southern service population. From central Muscovy's perspective, such distinctions by default continued to rest on traditional criteria, whose meaning had been transformed by southern conditions; by the latter part of the century, however, the southern versions had clearly been judged inadequate by the Moscow elite. Despite questionable family origins, southern hereditary servicemen at the beginning of the century had had approximately the same opportunities for advancement up the provincial echelons to Moscow rank as other provincial servicemen of similar caliber. The subsequent creation of new formation units in the south, the continued mixing of social classes in the new regiments, and the dilution of service land tenure were perhaps necessary in the south, but the consequences did not conform to Moscow's social standards. A decree of 1659 barred the lower echelons of southern hereditary service from entry into the Moscow ranks.[42]

From 1659 on, the position of most southern hereditary servicemen in the eyes of Moscow's elite became still more precarious. On the one hand, the few southerners with the traditional attributes of hereditary service remained in the old-style cavalry and were treated as men of their stature were treated elsewhere in Muscovy. But the claims of other southern servicemen to hereditary status were frequently disregarded. During the reforms of 1678, for example, southern servicemen were treated differently from their counterparts elsewhere in Muscovy, forced into infantry service against their will, at least until their circumstances improved. After the reforms the south's already limited access to the Moscow service elite was quickly terminated. Servicemen from Sevsk (as well as Belgorod) were forbidden access to the Moscow ranks in 1685, and the children of hereditary servicemen from both Belgorod and Sevsk were directed into the local forces. Finally, in 1686 southern hereditary servicemen then in the infantry were forbidden to advance even into the south's cavalry units.[43] In short, southern servicemen were treated as members of the hereditary class only if they had retained the marks of status consonant with Moscow usage, despite changing regional conditions. Few southerners fit this description, certainly not the descendants of early-seventeenth-century smallholders; because they did not, they were categorized on the basis of their wealth and service at the point of reform, with little regard for family claims or past military responsibilities.

As a result, by the early 1690s the south was home to many servicemen who, however they defined their own social positions, were unable to demonstrate them to the rest of the country. Even from outside their own regions, it was clear that these men were servicemen, not part of the dependent population; beyond that, it was difficult to distinguish hereditary from recruited servicemen among the mass of southern servitors. On the contrary, the resemblances between the two groups were obvious. Service land was no longer limited to hereditary holders in the south; in a slightly modified form, it had became more broadly accessible. With smaller land grants and the general lack of labor, there was also relatively little difference in economic position among the service population. Nor did their military duties predicate permanent distinctions. These changes effectively marginalized southern servitors and limited their access to the traditional hereditary service hierarchy. To central Muscovy's hereditary elite, there was little about these southerners that evoked common origins, standards, and aspirations.

While these changes were in progress, the central government initiated a practical reorganization of southern servicemen's roles. In principle, at least, the old-style self-supporting cavalry served the tsar in the army, while the peasantry and townspeople bore the burden of taxes; service households normally paid military dues.[44] This simple division of responsibilities may have remained at the basis of social relationships, but after Muscovy began hiring salaried troops, it proved increasingly inadequate for the state's fiscal needs. Moscow's efforts to extract revenue in the Belgorod and Sevsk military regions redefined the relationship between taxpaying and service. That redefinition would be the basis of a new social category for petty southern servicemen in the eighteenth century.

The shortage of peasants in isolated southern provinces prior to 1650 gave rise to financial incongruities in the region. Thus servicemen who settled on taxable lands and had no peasants of their own found themselves paying cash taxes for the postal system (iamskaia gon'ba) and for the captives' ransom (polonianich'i den'gi), obligations that continued when these taxes shifted to household assessments in 1646 and combined into a single tax in 1678.[45] Taxpaying service households did not, however, share in all the taxes of the southern peasantry, and their tax payments appear to have had no immediate social impact.[46]

Military dues had a more complex impact. Initially part of local defense and upkeep, and less important than military activity,[47] dues were in most respects a normal component of frontier service.[48] For southern garrison servicemen before 1650, such dues included farming court lands, filling emergency granaries, and repairing local fortifications. As military contributions were reorganized in the latter part of the century, the dues system redefined the balance between its payers' military and fiscal responsibilities, a process with enormous social and economic consequences.

By the late 1660s the contributions made by town servicemen no longer primarily supported the garrisons; instead, annual grain payments, carting, boat-building, and caring for horses were increasingly undertaken in support of the south's new campaign regiments (or at least in support of regional goals). The garrisons' military responsibilities in defense of the frontier remained their dominant function; nonetheless, garrisons directed a great deal more of their activity toward dues paying than did campaign servicemen.[49]

Because dues assessments were often status-blind, the payment of dues from the 1660s on did nothing to counteract the increasing resemblances between hereditary and recruited garrison servitors. Military dues payments were not specifically attached to any service or status group, nor was any group excluded from them.[50] For example, all members of the Dedilov and Tula garrisons shared (with the province's peasants) the task of hauling materials to Voronezh to prepare for a Don grain shipment in 1673.[51] Boat-building at Voronezh in the same year also drew on the entire garrisons of twenty-five cities; some town residents and peasants also contributed.[52] There were exceptions, of course: recruited servicemen predominated among laborers on court lands in some provinces.[53] The dragoons of the Komaritskii district certainly contributed grain, paid cash for the purchase of horses, supplied carts, and repaired fortifications with greater frequency than the rest of the Sevsk region's population; but this district's organization, which made the rapid extraction of labor, cash, and supplies relatively easy, were as likely a reason for this as the inhabitants' former peasant status.[54]

The general move to household assessments for southern dues and taxes was closely related to the growing status blindness of military contributions. After the 1646 census, for example, the captives' ransom tax was collected at a set rate per taxable household, regardless of that household's wealth or status. Dues payments shifted to household payments faster in the south than in most of Russia: every forty households provided one cart and every seventy households one boat, regardless of exactly which households were involved. These assessments did not, of course, mean that each contributing household in a given province actually paid the same amount, nor that the assessments per household were the same in different provinces. They did, however, represent an official abandonment of contributions differentiated by status and wealth.[55] Although individual exceptions to this general trend persisted,[56] supplies for local campaign regiments in general came from an undifferentiated population, which was dominated by garrison servicemen but which also included a few peasants and still fewer townspeople.

Grain contributions paid between 1663 and 1683 were clearly part of this transition to status-blind dues. On the one hand, from the inception of regional grain collections, eighth-grain was assessed and collected in equal amounts from each household; on the other, not all garrison service households or all local residents were affected. Eighth-grain contributors had access to land, usually to service land. Thus eighth-grain rolls were dominated by smallholders (in the early seventeenth-century sense of that word): garrison defenders from hereditary service households and their closest equivalents—steppe patrolmen, Cossacks, and Ukrainian migrants. But there was no implication that the grain collections were connected to hereditary service status. The few peasant households that these servicemen owned, as well as ex-peasants, musketeers and other nonhereditary servicemen holding land parcels, could also be subject to the collections.

Southern garrison servicemen did not fail to dispute the assessments of military dues that appeared after 1663. Some argued that it was inappropriate to collect dues from them in years when their military obligations took them away from their provinces; others complained of the new dues' failure to acknowledge the differences in wealth implicit in different service categories. More than a few simply petitioned for exemptions in years of particular hardship and poverty.[57] These disputes, however, were about the conditions under which dues should be collected and from whom in the service population. Perhaps because of their dominance on southern dues lists and their earlier experience with similar local collections, southern servicemen were little concerned that similar obligations had been attached to taxpayers, rather than servicemen, elsewhere in Russia.

The reforms of 1678–1682 represented a crucial stage in identifying new relationships among southern servicemen. The support of the campaign army provided by the south proved vital in the context of ongoing disputes with the Ottoman Empire. As frontier defense became increasingly bolstered by artillery, town servicemen's contributions and taxes could be increased. The net of assessment also widened; grain was drawn from every household, without reference to land, rank, or ability to pay. No distinctions of wealth or former status remained.[58] At first glance, the reforms seemed to institutionalize the situation implied by prereform military dues in the south: an undifferentiated group, consisting primarily of garrison servicemen, paid dues to support the campaign army.

Nothing so straightforward took place. For one thing, it seems probable that garrison servicemen could not contribute much more than they had before 1678. Southern military dues after the reforms still resembled the cash and in-kind taxes paid by peasants in the north or even in parts of the Sevsk region;[59] but most southern contributors also bore individual military responsibilities unlike any peasant's. Perhaps for this reason, annual dues from garrison households rose in value only by a relatively modest half-ruble per household over the entire last half of the seventeenth century, while the support these garrisons alone could provide for the campaign troops fell far short of what was needed.

Meanwhile, a half century of military pressure had given rise to large numbers of troops in the south ill suited to sustained service in the field army. Under the circumstances, the contributions of these troops to supply were apparently as valuable as any military help they could offer in the field. They swelled the ranks of southern households contributing grain, labor, and other support. Their military responsibilities were not eliminated by this new requirement. In 1683 and after, however, military commanders gradually called upon them to serve in the campaign regiments only one year out of every two or three. Eventually, many of the troops staffed forward garrisons or served in labor brigades rather than in field units. In the early 1690s some town servicemen even joined them in this service, just as the campaign troops had earlier joined garrison servicemen in paying dues.

The new dues-paying servicemen of the 1680s were difficult to fit into any previously existing category. They had no common status in established terms, for their number included cavalrymen, hereditary garrison servicemen, musketeers, soldiers, and peasants. The kinds of service they performed varied from cavalry to infantry, from garrison and labor duties to campaign warfare. Nor did they share an economic status (such as small landholding) because the new rolls included some who may have had the right to land but who were in actuality landless. Nevertheless, all of these men served and paid taxes and military dues concomitantly. This combination of responsibilities set them apart from other categories, as did their relative poverty. An older name was applied to this new and distinctive social category—*odnodvortsy*; a new census of southern petty servicemen launched after 1684 recorded their numbers and locations.[60]

This category of convenience created by the state was challenged by some of its members. For example, in 1686, smallholders of Mtsensk province challenged the grain collection orders that grain "should be taken from all Mtsensk *odnodvortsy*: from lancers and cavalrymen and soldiers and garrison servicemen." They were not all alike, as the orders assumed; those who lived in town (i.e., who had little or no land) lacked the wherewithal to pay.[61] On other, equally traditional bases, petitioners argued that dues paying and service far from home were incompatible, and that point was sometimes conceded. Thus the Komaritskii dragoons' contributions were described as "freeing the dragoons from [campaign] service," or "in lieu of infantry duty." In the late 1680s hereditary town servicemen were similarly "excused from service" in order to cart goods to Crimea-bound armies.[62] Such concessions, while by no means routine, emphasized the increasing importance of the dues component of smallholder service. Meanwhile, the smallholder census proceeded slowly and with difficulty.[63]

Though these smallholders were virtually identical to those of the Petrine period, the men of the 1680s did not yet constitute a legally defined and socially recognized grouping. They contributed to the ever-growing cost of military change in the late seventeenth century from their small holdings; they also bore reduced campaign and garrison duties. But the fiscal responsibilities and economic circumstances they shared were not precisely defined in law or by social usage. They rested instead on local understandings and the state's fiscal requirements. But, at least in the south, local understandings and usages had lost the elaborate underpinning of relationships among service, wealth, landholding, and family that gave them social and institutional substance and that linked them to the rest of Muscovy. Nor was there another obvious basis for social distinctions to replace those lost, such as membership in a particular military service. The upward mobility of smallholders was severely limited, and their relationship to the rest of Muscovite society remained unclear.

The *odnodvortsy* as a group were not more completely defined in law and practice until 1710–1724. Efforts to generate more serviceable, modern troops based in the southern regions led Peter I's government to try a variety of expedients dividing service and supply responsibilities; like his predecessors, he applied different rules there than elsewhere in Russia.[64] By the turn of the century smallholders and other dues payers of the 1680s were (still) routinely providing support to campaign regiments. In 1699–1700 new forms of payment were introduced. Instead of equal in-kind payments from each household, cash payments were levied on each adult male, using a sliding scale based on former service; that is, former lancers and cavalrymen paid most, while artillerymen's relatives and the occasional peasant paid least.[65] This assessment proved the forerunner to assessment in 1710 of the "soul tax" (podushnaia podat') on smallholders and peasants alike.[66] The soul tax did not relieve the smallholders of their military responsibilities, however; by 1724, in light of the continuing need for local defense against Tatars and others, smallholders took up service in their own land militia regiments, with landholding and other rights to support that effort. The increasingly rigid definition of smallholder duties and responsibilities provoked furious protest from the smallholders themselves. Many of them appealed (as had their predecessors) to older understandings of status to support their claims to hereditary service. But the Senate, drawing on a century's growing social distance between central Muscovy and the servicemen of Belgorod and Sevsk, refused to recognize their claims to elite status, although some of the claimants offered even serf ownership as proof. Some servicemen used the new category as a means of evading the new pressures on the nobility. Either way, legal definition reinforced the isolation of the anomalous servicemen of the south; they remained a separate entity in Russian society—neither peasant nor nobleman—well into the nineteenth century.[67]

Muscovy in the late seventeenth century was in the throes of large-scale social realignment, a process catalyzed by the acceptance of Russia's military revolution. One of the groups most dramatically affected by that process were poor servicemen of the southern provinces. By the early eighteenth century a new social category had been created, the odnodvortsy. These smallholders performed military service and held land in service tenure, yet none of the associated claims to lineage and elite service were attached to their positions. Instead, they paid taxes like the peasantry. The separation of the smallholders into a distinct category followed the gradual dissolution of linkages that had been assumed in an earlier Muscovite social system: landholding to lineage, status to a distinctive military function, and wealth to both. This dissolution clearly resulted from the interaction of state needs and local demands on the southern frontier in the late seventeenth century. The new definitions, however, were imposed by a reforming state for its own fiscal and military convenience. In this regard, the demands and failings of military supply played a key role in isolating petty southern servicemen from the social, military, and economic structures that had created them.

CONCLUSION

Beginning in the 1630s, Muscovy invested money, manpower, and organizational resources in a century-long transformation of its army. The program had dramatic and unforeseen consequences. Military change in the frontier provinces was an important component of Russia's military revolution, and the progress of that momentous transformation is charted here not in law codes and government instructions but as it was lived in the crucible of Russian army activity—on the southern frontier. This process of reform was initiated by the Muscovite state and executed in the south, for the most part, through the offices of the Military Chancellery. The image of the Muscovite government that emerges from these activities, however, is not that of a powerful centralized state, imposing its unfettered will in occasionally draconian ways on the provinces. Rather, whatever success seventeenth-century chancelleries enjoyed in introducing the desired reforms was achieved through a complex series of initiatives that involved compromising with and accommodating regional interests and local officials. The development of a modern army and its support systems, moreover, had unintended social consequences. As Muscovy's ruling stratum adjusted to the new conditions of military service, the traditional bases of elite membership were gradually eroded. The southern frontier provinces became an arena for redefinition of the country's nobility, as the status system tried to deal with the new fiscal and military roles acquired by southern servicemen during the seventeenth century. The changes to army, central state, and social structure alike presaged the legal and military transformations that would be enacted by Peter I's government.

The patterns of military change that emerged from Russia's military revolution differed in significant ways from those in European states further west. Even as related to the visibly shared goals of fielding and supporting trained modern troops, the techniques used in Russia to create and sustain such forces were frequently adaptations of existing Russian arrangements rather than imported European methods. Although these adaptations corresponded to the country's particular social structure and to an unproductive agricultural economy, the new pressures they embodied led, for example, toward a complete reordering of Russian social norms. It would be misleading to view these techniques as incongruous or unsuccessful because they failed to produce a trained, standing army on the western and central European model. For not only the instruments of change but also the goals of the military revolution differed from the dominant European model. Russia's drive to produce "modern" forces was constrained by two competing needs. First, after the rapid expansion of Russian forces during the Thirteen Years' War (nearly ten times faster than elsewhere in Europe), retaining 100,000 men or more under arms became imperative to confronting the Ottoman Empire. And second, Russia's long, open southern and eastern frontiers required heavy investment in defense in both old and new ways. These competing needs placed heavy demands upon Russia's population and intensified the economic pressures of military change, affecting even household organization; Moscow clearly judged the need to mobilize rapidly a necessary political risk, important enough to risk both the patience and the resources of its subjects.

These particular emphases to military change were writ large in the experience of the southern frontier provinces. Here, as elsewhere in Russia, the clear focus of reform lay in the creation of infantry campaign regiments. Infantry soldiers were, of course, key to the new tactics and strategy envisioned for modern forces. Especially after the loss of the best Muscovite cavalry during the Thirteen Years' War (1654–1667), the effectiveness of foot soldiers was repeatedly and convincingly demonstrated by the experiences of war. The emphasis on infantry reform had further advantages in that soldiers in most of Russia could be drawn heavily from the unfree population, where recruitment least challenged prevailing social norms. In the south, Muscovy responded with the enrollment of more and more free men in infantry regiments. With each succeeding effort at reform, the number of soldiers grew until the two southern army groups mustered more than 20,000 such troops in the 1680s. Filling infantry regiments was the insistent aim of Military Chancellery decrees, instructions, and reprimands. The central state exerted itself to provide for these soldiers the pay, provisions, weapons, and European officers that would make them effective fighting men. In short, Muscovy succeeded very rapidly indeed in generating both a large number of soldiers and, to a lesser degree, the resources to support and train them.

Even in the southern provinces, whose residents in traditional Muscovite terms lacked wealth, high status, and political influence, the central state approached military change with great prudence. Along the frontier the Military Chancellery could not rely on serfs for its new soldiers because the region lacked a significant dependent population. Instead, each wave of military reforms tried to fill infantry regiments from the south's marginal populations. In 1653, for example, a call for volunteers was first directed at the unregistered and fugitive serf populations; in 1678 the state drew upon wanderers, provincial musketeers, and other men whose value as military recruits was increasingly dubious. These groups, too, provided inadequate numbers, and Muscovy was forced to employ the active military population as foot soldiers. The enlistment of servicemen in infantry regiments, however, ran counter to the elaborate status system of the Russian elite, which valued cavalry service, remuneration in land, and hereditary position. Initially, the children of southern servicemen, who were technically not yet part of that system, were conscripted as soldiers. Later, when established servitors followed them, the ceremony of initiation and service in separate regiments were used to distinguish among infantrymen of different social strata. Hereditary servicemen were reassured that they would be able to return to the more prestigious cavalry. In the south this cautious dealing complicated the issues of how to pay and muster such troops, and it created new kinds of social questions, but it was rewarded by rapidly growing numbers of soldiers and a minimum of overt protest.

The economic and organizational obstacles to paying and supplying Russia's new formation forces as befitted modern troops were so formidable that Muscovy quickly acceded to paying and supplying only the infantry and doing so only for part of the year. Even this required a variety of special regional and national arrangements, not all of which were consonant with a standing army. Southern soldiers represented an exaggerated case of the general problem because the resources available to them, beyond those provided by state support, were often very limited. The southern regions themselves could contribute little toward supporting their troops; not only was the south near the front lines of battle for most of the century, but it had a cash-poor economy, a small taxable population, and an unproductive frontier agriculture. Many soldiers were paid in land, which provided them with off-duty sustenance, even if it limited their military training time and linked them to the old status system. The south's particular contribution was an adaptation of the military dues traditionally paid by servicemen. Grain paid in kind into emergency granaries for besieged garrisons developed into a regional system of depot granaries that provisioned the southern infantry regiments as they campaigned south and west of Muscovy's borders. By the late 1680s this system became part of a countrywide provisioning system, which fed Russian infantrymen while they were on duty in a way that reliance on cash payments and markets could not have. This innovative expansion of an old military dues system in the south placed a significant economic drain on its contributors and undercut their military effectiveness; the regional organization of the provisioning system also made it difficult to expand provisioning to other troops. Nevertheless, southern supply did sustain Russian military activity beyond the frontier during the late seventeenth century.

The creation and maintenance of infantry regiments was of course not the only goal of Russian military reformers; in the south it was simply the most marked of changes to the campaign army. Changes to army organization, to the politically charged status of the old-style cavalry, and to the central state structure, though exceedingly important, were less central to southern life and have not been the primary focus of this analysis. For Russia, military revolution meant more than the creation of new formation forces; frontier defense was an exceedingly important and often underestimated component in the reform equation. Russia's border forces and fortifications were frequently updated and revised, in competition with the more noticeable changes in the campaign army. The early-seventeenth-century defenders of the southern border were its settled, colonizing garrisons. The subsequent construction of defensive fortified lines across the south required immense investments of cash and military personnel; the Belgorod line, largely complete by the mid-1650s, and the Izium line, mostly complete by 1682, were so effective against Tatar raids that defense became a matter of garrisoning the fortified lines and towns rather than patrolling the territory and calling out the army. The garrison service, designated specifically for that purpose, drew a significant share of men from the south's limited manpower. Late in the century, artillery bolstered the fortifications and the garrison forces; defense was supported in other ways, including the payment of the Don Cossacks (in grain, cash, and other items) as auxiliary forces. In the next century the importance of the southern frontier was rediscovered by Peter I, who, after eliminating the garrison forces at the start of his reign, ended by restoring them as a reorganized frontier militia. The redesigning, updating, and maintenance of southern defenses in the latter part of the seventeenth century achieved no more wholesale successes than did reform to the campaign forces. Tatar raids rarely circumvented the defensive lines after 1660, but the defensive forces suffered economic distress, social dislocation, and manpower shortages from the more immediate needs of a country at war. Nevertheless, their persistence argues the importance of older-style defense even during decades of campaign army reform.

The explication of the southern case offers a unique opportunity for comparing the Russian military revolution and its impact with that transformation as experienced by a variety of European states to the west. Russia shared numerous military goals with its neighbors, and it faced broadly similar questions as it mobilized to implement reform. However, the Russian context (and particularly the concomitant enserfment of the peasantry) imposed different techniques for the extraction of men and resources, politically defined the limits of rapid military change, prolonged a heavy emphasis on an older kind of frontier protection, and created correspondingly diverse results. The reorganization of the Petrine period, which often formalized the economic and social shifts that had accompanied earlier army reform, made Russia into a European power. Those changes also redefined and limited the Russian elite, delineated new political ties, and redistributed fiscal and service burdens, in the name of military reform and a reconstituted frontier defense.

Furthermore, the southern case makes several important points about the nature of Russian government in the seventeenth century. The Muscovite state that implemented these dramatic military changes exhibited a certain willingness to accommodate regional interests. The need to staff southern fortress cities, for example, was a regional defensive imperative requiring that the southern provinces be shielded from searches for fugitive serfs, who were filling the garrisons. The central government intermittently provided that protection until quite late in the seventeenth century, despite strong pressures to rescind it. Policies that accommodated regional goals did not always emerge from competing central governmental interests. Occasionally, the wishes of the southern elite itself helped redefine those policies. Thus southern service cities were strengthened as part of regional defensive policy; the acquisition of land in a frontier province was officially prohibited to anyone not serving its garrison, although the restrictions were applied to high-ranking Moscow servicemen more than to prominent southerners. The persistence of elaborate symbolic distinctions between hereditary and recruited servicemen in the infantry over a half century also reflects the government's willingness to accommodate local concerns about traditional status. Similarly, despite a countrywide effort to standardize the requirements for cavalry and infantry service in 1678, the Military Chancellery protected the existence of elite southern cavalry regiments in clear violation of those standards. The result of these and other regional adjustments to the reforms of 1678–1682, which were clearly intended to standardize service qualifications and centralize military governance, was to lower significantly the military quality of southern troops.

An important element to the success of the Military Chancellery in carrying out official policies lay in the chancellery's willingness to overlook noncompliance with its orders both by local officials and, more broadly, by southern servicemen. The payment of the grain dues that provisioned the Russian infantry offers a case in point. If a servitor did not bring his contribution to the granary, his failure was often ignored by local officials. If his noncompliance was recorded in local account books, Moscow rarely ordered the enforcement of sanctions, and, even then, regional and local officials might not undertake them. Moscow, although clearly aware of the difference between orders given to men from the capital and those left to local representatives, did not always act to rectify matters. Such leniency applied not only to unimportant matters but to undeniably crucial affairs as well. Desertion from military duty or failure to appear for musters, for example, often failed to bring severe sanctions from military authorities.

This is not to suggest that the Military Chancellery or the personnel of other central Muscovite chancelleries yielded in the seventeenth century to political pressure from the great clans or to organized protest from southern residents. The character of political decision making in Muscovy has to be judged largely by its consequences; detailed records of the processes leading to chancellery policies are lacking. But there is no record of prolonged clan interest in southern affairs. Although there were incidents of public protest in the south over local malfeasance, unduly heavy taxation, and similar matters, there was no vehicle for their becoming more than isolated occurrences. Rather, the Military Chancellery's behavior can be attributed broadly to southern conditions. Frontier life provided southerners with an opportunity to move on, to renegotiate their relationship to government by putting themselves temporarily out of its reach. Southerners took advantage of that opportunity in considerable numbers, especially in provinces closest to the edge of settlement. Even if migrants did not leave written records articulating these sentiments, their migration was interpreted in this way by the Military Chancellery, which, under the pressure of military change, fiscal shortcomings, and constant fighting, needed a cooperative and predictable populace to draw upon. The chancellery's leniency and adaptability can be understood as a form of forced recognition of demands by crucial southern service populations.

The common understanding of the Russian state in this period, as highly centralized and focused on the court and on Moscow, does not easily allow for such behavior. In the south, however, the Muscovite state could not be said to have exercised its authority through representatives unresponsive to the concerns of the governed; instead, it responded as best it could to pressing local needs and granted some leeway to provincial officials and their populations. This pattern cannot realistically be attributed to divided leadership, laxity, corruption, or other products of a temporarily weakened autocracy. Muscovy's recognition of southern interests, peculiarities, and diversity was a persistent, if occasional, feature of Muscovite activity for the best part of a century; it hints at an intricate interaction of local and regional elites with each other, with their counterparts in Moscow, and with agents and agencies of central bureaucratic power. The example of southern military change strongly suggests the need to reexamine the components and characteristics of the highly centralized state as usually depicted in Russian historiography. Just to cite one possibility, it may be that the process of centralization in Russia marched no more in lockstep with efforts at political and cultural standardization than it did in early modern France.

Issues about the nature of local and regional power are also implied by the changing organization of Muscovite authority in this period, which reflects a particular preoccupation with weighing important regional differences against the advantages of standardization. That is, in the early seventeenth century the south was ruled, as was most of Muscovy, by a series of geographically overlapping functional jurisdictions. The Service Land Chancellery dealt with land grants to hereditary servicemen, the Musketeers' Chancellery collected grain from those lands, and so on. This arrangement articulated authority in a way that made it singularly difficult to adjust policy from the center to the atypical characteristics of the frontier provinces. After 1650 the dominance of the Military Chancellery's Belgorod and Sevsk desks gave a kind of territorial unity to the governance of the south, and the Chancellery over the next decades proved adept at using at least some of the frontier's unique characteristics, although by 1678 the pressure to standardize many aspects of military life was great. The shortcomings of an army that operated with an old-style command structure, new formation regiments, and decentralized financial institutions were manifest. The regional structure of army administration was duplicated and proliferated, so that most of Muscovy was encompassed by similar military-administrative regions; the entire army was simultaneously transferred to a new formation command structure. Not only old-style troops but new-style officers complained bitterly, and the consolidation was not successfully implemented. At least in the south, reform produced troops that were militarily disappointing. The balance of needs and interests among local officials, central chancellery representatives, town elites, and an atypical southern service population was not successfully achieved by standardizing the organization of state power. This vacillation between distinctive and standardized articulation of central authority, it should be noted, corresponds inversely to the presence of "powerful" and "weak" leadership in Moscow, as that is usually understood.

Like military transformation elsewhere in Europe, the implementation of military change by the Russian state produced unintended social consequences. Throughout the country important characteristics of traditional Muscovite society were irrevocably transformed during the seventeenth century. Clan politics among the great families around the tsar altered, for example, as clan leaders prepared to move into the offices of an increasingly bureaucratic state. Existing social understandings for the ruling stratum of Russia were undermined by new kinds of military service, so that new definitions of elite status had to be developed. Categories throughout the social spectrum were redrawn and rigidified. These changes were not merely the minor adjustments that might be expected over time to any system of social understandings but major recategorizations that transformed the nature of the Russian social system.

The broad social redefinitions at the turn of the eighteenth century were not without their casualties. The population of the southern frontier, with its disproportionate representation of small, independent landholders and its few dependent serf households, did not evolve socially, economically, or militarily in step with the Muscovite metropolis during the seventeenth century. The incongruity between metropolitan and southern social status was sufficient to marginalize the southern smallholders, who were brusquely rejected by Moscow's elite with the creation of new legal and social categories early in the eighteenth century. The emergence in the south of a new social group, barred from the central service elite, was not the intended result of a long-term policy of military change. The Muscovite state used southern servicemen to the best of its ability—to avoid social disruption, to fill military needs, and to protect a valuable and vulnerable frontier—but it did not intentionally marginalize them. Social redefinition may have begun with deliberate military policy, but that policy interacted in myriad, subtle ways with regional political considerations, the needs of an atypical southern population, and the economic conditions of the frontier before culminating in the realignment of the elite status system. The new system moved Russia inexorably toward a new relationship between state and the nobility that would crystallize in the eighteenth century.

APPENDIX

Table 1
COULD MUSCOVY AFFORD TO PAY?

Formation	1663 "Salaries"	Number of Men Enrolled During		
		1663	1680	1687
Cavalry (*reitary*)	2 ch. rye 2 ch. oat	2,400	3,661	6,380
Dragoons	1/2 ch. rye 1/2 ch. oats	5,000	-------	-------
Infantry (*soldaty*)	1 ch. rye	9,202	16,003	17,028
Musketeers (*Moscow*)	4 ch. rye	600	746 (?)	-------
TOTAL Salaries (*issuing chetverti*)	rye oats	18,902 6,650	26,309 7,322	29,788 12,760

TOTALS OF ALL CATEGORIES OF GRAIN PAYMENT

Total Salaries (*dep. ch.*)		19,164	25,223	31,911
Don shipment to Cossacks (*dep. ch.*)		4,500	6,000	6,500
Kievan shipment (*dep. ch.*)		-------	12,000	18,851
TOTAL (*dep. ch.*) (*tons*)		23,664 2,556	43,223 4,668	57,262 6,184
Annual Grain Dues Assessments (*dep. ch.*)		31,482	46,000	-------
Approximate Returns (*dep. ch.*)		16,371	36,800	

Sources: RGADA f. 210 Belgorod kn. 100, ll. 4–100, 177; Belgorod kn. 152, ll, 458–end; Hellie, *Enserfment*, pp. 228, 271–2; Vazhinskii, "Uselenie," pp. 57, 62; Vazhinskii, "Sbory," pp. 31–32; Zagorovskii, *Belgorodskaia*, pp. 154–155.

Table 2
Emergency Grain Levies

Date	Total Levy	Ch. from South	Contributors	Ports of Departure
1663	17,500*	entire	peasants, towns, s. garrisons	Voronezh, Belgorod, Putivl, Smolensk
1677	15,000*	entire	peasants, towns of Sevsk region, Sevsk dragoons	Sevsk
1682			southern residents	Don cities
1686[†]	91,602	5,800*	peasants, towns, both s. regions	Briansk, Sumy, Khotmyzhsk, Akhtyrka, etc.
1688				Novobogoroditsa
1691	20,000	entire	Sevsk dragoons	Sevsk
1692	20,000	entire	Sevsk dragoons	Sevsk
1693	14,000	entire	peasants, towns, s. servicemen	Kursk, Akhtyrka, Khotmyzhsk
1694	20,000	entire	Sevsk towns, peasants	
1695		entire	peasants, towns, s. servicemen	Korotoiak, Voronezh
	94,687	19,100*	Sevsk peasants	Voronezh, Korotoiak, Ostrogozhsk
1696	9,922	entire	regiments of Slobod. Ukraine	Valuiki
1697[†]	106,737	27,342	Sevsk peasants, Belg. servicemen	Briansk
1698	160,890	37,000*	Sevsk dragoons, garrisons, regs. of Slobod. Ukraine	Voronezh, Romanov on Steppe
1699	198,780		Sevsk dragoons, peasants, Belgorod garrisons	Korotoiak
1700	124,494		peasants, Sevsk dragoons, Belgorod garrisons	

(*chetverti* × 0.108 = tons)
* These entries are calculated.
[†] These are total levy sizes, not just on-demand grain, because the individual components were hard to identify.

Sources: RGADA f. 210, Belgorod kn. 78, ll. 2–60; Belgorod kn. 163, ll. 1ff; Belgorod kn. 174; Belgorod stb. 1267; Belgorod stb. 1314; Novombergskii, *Prodovol'stvennoe*, vol. 1, nos. 307–10, 324–36, 346–72, 377–78, 381–82, 385, 396, 436–40, 445–46, 458, 487; Vazhinskii, "Sbory," pp. 27–37, 40; *AI*, vol. 4, no. 299.

Table 3
SERVICEMEN IN CAMPAIGN AND GARRISON SERVICE

	1668	1671	1675	1679	1681	1687
Belgorod army	15,000	14,000	19,452	23,000	33,268*	27,000
Belgorod garrisons	(11,782)	(16,857)	36,730	41,247	36,553	39,674
Sevsk army	20,500	15,587	15,888	27,117*	16,641	
Sevsk garrisons					5,842	7,692

POPULATION OF BELGOROD AND SEVSK REGIONS

Year	1650	1678	1700–1710
Service pop.	275,000	416,600	474,000
Total	532,500	934,100	2,090,400

All Belgorod army figures exclude Ukrainian regs.
* Includes Tambov forces
† calculated

Sources: Table 1; Chernov, *Vooruzhenye sily;* Ustrialov, *Tsarstvoyanie,* vol. 1, Appendix; Zagorovskii, *Iziumskaia,* pp. 39–40; RGADA f. 210 Belgorod kn. 79, 95, 100; Belgorod stb. 691; Sevsk kn. 15; Davies, "Prikaz stb. 859"; Bagalei, *Materialy* (1886), no. 22; Hellie, *Enserfment,* p. 271; *DAI,* vol. 9, nos. 46, 106; M. V. Klochkov, *Naselenie Rossii pri Petre velikom po perepisiam togo vremeni* (St. Petersburg, 1911); Iu. A. Tikhonov, *Pomeshchich'e kres'tiane v Rossii* (Moscow, 1974), p. 98; V. M. Vazhinskii, *Zemlevladenie,* pp. 54, 56, 65–66; Vazhinskii and Ia. E. Vodarskii, "K voprosu o razmeshchenii sluzhilykh liudei i ikh krepostnykh na iuge Rossii," *Voprosy istoricheskoi geografii i istorii geografii* (Moscow, 1973), pp. 117–30; Vazhinskii, *Naselenie.*

Table 4
MEN IN GARRISON SERVICE

TOTALS

Belgorod Totals	1676	1678		1682	1686	1695
All garrisons (66)	36,730	41,247		36,553	37,356	23,404
Hereditary servicemen	16,326	17,675		15,118		
Retired hereditary servicemen	885	1,282		1,067		
% Hereditary servicemen	39.5	48		41		
% Retired hereditary servicemen	5	7		7		

Sevsk Totals		1678	1679	1682		
All garrisons (12)		5,745	5,842	7,692		
Hereditary servicemen		783	1037	745		
Retired hereditary servicemen		305	549	353		
% Hereditary servicemen		15	18	10		
% Retired hereditary servicemen		39	53	47		

(*Continued on next page*)

169

Table 4—*Continued*

BY TOWN

belgorod towns Source (bk. no.)	1677 b95	1678 m93	1679 m103	1682 m126	1686 b132–33	1695 b1408/b1557
Akhtyrka	1100ᵁ	884ᵁ		346ᵁ	383ᵁ	
Andreev. Lozy				130ᵁ	91ᵁ	
Balakleia	275ᵁ	135ᵁ		104ᵁ	256ᵁ	
Belgorod	1102	1068	719	1230	1278	638
Belokolodets	291	279		342	268	232
Belopol'e	454ᵁ	900ᵁ		596ᵁ	495	
Bogodukhov	606ᵁ	500ᵁ			294ᵁ	
Bolkhovets	430	380	440	440	404	120
Borovlia		974ᵁ		395ᵁ	343	
Chern'	136	169		170	296	10
Cherniavsk	465	448		450	580	—/425
Chuguev	559	529		531	488	
Dankov	186	245		561	563	436/565
Dobryi	1513	1402		1113	1118	260
Efremov	437	476		894	822	325
Elets	1241	1197		1573	2246	1693/1914
Epifan'	213	220		97	128	
Gorodnoi	222ᵁ	275ᵁ		158		
Iablonov	636	670		877	829	454
Izium	218				744ᵁ	
Karpov	661	700		874	711	
Khar'kov	151	1399		1211	962	310
Khotmyzhsk	490	419		·418	561	234
Kolontaev	680ᵁ	814		216	194	
Korocha	658	645		660	596	454
Korotoiak	1192	1298		1324	1236	673/1233
Kostensk		348		441	421	156/418
Kozlov	4786	4501		4385	3735 (kn.36)	3949
Krasnopol'e	768	593ᵁ		165	175	
Krasnyi Kut	553	531ᵁ		195ᵁ		
Kursk	1463	1488			1679(kn.143)	
Lebedian'	429	356		531	509	403/856
Lebedin	1022ᵁ	1011ᵁ		664ᵁ	452ᵁ	
Livny	122	1007		1203	1213	566/1628
Maiatsk	92	211		182	140	
Miropol'e	549	588		207	175	
Mtsensk	360	473		614		53
Murafa	193ᵁ	306		95ᵁ	98ᵁ	
Nizhegol'sk	142	153		207	105	
Novosil	481	647		403	458	
Novyi Gorodok					274	
Novyi Oskol	596	512		707	669	549/639
Oboian	971	905		848	851	700
Oleshnia	178	261		294	219	140
Ol'shansk	560	508		525	493	282/453
Orlov gorodok	258	221		515	218	160/214
Ostrogozhsk	684	350		235	212	145/207
Perekop				218		

ᵁ indicates predominantly Ukrainian population

Table 4—*Continued*

	1677	1678	1679	1682	1686	1695
Saltov	109	209		168	223	
Sennoe		546		123	85	
Sokol'sk	744	698		700	504	438
Soliannyi				151	62	
Staryi Oskol	754	650		741	1220	1240
Sudzha	766	499		422	330	
Sumy		247		60	270	see Elets
Talitsa	225	273		214	209	
Tsarev-Borisov	(243)	170		51	271	
Uryv	53	63		62	53	see Korotoiak
Userd	466	414		488		712/534
Usman'	1044	1021		1241	889	816/1524
Valki	290	606		446	318	
Valuiki	570	634		468	629	185
Verkhososensk	350	303		393	605	294/384
Vol'nyi	357	414		375	362	159
Voronezh	1889	1823		2240/360	1990	728/1895
Zemliansk	746	712		564	736	982/710
Zmiev	275ᵁ	639		302	323	

Sevsk towns	1678		1679		1682	
Source (bk. no.)	m93		m103		m126	
	hrdty	**srvc**	**hrdty**	**srvc**	**hrdty**	**srvc**
Belev	558/308	18†	565/350	16†+1	819/33	21†
Bolkhov	812/531	18†	960/661	15†	960/661	31†
Briansk	507/72	16†	903	15†	795/48	0
Kamennoe	320	203	320	203	249	145
Karachev	480	8†+166*	432	5†+166*	469	22†
Kromy	357	62†	314	52†	616	14†+70
Nedrygailov	398	105	396	105	220	96
Orel	491	148†	404	388†	477	0
Putivl	686	14†+14*	651	14†+13*	1840	122†
Rylsk	375	94*	425	44†	431	103†+81*
Sevsk	761	7†	472	0	605	40†
Trubchevsk					211	0

* Indicates Cossacks with service lands
† Indicates retired servicemen

Table 5
ARTILLERY AND AMMUNITION IN SOUTHERN FORTRESSES

TOTALS

Usable Artillery Pieces Available in Belgorod Regional Fortresses

1668	1672	1678	1682	1686
130	365	636	627	588
n=15	n=25	n=62	n=60	n=55
		563	550	588
		n=55	n=55	n=55

Usable Artillery Pieces Available in Sevsk Regional Fortresses

1678	1679	1682
204	216	270
n=11	n=11	n=12
		252
		n=11

USABLE ARTILLERY AND AMMUNITION IN SOUTHERN FORTRESSES
Entries = no. artillery pieces / no. usable shots

Belgorod towns bk. no.	1668 b57	1671 b77	1672 b82	1678 m93	1682 m126	1686 b132–33
Akhtryka				9/398	9/398	9/398
Andreev. Lozy					6/132	2/32
Balakleia				3/90	5/100	5/935
Belgorod		50/3909	51/6715	45/8601	39/7046	24/4771
Belopol'e				4/395	8/193	4/395
Bogodukhov				2/50		2/45
Bolkhovets		11/1266	15/996	21/835	16/1484	11/30
Borovlia	5/450	5/406	5/440	3/267	5/450	5/440
Chern	6/210		13/n.a.	22/1060	13/603	16/810
Cherniavsk	3/1457	8/1384		3/1300	8/1322	9/1615
Chuguev				17/2003	7/630	12/—
Dankov	8/1123	7/207	8/2243	13/1344	24/2233	24/2137
Dobroe				13/1295	13/1295	15/1340
Efremov	13/738			11/744	10/743	10/743
Elets	11/1240	25/1510	18/2520	22/3336	21/2813	20/1470
Epifan'	5/770	2/199	4/193	5/620	5/220	20/220
Gorodnoi				3/74	3/n.a.	
Iablonov			30/2744	30/2359	28/2799	15/2239
Izium					5/n.a.	4/1222
Karpov			18/n.a.	5/110	16/n.a.	17/870
Khar'kov				11/346	11/354	14/—
Khotmyzhsk			15/300	20/1335	13/1555	14/1538
Kolontaev				2/150		
Korocha			15/1548	15/1518	21/1977	14/1268
Korotoiak				15/1230	14/1300	13/810
Kostensk				7/518	7/518	7/518
Kozlov				19/2189	20/1605	
Krasnopl'e				3/300	3/300	3/300

Table 5—*Continued*

	1668	1671	1672	1678	1682	1686
Krasnyi Kut				6/211		
Kursk	9/640	18/1408		14/2203		
Lebedian'	11/311	20/350		15/429	14/340	13/364
Lebedin	9/250	8/n.a.	8/800	9/873	9/883	9/800
Livny		12/396	1a3/n.a.	15/510	13/425	
Maiatsk				3/210	4/267	4/201
Miropol'e			8/450	3/384		
Mtsensk	27/1290	18/1445	6/577	19/1697	19/2277	
Murafa				1/96	1/n.a.	
Nizhegol'sk				6/422	6/211	6/—
Novosil	6/782	11/—	13/n.a.	15/1700	11/904	19/1525
Novyi Gorodok						2/100
Novyi Oskol			26/2179	26/2184	19/1178	21/1539
Oboian		10/n.a.	10/1000	19/2000	11/1100	9/999
Ol'shansk				3/250	8/850	8/708
Oleshnia			7/n.a.	9/308	9/393	9/393
Orlov gorodok				6/691	6/761	6/680
Ostrogozhsk				10/1188	12/1098	14/1143
Perekop					2/n.a.	2/200
Saltov				2/192	2/n.a.	2/192
Sennoe				3/296	3/290	
Sokol'sk				9/790	8/705	9/880
Soliannyi			2/226	1/62	4/236	
Staryi Oskol		16/2211	11/745	11/745	11/743	14/941
Sudzha	3/300	3/260	3/260	3/283	3/283	3/283
Sumy		12/890		12/1000	13/831	13/831
Talitsa	8/n.a.	8/430	8/522	8/832	7/642	8/632
Tsarev-Borisov				2/—	4/208	7/238
Uryv				3/106	3/270	5/90
Userd			5/339	5/548	5/539	
Usman'				20/1286	21/1779	18/2100
Valki				2/100	2/90	2/100
Valuiki				8/6676	19/6670	18/6622
Verkhososensk			8/287	3/120	5/450	8/738
Vol'nyi			10/700	9/908	11/1272	10/1060
Voronezh				24/1478	22/3000	23/3279
Zemliansk	6/n.a.	6/400		6/391	8/531	8/590
Zmiev				4/50	5/150	4/250

			1678	1679	1682
SEVSK TOWNS					
(bk. no.)			m93	m103	m126
Belev			14/1004	25/41	25/1004
Bolkhov			18/1722	16/2123	17/2463
Briansk			8/926	12/1873	8/1973
Kamen/Putvl'			11/1120	17/1125	17/1125
Karachev			7/n.a.	14/1026	14/1802
Kromy			8/515	10/296	3/296
Nedrygailov			8/313	2/49	5/321
Orel			24/2295	11/231	27/3402
Putivl'			21/3109	25/3030	41/4275
Ryl'sk			26/2083	28/2444	48/2984
Sevsk			59/8703	59/n.a.	50/7790
Trubchevsk					18/1441

NOTES

INTRODUCTION

1. See, for example, J. Teodorczyck, "L'armée polonaise dans la première moitié du XVIIe siècle," in *Histoire militaire de la Pologne: Problèmes choisis*, ed. W. Bieganski (Warsaw, 1970), pp. 95–113; Geoffrey Parker, *The Military Revolution: Military Innovation and the Rise of the West, 1500–1800* (Cambridge, 1988), p. 37.

2. Richard Hellie, *Enserfment and Military Change in Muscovy* (Chicago, 1971), pp. 271–72; Parker, *Military Revolution*, p. 24. But see also Simon Adams, "Tactics or Politics? The Military Revolution and the Hapsburg Hegemony, 1525–1648," in *The Tools of War: Instruments, Ideas, and Institutions of Warfare, 1445–1871*, ed. John A. Lynn (Urbana, Ill., 1990), pp. 44–47, where it is argued that these large armies were not intended to be regular commitments.

3. André Corvisier, in "Guerre et mentalités au XVII siècle," *XVII siècle* 1985 (July–September): 220, underestimates Russian military activity in the latter part of the century, omitting the Crimean campaigns of the late 1680s and the persistent fighting in Ukraine during the 1670s. The Ukrainian campaigns were responsible for some of the highest levels of recruitment into the army Muscovy experienced in the seventeenth century. V. M. Vazhinskii, "Usilenie soldatskoi povinnosti v Rossii v XVII veke po materialam iuzhnykh uezdov," *Iz istorii tsentral'no-chernozemnogo kraia: Izvestiia Voronezhskogo pedinstituta* 157 (1976): 63–64.

4. For Russia, the ratio of military effectives to population in the 1680s was about 1:50. John H. L. Keep, *Soldiers of the Tsar: Army and Society in Russia, 1462–1874* (Oxford, 1985), p. 89; André Corvisier, *Armies and Societies in Europe, 1494–1789*, trans. A. T. Siddall (Bloomington, Ind., 1979), p. 113. According to Corvisier, only Prussia and Sweden were more highly mobilized.

5. Jean Chagniot, "Guerre et société au XVII siècle," *XVII siècle* 1985 (July–September): 250; Caroline Finkel, *The Administration of Warfare: The Ottoman Military Campaigns in Hungary, 1593–1606*, Beihefte zur Weiner Zeitschrift für die Kunde des Morgenlandes, vol. 14 (Vienna, 1988), pp. 23–25, 48–49.

6. A brief overview of this relationship is offered in Richard Hellie, "Warfare, Changing Military Technology, and the Evolution of Muscovite Society," in Lynn, ed., *Tools of War*, pp. 74–99.

7. Brian M. Downing, *The Military Revolution and Political Change: The Origins of Democracy and Autocracy in Early Modern Europe* (Princeton, 1990), pp. 9–10, argues that the ability to muster nondomestic resources for military reform in this period encouraged the persistence of constitutional government in western Europe.

8. Charles Tilly, *As Sociology Meets History* (New York, 1981), pp. 115–16; Yves-Marie Bercé, "Guerre et état," *XVII siècle* 1985 (July–September): 263; Jean Meyer, " 'De la guerre' au XVII siècle," ibid., p. 286.

9. Parker, *Military Revolution*, p. 62. Alain Guéry, "Les finances de la monarchie française sous l'Ancien Régime," *Annales: ESC* 1978 (March–April): 219, points out that France lacked precise budgets at this time and relied on extraordinary or privately run collections to make up immediate shortfalls. See also Bercé,

"Guerre et état," p. 257. Muscovy also lacked state budgets until 1680, but this was not as clearly connected to the use of private collectors of tax revenues.

10. *PSZ*, vol. 1, no. 584; see *AMG*, vol. 3, no. 235, for instances of government payments being made in goods rather than in cash; cf. Stanislas Hoszowski, "L'Europe centrale et la révolution des prix," *Annales: ESC* 1961 (May–June): 441–56, which addresses the leveling of prices in the early seventeenth century.

11. K. V. Bazilevich, "Elementy merkantilizma v ekonomicheskoi politiki pravitel'stva Alekseia Mikhailovicha," *Uchenye zapiski MGU* 41 (1940): 3–34. Muscovy did, in a fashion, rely on tax farming and, like other European states, tried gradually to eliminate this method for collecting taxes over the seventeenth century. Relatively little is known about this process. Paul Alexander Bushkovitch, *The Merchants of Muscovy, 1580–1650* (Cambridge, 1980), pp. 158–59.

12. John Brewer, *The Sinews of Power: War, Money, and the English State, 1688–1783* (New York, 1989), p. 30; Carol B. Stevens, "The Politics of Food Supply" (Ph.D. diss., University of Michigan, 1985), pp. 29–30.

13. Bercé, "Guerre et état," pp. 259–60; Parker, *Military Revolution*, pp. 76, 80, summarizing Geoffrey Parker, *Army of Flanders and the Spanish Road, 1567–1659: The Logistics of Spanish Victory and Defeat in the Low Countries' Wars* (Cambridge, 1977), chaps. 2–3, 7–8; G. Perjès, "Army Provisioning, Logistics, and Strategy in the Second Half of the Seventeenth Century," *Acta Historica Academiae Scientiarum Hungaricae* 16 (1970): 35–46.

14. There is an extensive literature on the redirection of food resources and its political impact in France, including Steven Kaplan, *Bread, Politics, and Political Economy in the Reign of Louis XV*, 2 vols. (The Hague, 1976); in a theoretical context, Charles Tilly, "Food Supply and Public Order in Modern Europe," in *The Formation of National States in Western Europe*, ed. Tilly (Princeton, 1975), pp. 383, 392–96; Jean Meuvret, "Le commerce des grains et des farines à l'époque de Louis XIV," *Revue d'histoire moderne et contemporaine* 3 (1956): 169–203. That the movement of grain under state control did not take place on the marketplace may explain the absence of the food riot as a political phenomenon in early modern Russia. Cf. Louise Tilly, "The Food Riot as a Form of Political Conflict in France," *Journal of Interdisciplinary History* 2 (1971): 23–57, with A. N. Speranskii, "K voprosu o sushchnosti i kharaktere Psovskogo vostaniia, 1650 g.," *Istorik-marksist* 57 (1936): 124–38; Mikhail Nikolaevich Tikhomirov, *Pskovskoe vosstanie 1650 goda* (Moscow, Leningrad, 1935), and Tikhomirov, "Pskovskii miatezh XVII veka," in *Klassovaia bor'ba v Rossii XVII veka* (Moscow, 1969), pp. 352–96; A. Vasil'ev, ed., "Dokument o vosstanii 1650 goda vo Pskove," *Istoricheskii Arkhiv* 1 (1936): 67–72, the last three works for material about the Pskov riots taking place as grain bound for Sweden was shipped through the city.

15. See, for example, Hellie, *Enserfment*; Keep, *Soldiers*; A. V. Chern'ov, *Vooruzhennye sily Russkogo gosudarstva v XV–XVII vekakh* (Moscow, 1954); Gustave Alef, "VII: Muscovite Military Reforms in the Second Half of the Fifteenth Century," in *Rulers and Nobles in Fifteenth Century Muscovy* (London, 1983), pp. 73–108.

16. In western Europe the military revolution proved a politically and socially dramatic process. Michael Roberts, who coined the phrase "military revolution," argued that it fundamentally changed the impact of war on European societies, spreading war's burdens deeper and wider than ever before. Indeed, military

revolution in western Europe has been linked to a variety of important changes, from the reduction of civilian violence in France, to the instigation of fiscal transformation in Great Britain, to the reinforcement of the Junker hold on the Prussian social hierarchy. More recently, Brian Downing has argued that the character of western European governments in the early modern period was determined by their ability to pay for military change. Corvisier, "Guerre et mentalités," pp. 229–30; Brewer, *Sinews of Power*, p. xvii; Downing, *Military Revolution*, p. xi; Hans Eberhard Mueller, *Bureaucracy, Education, and Monopoly* (Berkeley, 1984), pp. 40–42.

17. Our knowledge of changes in the army structure in the late seventeenth century is very slim. Hellie, "Warfare," p. 92.

18. John H. L. Keep, "The Muscovite Elite and the Approach to Pluralism," *Slavonic and East European Studies* 14 (1970): 207–8, 215.

19. Recent work emphasizes the ways in which Siberia was forced into an all-Russian mold rather than the ways in which it retained and articulated its separateness. See N. I. Nikitin, *Sluzhilye liudi v zapadnoi Sibiri* (Novosibirsk, 1988).

20. See, for example, A. A. Novosel'skii, "Praviashchie gruppy v sluzhilom gorode XVII veka," *Uchenye zapiski RANION* 5 (1929): 315–35; Ann Kleimola, "Holding on in the Stamped-over District: The Survival of a Provincial Elite" (Paper delivered at the Conference on the Role of the Frontier in Rus'/Russian History, Chicago, 29–31 May 1992); Janet Martin, "The Novokreshcheny of Novgorod" (Paper delivered at the 21st National American Association for the Advancement of Slavic Studies Convention, 4 November 1989); and forthcoming work by Valerie Kivelson and Brian Davies.

CHAPTER 1: MUSCOVY AND ITS SOUTHERN PROVINCES

1. Hellie, *Enserfment*, p. 166, which is quoted in Parker, *Military Revolution*, p. 38. More recently, Richard Hellie has referred to the process as the "military revolution." Hellie, "Warfare," p. 74.

2. Alef, "Military Reforms," pp. 79–81, 106.

3. David Kirby, *Northern Europe in the Early Modern Period: The Baltic World, 1492–1772* (London, New York, 1990), pp. 147–50, 170–77.

4. Hellie, *Enserfment*, chaps. 11, 13, describes the process of adaptation in some detail.

5. Keep, *Soldiers*, p. 21, 36; Robert O. Crummey, *Aristocrats and Servitors: The Boyar Elite in Russia, 1613–1689* (Princeton, 1983), p. 36.

6. See, for example, the approach of Edward L. Keenan, "Muscovite Political Folkways," *Russian Review* 45 (1986): 115–81.

7. Keep, *Soldiers*, p. 13, quotes Sigismund von Herberstein, Adam Olearius, and Giles Fletcher.

8. John LeDonne, *Absolutism and the Ruling Class: The Formation of the Russian Political Order, 1700–1825* (Oxford, 1991), pp. viii, xii.

9. The term "upper service class" is Richard Hellie's. See Hellie, *Introduction to Muscovite Society* (Chicago, 1967), p. 16.

10. Ia. E. Vodarskii, *Naselenie Rossii v kontse XVII–nachale XVIII vv.* (Moscow, 1977), pp. 68, 71, 89; H. L. Eaton, "Early Russian Censuses and the Population of Muscovy, 1550–1650" (Ph.D. diss., University of Illinois, 1971), pp. 76, 85, 86.

11. B. H. Slicher van Bath, "Yields of Different Crops in Relation to the Seed,

c. 870–1820," *Acta historiae Neerlandica* 2 (1967): 34, 36, 52, 57, 60–61. Muscovite yields were in places so low as to be barely adequate for the support of a nonagricultural population. Hellie, *Enserfment*, p. 255.

12. Vodarskii, *Naselenie*, p. 192; Eaton, "Censuses and Population," p. 160; H. L. Eaton, "Decline and Recovery of Russian cities from 1500 to 1700," *Canadian-American Slavic Studies* 1977 (Summer): 220–52.

13. One could speculate that the Dutch were present because the Dutch Republic had its own defensive wall of wooden fortifications, built in 1605–1606. Parker, *Military Revolution*, p. 38; V. P. Zagorovskii, *Belgorodskaia cherta* (Voronezh, 1969), pp. 64–66.

14. Stevens, "Food Supply," table 4, p. 69.

15. Alan W. Fisher, "Muscovite-Ottoman Relations in the Sixteenth and Seventeenth Centuries," *Humaniora Islamica* 1 (1973): 214; Linda Gordon, *Cossack Rebellions: Social Turmoil in the Sixteenth-Century Ukraine* (Albany, N.Y., 1983), pp. 89–90.

16. The Habsburg Empire further southwest was part of this configuration but participated directly in the competition for the territory south of Muscovy largely through its support of the Poles. Cf. William H. McNeill, *Europe's Steppe Frontier, 1500–1800* (Chicago, 1964), pp. 14, 26, 140–42.

17. See table 3 of appendix; Zagorovskii, *Belgorodskaia*, pp. 27, 141; E. A. Razin, *Istoriia voennogo iskusstva*, 3 vols. (Moscow, 1955–1961), vol. 3, p. 228. The Belgorod garrison service fell to between 10,000 and 11,000 men in the mid-1660s, but this had to do in part with administrative division of the southern provinces and the pressures of a costly war; it was, in any case, temporary. These themes are elaborated in chapter 6.

18. Kleimola, "Holding On," p. 6, describes the organization of garrison service on the Riazan' frontier; Janet Martin, "Frontier Policies of the Muscovite State" (Paper delivered at the Conference on the Role of the Frontier in Rus'/Russian History, Chicago, 29–31 May 1992), p. 13, discusses the settlement of servicemen for defense purposes near the Novgorod frontier in the 1580s. Siberian garrisons were similarly organized, though the designation "town service" was not used.

19. V. P. Zagorovskii, "Nekotorye osobennosti kolonizatsionogo protsessa iuzhnoi okrainy Rossii v XVII veke i ego periodizatsiia," *Iz istorii Voronezhskogo kraia*, vyp. 3 (1969), p. 85; Vodarskii, *Naselenie*, p. 172; V. M. Vazhinskii, *Zemlevladenie i skladyvanie obshchiny odnodvortsev v XVII veke po materialam iuzhnykh uezdakh*, (Voronezh, 1974), esp. pp. 50–51. As I have noted elsewhere, however, many of these studies fail to consider the different speeds of colonization and settlement and the variety of colonizing settlers. Stevens, "The Politics of Food Supply," p. 38.

20. One town, Tsarev-Borisov, actually disappeared altogether. Zagorovskii, *Belgorodskaia*, p. 25.

21. Rossiiskii gosudarstvennyi arkhiv drevnikh aktov, f. 210, Razriadnyi prikaz, Sevskii stol, kniga 18, list 70 (hereafter, RGADA, f. 210, Sevskaia kn. 18, l. 70); A. A. Novosel'skii, "Raspad zemlevladeniia sluzhilogo goroda v XVII veke," in AN SSSR II, *Russkoe gosudarstvo v XVII veke: Novye iavleniia v sotsial'no-ekonomicheskoi, politicheskoi, i kul'turnoi zhizni* (Moscow, 1961), p. 239.

22. V. A. Aleksandrov, "Streletskoe naselenie iuzhnykh gorodov Rossii v

XVII veke," in AN SSSR, Arkheograficheskaia komissiia, *Novoe o proshlom nashei strany: Pamiati akademika M. N. Tikhomirovu* (Moscow, 1967), p. 239.

23. V. L. Kotel'nikov, "Ob izmenenii geograficheskoi sredy sel'sko-khoziaist-vennoi deiatel'nosti cheloveka," *Izvestiia vsesoiuznogo geograficheskogo ob-shchestva* 82 (1950): 144. A mid-seventeenth-century visitor, contemplating similar black-earth soils further to the southwest, wrote: "The fertility of the land produces grain in such abundance that they do not know what to do with it [the crop]." Guillaume le Vasseur de Beauplan, *Description de l'Ukranie depuis les confins de la Moscovie jusqu'à la limite de la Transylvanie* (Paris, 1861), p. 19. An English language version of the above is Beauplan, *A Description of Ukraine Containing Several Provinces of the Kingdom of Poland* (New York, 1959).

24. AN SSSR, Institut Russkogo iazyka, *Pamiatniki iuzhno-velikorusskogo narechiia*, vol. 1, *Otkaznye knigi* (Moscow, 1977), p. 55; Vazhinskii, *Zemlevlade-nie*, p. 98.

25. I. Stebelsky, "Agriculture and Soil Erosion in the European Forest Steppe," in *Studies in Russian Historical Geography*, ed. James H. Bater and R. A. French, 2 vols. (London, 1983); vol. 1, pp. 45–64, provides a recent summary of extensive Soviet, European, and American literature on the subject. For a discussion of available agricultural technology, see A. G. Sliusarskii, *Sotsial'no-ekonom-icheskoe razvitie Slobozhanshchiny v XVII–XVIII vekakh* (Khar'kov, 1964), p. 185; R. E. F. Smith, *Peasant Farming in Muscovy* (Cambridge, 1977), p. 10; E. I. Indova, "Zemledel'cheskaia praktika v tsentral'noi Rossii XVII veka," *Materialy po istorii sel'skogo khoziaistva i krest'ianstva SSSR* 7 (1969): 33.

26. Jacqueline Kauffman-Rochard, *Les origines d'une bourgeoisie Russe, XVI–XVII siècles: Marchands de Moscovie* (Paris, 1969), frontispiece map; cf. V. M. Vazhinskii, "Torgovye sviazi iuzhnykh gorodov v tret'oi chetverti XVII veka," in AN SSSR II, *Goroda feodal'noi Rossii*, ed. N. V. Ustiugov and V. I. Shunkov (Moscow, Leningrad, 1966), pp. 287–307; cf. AN SSSR, Institut Russkogo iazyka, *Pamiatniki iuzhno-velikorusskogo narechiia*, vol. 2: *Tamozhennye knigi* (Moscow, 1982), pp. 246–51; RGADA, f. 137, Mtsenskaia kn. 1, for the high proportions of local traders remaining even in border trading towns as late as 1691.

27. Vazhinskii, *Zemlevladenie*, p. 97, lists 26.7 percent of cultivated land and 23 percent of haying land as belonging to *odnodvortsy*, a term that in the early seventeenth century referred to hereditary servicemen without peasants; however, this figure excluded court land and land held by musketeers and other lower service class servicemen. The acreage of the court land unquestionably exceeded that of the lower service class servicemen, though some of it was untenanted; recruited servicemen constituted only about one-fourth of most garrisons. When they received land, it was in small plots. See, for example, Zagorovskii, *Belgorodskaia*, p. 27.

28. Eaton, "Censuses and Population," chap. 12.

29. Zagorovskii, *Belgorodskaia*, p. 127.

30. I. N. Miklashevskii, *K istorii khoziaistvennogo byta Moskovskogo gosu-darstva*, pt. 1: *Zaselenie i sel'skoe khoziaistvo iuzhnoi okrainy XVII veka* (Moscow, 1894), p. 15 n. 2.

31. Vazhinskii, *Zemlevladenie*, p. 59.

32. Hellie, *Enserfment*, p. 129.

33. A. A. Novosel'skii, "Vol'nye i perekhozhye liudi v iuzhnykh uezdov Russkogo gosudarstva v XVII v," *Materialy po istorii sel'skogo khoziaistva i krest'ianstva SSSR* 5 (1962):75, 77.

34. Brian L. Davies, "From Village into Garrison," *Russian Review* 1992 (October): 481–501, makes this argument for Kozlov province.

35. L. V. Cherepnin, "Klassovaia bor'ba na iuge Moskovskogo gosudarstva v 1682," *IZ* 4 (1938): 41–75; *PSZ*, no. 482, for example.

36. Zagorovskii, *Belgorodskaia*, pp. 117, 124–47.

37. Novosel'skii, "Raspad," pp. 240–49.

38. A. A. Novosel'skii, "Rasprostranenie krepostnicheskogo zemlevladniia v iuzhnykh uezdakh," *IZ* 4 (1938): 23–24.

39. Zagorovskii, *Belgorodskaia*, pp. 120–21; see chapter 2.

40. Zagorovskii, *Belgorodskaia*, pp. 145, 154–55. Prior to 1653 individual men may have been called to serve in the steppe cavalry army from southern lands, but most served in the garrison forces of local fortresses. There were also some new formation dragoon regiments in the southern provinces before 1653, but they were used for frontier defense, not campaigning. Davies, "Village," p. 481.

41. *AMG*, vol. 1, no. 1, cited in Kleimola, "Holding On," p. 6. Siberia had only garrison forces; central Muscovite garrison servicemen had few strenuous military duties, and these forces were the preserve of retirees and nonmilitary men. Beliaev, I. S., ed., "Dlia sravnitel'noi statistiki drevnei Rusi: Smetnye rospisi gorodovoi sluzhby 7194 (1686)," *ChOIDR*, god 3, pp. 39–40; Hellie, *Enserfment*, p. 192; Nikitin, *Sluzhilye liudi*, chap. 1.

42. See introduction, note 4; see table 3 of appendix for population size. Russia as a whole mustered 1.5–2 percent of its population under Peter I. Corvisier, *Armies*, p. 113.

43. Stevens, "The Politics of Food Supply," p. 119; RGADA, f. 210, Belgorodskaia kn. 79, ll. 310–29.

44. Vazhinskii, *Zemlevladenie*, pp. 55–58; Dmitrii Ivanovich Bagalei, "K istorii zaseleniia stepnoi okrainy Moskovskogo gosudarstva," *ZhMNP* 1886 (June): 271–73; D. I. Bagalei, *Materialy dlia istorii kolonizatsii i byta stepnoi okrainy Moskovskogo gosudarstva v XVI–XVIII stoletiiakh* (Khar'kov, 1886) p. 152.

45. For more detail, see Stevens, "Food Supply," table 2, p. 54. A final population shift, the migration of poor servicemen further south, was observed in the 1690s. Vazhinskii, *Zemlevladenie*, pp. 48, 56, 60–65.

46. The ratio of servicemen to total number of households would be inaccurate because some families had more than one adult male in active service.

47. Richard Hellie, "Ulozhenie Commentary: Preamble and Chapters 1–2," *Russian History* 15 (Summer–Fall–Winter 1988), 197.

48. V. M. Vazhinskii, "Melkoe sluzhiloe zemlevladenie odnodvortsev" (Dok. diss., Moscow State University, 1975), pp. 62–67.

49. Peasant populations in these northern provinces would begin growing again toward the end of the century. Vodarskii, *Naselenie*, appendix 7; Novosel'skii, "Rasprostranenie," pp. 21–22.

50. See Keep, *Soldiers*, p. 22, for a description of the service-military hierarchy in its entirety.

51. Whether the cash entitlement was to come from the central treasury or

from local sources (*iz cheti, s gorodom*) was also frequently specified. For example, see RGADA, f. 210, Sevskaia kn. 14, ll. 33–37.

52. Vazhinskii, *Zemlevladenie*, p. 110.

53. RGADA, f. 210, Sevskaia kn. 18, ll. 223–50, in an example from later in the century, lists hereditary servicemen with only 15 percent of their entitlements.

54. Miklashevskii, *K istorii khoziaistvennogo byta*, pp. 145–46; V. M. Vazhinskii, *Sel'skoe khoziaistvo v chernozemnon tsentre Rossii v XVII veke* (Voronezh, 1983), pp. 23, 25.

55. Musketeers' land parcels did not always turn out to be smaller than the land actually farmed by hereditary servicemen. M. D. Rabinovich, "Sud'ba sluzhilykh liudei starykh sluzhb i odnodvortsev v period oformlenii reguliarnoi Russkoi armii v nachale XVIII veka" (Kand. thesis, Moscow State University, 1953), p. 443.

56. L. Tverskoi, *Russkoe gradostroitel'stvo do kontsa XVIII veka: Planirovka i zastroika Russkikh gorodov* (Leningrad, 1953), pp. 166–67; A. S. Lappo-Danilevskii, "O velichine dvorovykh i ogorodnykh mest drevnerusskogo goroda po nekotorym dannym v pervoi polovine XVII veka," *Zapiski Russkogo arkheologicheskogo obshchestva*, n.s., vol. 3, vyp. 3–4 (1888), pp. 307–16.

57. For example, see RGADA, f. 210, Belgorodskii stb. 772, ll. 142–48.

58. An extensive literature exists on this and other aspects of the military revolution, of which Geoffrey Parker, *The Military Revolution*, is but one recent example. Similar status problems faced the Ottoman Empire as it modernized its armed forces.

59. Elsewhere, infantry drafts took peasants, but the conscripts were often supported by cash payments from the serfholders, not by land confiscated from serfholders and transferred to former peasants. For example, see *AMG*, vol. 3, nos. 376, 504; *DAI*, vol. 8, no. 40, cited in F. I. Kalynchev, *Pravovye voprosy voennoi organizatsii Russkogo gosudarstva vtoroi poloviny XVII veka* (Moscow, 1954), p. 71; Hellie, *Enserfment*, p. 360; Chernov, *Vooruzhennye sily*, p. 145.

60. *AMG*, vol. 2, p. 306; Zagorovskii, *Belgorodskaia*, p. 146; Hellie, *Enserfment*, pp. 192–96.

61. The Military Chancellery's powers in the south were significant from the late sixteenth century, but increases in those powers were pronounced during the construction of the Belgorod Defensive Line and again as regional campaign armies were formed. Peter B. Brown, "Early Modern Russian Bureaucracy: The Evolution of the Chancellery System from Ivan III to Peter the Great, 1478–1717" (Ph.D. diss., University of Chicago, 1978), pp. 469–70.

62. The evidence on this point is indirect; I find no traces of direct demands for accommodation, but there is ample evidence that men of hereditary status tried to avoid infantry service and preserve recognition of their particular standing. RGADA, f. 210, Belgorodskaia kn. 94, ll. 382, 386, 400–3; kn. 95, ll. 142–47, for example.

63. *AMG*, vol. 2, no. 617; A. Birzhe, ed., "Volnenie krest'ian Belgorodskikh metropolichikh dereven' v 1682 godu," *Krasnyi arkhiv* 79 (1939): "Petition from T. Ushakov," lists soldiers and cavalrymen formerly receiving food payments (*na prokorm*), who were asking for formal initiation; they did receive lands. The northern cavalry was more exclusively made up of hereditary servicemen because interlopers were purged after the war was over. Hellie, *Enserfment*, p. 198.

64. For example, see RGADA, f. 210, Sevskaia kn. 14, ll. 134–66, 209–22; I. V. Arsen'ev, ed., *Dedilov i ego uezd v voennom otnoshchenii po neizdannym*

aktam XVII veka (Kiev, 1913), nos. 8, 19, 34; A. V. Chernov, "TsGADA kak istoch-nik po voennyi istorii Russkogo gosudarstva do XVII veka," *Trudy MGIAI* 4 (1948): 135.

65. Zagorovskii, *Belgorodskaia,* pp. 154–55.

66. Hellie, *Enserfment,* pp. 215–16; Keep, *Soldiers,* pp. 82, 85–86.

67. RGADA, Smotr kn. 35, ll. 186–95.

68. RGADA, f. 210, Sevskaia kn. 16, ll. 473–85, offers an example of a re-cently initiated Russian officer, but a typical relationship between an officer's mili-tary and economic status and his entitlement has proven difficult to formulate.

69. RGADA, f. 210, Sevskaia kn. 18, ll. 52–53, lists *gorodovye kopeishchiki* as well as *dvorovye reitary.*

70. The function of initiation as described here extends and, to a certain degree, contradicts Kalinychev, *Pravovye voprosy,* p. 55. For examples of the vary-ing information contained in initiation testimonies, cf. *PSZ,* vol. 2, no. 744, with *AIuB,* vol. 3, no. 341. Different conditions for initiations are described in Keep, *Soldiers,* p. 32, and N. Vtorovoi and K. Aleksandrov-Dol'nik, eds., *Drevnie gramoty i drugie pismennye pamiatniki, kasaiushiesia Voronezhskoi gubernii i chastiu Azova: Voronezhskie akty,* 3 vols., 2d ed. (Voronezh, 1851–1853), vol. 1, no. 173 (1671). For an example of muster and initiation procedure, see RGADA, f. 210, Sevskaia kn. 18, ll. 52–70, 216–35.

71. The *sotni* were not eclipsed until after the reforms of 1678–1682.

72. V. P. Alekseev, *Biudzhet razriada v 1650–1652: Novyi dokument k ist-orii zemskogo sobora, 1648–1649* (Moscow, 1900), p. 8–10; M. V. Dovnar-Zapol'-skii, ed., *Materialy dlia biudzheta razriadnogo prikaza* (Moscow, 1900); Pavel Ni-kovaevich Miliukov, *Gosudarstvennoe khoziaistvo Rossii v pervoi chetverti XVII stoletiia i reforma Petra velikogo,* 2d ed. (St. Petersberg, 1905), p. 71–74.

73. Brown, "Bureaucracy," pp. 469–70; Brown, "The Pre-1700 Origins of Peter the Great's Provincial Administrative (*Guberniia*) Reform: The Significance of the Frontier" (Paper delivered at the Conference on the Role of the Frontier in Rus'/Russian History, Chicago, 29–31 May 1992), esp. pp. 16–20.

CHAPTER 2: FOOD AND THE MILITARY BEFORE 1663

1. Jacques Bertin et al., *Atlas des cultures vivrières* (Paris, 1971), Russian area maps; Smith, *Peasant Farming,* pp. 33–35; L. N. Vdovina, "Pishcha i utrav," in *Ocherki Russkoi kul'tury XVII veka,* 2 vols. (Moscow, 1979), vol. 1, pp. 219–20.

2. For example, see N. A. Gorskaia, "Obrabotka zerna i zernoproduktov v tsentral'noi chasti Russkogo gosudarstva vo vtoroi polovine XVI–nachale XVII vv.," *Materialy po istorii sel'skogo khoziaistva i krest'ianstva SSSR* 6 (1965): 36–54; N. Ia. Novombergskii, ed., *Ocherki vnutrennego upravleniia Moskovskoi Rusi XVII stoletiia: Prodovol'stvennoe stroenie: Materialy,* 2 vols., vol. 1 (Tomsk, 1914), nos. 394, 399.

3. Smith, *Peasant Farming,* pp. 256–59. Lower estimates, ranging upwards from one pound of bread daily, presume a more varied diet. See Fernand Braudel, *The Structures of Everyday Life,* 2 vols., trans. Sian Reynolds (New York, 1981), vol. 1, p. 132. Three pounds of bread daily could be baked from 3.28 *chetverti* of grain a year. Smith, ibid., uses 3 *chetverti* of rye with supplements from other grains.

4. See, for example, the list of professions from the Muscovite marketplace in 1638 in I. S. Beliaev, ed., *Rospisnoi spisok goroda Moskvy, 1638 goda*, vol. 1 of *Trudy Moskovskogo otdela voenno-istoricheskogo obshchestva* (Moscow, 1911), pp. xvii–xx; Vdovina, "Pishcha," pp. 219–21.

5. After 1652, in particular, there were attempts to increase income from distilled spirits. M. Ia. Volkhov, *Ocherki istorii promyslov Rossii, vtoraia polovina XVII–pervaia polovina XVIII vekov: Vinokurennoe proizvodstvo* (Moscow, 1979), p. 31; Gorskaia, "Obrabotka," p. 61; C. B. Stevens, "Trade and Muscovite Economic Policy toward the Ukraine: The Movement of Cereal Grains during the Second Half of the Seventeenth Century," in *Ukrainian Economic History: Interpretive Essays*, ed. I. S. Koropeckyj (Cambridge, Mass., 1991), pp. 180–82.

6. See, for example, R. E. F. Smith and D. Christian, *Bread and Salt: A Social and Economic History of Food and Drink in Russia* (Cambridge, 1984), pp. 74–78, 88. There was some imported, and still less domestic, wine (in the twentieth-century sense of that word). Sliusarskii, *Sotsial'no-ekonomicheskoe*, pp. 215–16.

7. G. G. Gromov, "Zhilishche," in *Ocherki Russkoi kul'tury XVII veka*, vol. 1, pp. 191–92, 196–97. Urban households also had such storage areas. RGADA, f. 210, Belgorodskaia kn. 76, l. 11.

8. G. K. Kotoshikhin, *O Rossii v tsarstvovanie Alekseia Mikhailovicha*, trans. and annotated by Benjamin Uroff (Ph.D. diss., Columbia University, 1970), p. 113; A. I. Zaozerskii, *Tsarskaia votchina XVII veka: Iz istorii khoziaistvennoi i prikaznoi politike tsaria Alekseia Mikhailovicha* (Moscow, 1937), pp. 20–21. It should be repeated that Muscovite yields were in places so low as to be barely adequate for the support of any nonagricultural population. Hellie, *Enserfment*, p. 255.

9. Novombergskii, *Prodovol'stvennoe*, vol. 1, nos. 13–14, 47; vol. 2, nos. 386–89; Arcadius Kahan, "Natural Calamities and their Effect upon Food Supply in Russia," *JGOE* 1968 (September): 371–72.

10. A point also amply made in west European historical literature. C. Tilly, "Food Supply and Public Order," pp. 383, 392–96.

11. Borivoj Plavsic, "Seventeenth-Century Chanceries and Their Staffs," in *Russian Officialdom*, ed. Walter Pintner and Don Rowney (Chapel Hill, N.C., 1980), p. 37; Hellie, *Enserfment*, pp. 163, 271; Smith, *Peasant Farming*, pp. 256–59; and most recently, Dianne L. Smith, "Muscovite Logistics, 1462–1598," *SEER* 1993 (January): 35–65.

12. Eaton, "Decline and Recovery," pp. 220–52.

13. For example, see P. O. Bobrovskii, *Perekhod Rossii k reguliarnoi armii* (St. Petersburg, 1885), pp. 80–98. In chapter 1, Bobrovskii discusses other European systems. See also Chernov, *Vooruzhennye sily*, pp. 179–80.

14. Because it lacked a large taxpaying population of townspeople and peasants, the south contributed limited cash revenues at midcentury. Some servicemen did pay limited taxes, and most made other contributions in the form of labor dues: boat-building, fortification repair, and the like. Vazhinskii, *Sel'skoe khoziaistvo*, p. 77, calculates the cash equivalent of all service responsibilities.

15. P. N. Miliukov, *Spornye voprosy finansovoi istorii Moskovskogo gosudarstva* (St. Petersburg, 1892), pp. 92–95; Miliukov, *Gosudarstvennoe khoziaistvo*, pp. 40–42, 120.

16. More accurately, the organization run by the Musketeers' Chancellery is

the only national supply system I have been able to discover in the literature on seventeenth-century Russia.

17. Note on dry measures: The dry measure used for issuing grain from government granaries was a *razdatochnaia chetvert'*. In this text, 1 issuing *chetvert'* = 162 pounds prior to 1678 and 216 pounds thereafter. The dry measure used for depositing grain payments into the granaries was the deposit *chetvert'* (*priemnaia chetvert'*); it was 1.3 times the issuing *chetvert'* (RGADA, f. 210, Belgorodskaia kn. 78, ll. 283–84). In this text, 1 deposit *chetvert'* = 216 pounds until 1678 and 288 pounds thereafter. These conversions are necessarily approximate. The *chetvert'* was the principal dry measure for grain. It had numerous subdivisions (1 *chetvert'* = 2 *osminy* = 4 *poluosminy* = 8 *chetveriki*). When an official deposit *chetvert'* (*priemnaia chetvert'*) was standardized for the south ca. 1650, it weighed 6 *pudy* (216 lbs.); between 1673 and 1678, it was raised to 8–9 *pudy* (288–325 lbs.). RGADA, f. 210, Sevskii stb. 5, ll. 1–8. Earlier *chetverti* were not standardized, varying by a factor of up to eight just within the southern provinces, but have been converted to their equivalents in post-1650 deposit chetverti in the text. Dry measure equivalents are .75–1.5 bushels for rye; 1.125–2.25 bushels for oats. Bushel weights are from U.S.D.A., *Agricultural Statistics for 1980* (Washington, 1980), pp. v–vii; V. M. Vazhinskii, "Razvitie rynochnykh sviazei v iuzhnykh uezdakh Rossii" (Kand. thesis, Moscow State University, 1963), p. 15.

18. The musketeers' grain tax, as structured by the reforms of 1678–1682, became a principal contributor to Peter I's Provisions Chancellery in 1700. *PSZ*, vol. 4, no. 1764. A full-fledged commissariat was not established until sometime after 1700, however. V. N. Avtokratov, "Pervye komissariatskie organy Russkoi reguliarnoi armii, 1700–1710 gg.," *IZ* 68 (1961): 163–88.

19. Provincial musketeers consistently numbered about 30,000 after the 1630s. The number of Moscow-ranked musketeers dropped to 4,000 in 1630. Thereafter, the number of Moscow-ranked troops grew, although they ceased to be stationed exclusively in Moscow. Chernov, *Vooruzhennye sily*, pp. 127–28, 162; Hellie, *Enserfment*, p. 202.

20. See, for example, S. B. Veselovskii, *Soshnoe pis'mo: Issledovanie po istorii kadastra i pososhnogo oblozheniia Moskovskogo gosudarstva*, 2 vols. (Moscow, 1915–1916), vol. 1, pp. 415–17; Chernov, *Vooruzhennye sily*, pp. 160–61; Novombergskii, *Prodovol'stvennoe*, vol. 1, no. 286; Hellie, *Enserfment*, p. 126; Miliukov, *Spornye voprosy*, pp. 92–95. Miliukov argues that there were actually two distinct taxes; one was the cash tax from the north, whose assessments were based on cultivated acreage (*sokha*), and the other was another form of musketeers' grain, which was collected in kind from a grouping of peasant households, here about ten (*zhivushchaia chetvert'*). In 1672 musketeers' grain in Voronezh province was based on a mixture of the two assessments (*zhivushchaia chetvert' soshnogo pis'ma*). L. B. Veinberg and A. Poltoravskaia, eds., *Materialy dlia istorii Voronezhskoi i sosednykh gubernii*, 2 vols. (Voronezh, 1887, 1891), vol. 1, *Voronezhskie akty*, no. 66, pp. 84–86.

21. There were exceptions. The Novogord area, for example, retained and distributed locally the grain it collected for the musketeers' grain tax. Other areas, such as Kazan' and the extreme north, did not contribute to this tax at all. I. A. Golubtsov, "K istorii podatnoi reformy, 1679–1681," *Istoricheskii Arkhiv* 1959 (September–October): 157; Brown, "Bureaucracy," p. 490.

22. Miliukov, *Gosudarstvennoe khoziaistvo*, pp. 40–42, 58–59; Miliukov, *Spornye voprosy*, pp. 90–95; Veselovskii, *Soshnoe pis'mo*, vol. 1, pp. 415–17.

23. Musketeers' grain was used to pay new formation troops based or paid in Moscow. Miliukov, *Gosudarstvennoe khoziaistvo*, pp. 43–58, 120, n. 2; S. G. Strumilin, "K voprosu ob ekonomike Petrovskoi epokhi," in *Ocherki ekonomicheskoi istorii Rossii i SSSR* (Moscow, 1960), p. 307; *PSZ*, no. 1764. E. D. Stashevskii, *Smeta voennykh sil Moskovskogo gosudarstva v 1663 g.* (Kiev, 1910), pp. 20–29, also cited in Hellie, *Enserfment*, p. 227, mentions that 70,000 *chetverti* of musketeers' grain should have been collected in 1663. Even supposing it were entirely distributed to musketeers (which it was not), this allows a maximum of 1–2.6 *chetverti* annually per musketeer, which was a low salary for all but the provincial musketeers.

24. The number of musketeers in the south rose to 8,500 during the construction of the Belgorod Defensive Line. Aleksandrov, "Streletskoe naselenie," p. 238; Zagorovskii, *Belgorodskaia*, pp. 27, 141, 155.

25. P. P. Epifanov, "Ocherki iz istorii armii i voennogo dela v Rossii," (Dok. diss., Moscow State University, 1969), pp. 35–38; *AAE*, vol. 4, no. 280; Keep, *Soldiers*, p. 71.

26. On the consolidation of civilian governmental powers in the south by the Military Chancellery, see Brown, "Bureaucracy," p. 470.

27. A decree of 1661–1662 lists residents of the "Ukrainian, field, and Seversk towns" as the southern payers of musketeers' grain. The "field" (*polevye*) towns were geographically within what became the Belgorod Military-Administrative Region, but the term predates the building of the Belgorod Defensive Line and so refers only to towns of that vintage. The Ukrainian towns were just south of the older Tula defensive line; the Seversk towns lined the southwest border and eventually became part of the Sevsk Military-Administrative Region. Another source mentions only the Ukrainian and Seversk towns. Veinberg and Poltoravskaia, *Materialy . . .* , vol. 1, *Voronezhskie akty*, no. 66; Novombergskii, *Prodovol's-tvennoe*, vol. 2, no. 372. There are numerous other reports of musketeers' payments from the same towns. Ibid., vol. 1, nos. 145, 168, 263.

28. Eaton, "Censuses," pp. 197–200; Miliukov, *Gosudarstvennoe khoziais-tvo*, pp. 4–5; or cf. Vodarskii, "Naselenie," pp. 198–212.

29. This estimate of southern musketeers' tax payments is derived from intermittent tax records from the appropriate provinces. Annual contributions from Belgorod, Voronezh, Putivl', Belev, Tambov, and Usman' for various years between 1660 and 1672 amounted to a total of 312 tons (2,890 six-pud deposit *chetverti*); because tax rolls were rarely corrected over that period, they have been simply added together. The other 860 *chetverti* are estimated payments from other provinces within the southern regions. Some of these, such as Valuiki, Livny, and Oskol, had almost no peasants and therefore would have paid little tax. RGADA, f. 137, Voronezhskaia kn. 1; RGADA, f. 210, Belgorodskaia kn. 79, ll. 235–39; Novombergskii, *Prodovol'stvennoe*, vol. 1, nos. 145, 168, 263.

30. Novombergskii, *Prodovol'stvennoe*, vol. 1, no. 263. Musketeers' grain in the south was collected at a rate of 2.33 deposit *chetverti* of each grain per grouping of peasant households (called a *zhivushchaia chetvert'*) from ecclesiastical land and at 1.75–2.25 deposit *cheverti* per grouping from hereditary and service lands. Veinberg and Poltoravskaia, *Materialy . . .* , vol. 1, *Voronezhskie akty*, no. 66; Vtorovoi

and Aleksandrov-Dol'nik, *Drevnie gramoty*, kn. 3, no. 156, pp. 143–47; Miliukov, *Spornye voprosy*, pp. 102–3. In Belgorod province in 1668 musketeers' taxpayers contributed one-half the amount per household that their free neighbors paid to other collections. RGADA, f. 210, Denezhnaia kn. 312, l. 26.

31. *PSZ*, nos. 509, 522; Miliukov, *Spornye voprosy*, pp. 102–3; Veinberg and Poltoravskaia, *Materialy . . .* , vol. 1, *Voronezhskie akty*, no. 66.

32. The taxpayers were responsible for transporting the grain to Moscow. See RGADA, f. 210, Belgorodskaia kn. 78, ll. 2, 29–30, 63–64, for example.

33. See RGADA, f. 210, Belgorodskaia kn. 78, ll. 247–317, for example. The Belgorod city granaries paid the local Moscow-ranked musketeers (*strel'tsy*) 70 percent of their available grain in 1669–1670. Granary income for that year derived from local and regional taxation only; there is no mention of musketeers' grain. Belgorodskaia kn. 78, ll. 317–end; Belgorodskaia kn. 79, ll. 347–50ob.

34. RGADA, f. 210, Belgorodskii stb. 618, ll 497–511; also see notes 35, 47 below.

35. RGADA, f. 210, Belgorodskii stb. 772, ll. 142–48; Belgorodskii stb. 643, ll. 224–36; Novombergskii, *Prodovol'stvennoe*, vol. 1, nos. 71, 230; Miklashevskii, *K istorii khoziaistvennogo byta*, p. 145 n. 2.

36. These are issuing *chetverti* (162 lbs. rye). RGADA, f. 210, Belgorodskii stb. 643, ll. 244–332 (for 1668–1670); Belgorodskii stb. 772, ll. 142–48 (for 1672–1673); Novombergskii, *Prodovol'stvennoe*, vol. 2, no. 264 (for 1681–1689). Belgorodskaia kn. 100, ll. 35ob.–39, mentions salaries from 4 rubles and 891 pounds grain (5.5 *chetverti*) up to 5 rubles and 1,728 pounds grain (8 *chetverti*) in 1682, while Belgorodskaia kn. 79, ll. 271–81, 330, gives lower salary levels of 729 to 891 pounds grain (4.5–5.5 *chetverti*) annually. The title of a commanding officer in a musketeer regiment was "head" (*golova*) until 1680, when he became a colonel (*polkovnik*). *PSZ*, no. 812. The cash amount of these salaries is substantially the same as those quoted for musketeers at the beginning of the seventeenth century, although the rye was often later supplemented by an equal amount of oats. *AAE*, vol. 3, no. 148.

37. RGADA, f. 210, Belgorodskaia kn. 76, 115, 156.

38. On location of granaries, see Novombergskii, *Prodovol'stvennoe*, vol. 1, nos. 17, 31; Miklashevskii, *K istorii khoziaistvennogo byta*, p. 57. On uses of grain, see Novombergskii, *Prodovol'stvennoe*, vol. 1, no. 3 (Oskol town accounts for 1634), no. 71 (musketeers' land). On Boboriko, see note 39 below.

39. Novombergskii, *Prodovol'stvennoe*, vol. 1, nos. 46, 49.

40. Bagalei, *Materialy* (1886), no. 40; Bagalei, *Materialy dlia istorii kolonizatsii i byta Khar'kovskoi i otchasti Kurskoi i Voronezhskoi gubernii* (Khar'kov, 1890), nos. 35, 38; Novombergskii, *Prodovol'stvennoe*, vol. 1, nos. 4, 7, 27, 39; on insistence that military men farm, and do so before Tatar attack, see *PSZ*, nos. 49, 87; Novombergskii, *Prodovol'stvennoe*, vol. 1, nos. 5, 16.

41. The use of the word *zhalovan'e* does not imply a regular salary in a set amount. Contributions to the support of individuals at the local level could be nearly annual, especially to the church, but their recipients were not exactly salaried. Amounts varied and petitions were often necessary before payment was made. Grain loans were interest-free, but effort was exerted to collect them on time; the bookkeeping, undertaken by a granary head (*golova*) and sworn deputies (*tseloval'niki*), was often meticulous. Novombergskii, *Prodovol'stvennoe*, vol. 1, nos. 3, 5, 6, 8, 11, 15, 30, 35, 36, 42, 43, 53, 80, 91, 134, and others.

42. On the Siberian frontier, where food supply problems were even more pressing, arable tenth was also adapted to local conditions. James H. Gibson, *Feeding the Russian Fur Trade: The Provisionment of the Okhotsk Seaboard and the Kamchatka Peninsula, 1639–1856* (Madison, Wis., 1969), p. 156. For other similarities between Siberia and the south, see Nikitin, *Sluzhilye liudi*, pp. 195–97.

43. Arable tenth obligations could apply to musketeers and Cossacks, as well as other members of the garrison. S. Tkhorzhevskii, "Gosudarstvennoe zemlevladenie na iuzhnoi okraine Moskovskogo gosudarstva v XVII veke," *Arkhiv istorii truda v Rossii* 8 (1923): 64–72. Working on arable tenth was enormously time-consuming. Miklashevskii, *K istorii khoziaistvennogo byta*, pp. 223–24.

44. The same parallel might be drawn between construction work on the defensive line and work performed by peasants elsewhere in Russia. Zagorovskii, *Belgorodskaia*, pp. 86, 88; Zagorovskii, *Iziumskaia cherta* (Voronezh, 1980), p. 128. Records show no awareness on the part of servicemen of these parallels.

45. Zaozerskii, *Tsarskaia votchina*, pp. 20–23; G. K. Kotoshikhin, *O Rossii v tsarstvovanie Alekseia Mikhailovicha: Sovremennoe sochinenie*, ed. and with commentary by A. E. Pennington (Oxford, 1980), p. 150.

46. RGADA, f. 210, Belgorodskii stb. 618, l. 478; Novombergskii, *Prodovol'stvennoe*, vol. 1, nos. 19–24, 27, 39, 41, 84; vol. 2, nos. 302, 359, 360.

47. Novombergskii, *Prodovol'stvennoe*, vol. 1, nos. 65–66, 127–28; Miklashevskii, *K istorii khoziaistvennogo byta*, pp. 215–16, 280–81.

48. RGADA, f. 210, Belgorodskaia kn. 152, ll. 130, 133; Novombergskii, *Prodovol'stvennoe*, vol. 1, nos. 12, 35, 39, 74, 99, 129, 131, 158, 170, 184, 185, 193–216, 270; Miklashevskii, *K istorii khoziaistvennogo byta*, pp. 235–36. A full granary was the responsibility of the resident military governor. F. P. Shelekhov, "Glavnoe intendantskoe upravlenie. Istoricheskii ocherk," in *Stoletie voennogo ministerstva, 1802–1902* (St. Petersburg, 1903), vol. 5, pt. 1, p. 5; *PSZ*, no. 1540.

49. Kursk taxes were assessed on groupings of peasant households (*zhivushchaia chetvert'*), which Kursk atypically had. Novombergskii, *Prodovol'stvennoe*, vol. 1, nos. 149, 270.

50. RGADA, f. 210, Belgorodskaia kn. 152, ll. 129–34; V. P. Zagorovskii, "Zemledel'cheskoe naselenie v pridonskikh uezdakh na Belgorodskoi cherte i vozniknovenie pervykh sel 'za chertoi,' " *EAIVE* 1964 (1966): 202; A. A. Novosel'skii, "Dvorstovye krest'iane Komaritskoi volosti vo vtoroi polovine XVII veka," in AN SSSR II, *Voprosy istorii sel'skogo khoziaistva, krest'ianstva, i revoliutsionnogo dvizheniia v Rossii* (Moscow, 1961), p. 67; Sliusarskii, *Sotsial'no-ekonomicheskoe*, pp. 192, 209–11, 216–17; Novombergskii, *Prodovol'stvennoe*, vol. 1, nos. 55, 58, 100, 123, 133, 163, 214, 244, 303. Again, payments similar to tenth-grain in the south are reported in Siberia. M. I. Navrot, "Okladnaia kniga Sibiri, 1697," *Problemy istochnikovedeniia* 5 (1956): 187.

51. For example, the volume of replacement taxes for five major tracts of arable court land listed in Miklashevskii, *K istorii khoziaistvennogo byta*, p. 235; Novombergskii, *Prodovol'stvennoe*, vol. 1, nos. 123, 203.

52. Cf. E. V. Anisimov, *Podatnaia reforma Petra I: Vvednie podushnoi podati v Rossii, 1719–1728 gg.* (Leningrad, 1982), p. 166.

53. Zagorovskii, "Zemledel'cheskoe," p. 203; Zagorovskii, *Belgorodskaia*, pp. 246–48; Vazhinskii, "Melkoe," p. 180.

54. V. M. Solov'ev, "Goroda Belgorodskoi cherty nakanune krest'ianskoi

voiny 1670-1671," *Problemy istorii SSSR* 10 (1979): 47; Miklashevskii, *K istorii khoziaistvennogo byta*, p. 280; Novombergskii, *Prodovol'stvennoe*, vol. 1, nos. 5, 8, 11, 15, 30, 34-36, 42-44, 48, 53, 61, 64, 70, 80, 84-86, 90-92, 96-98, 113-14.

55. Novombergskii, *Prodovol'stvennoe*, vol. 1, nos. 4, 10, 12, 17, 19, 25-27, 29-31, 40, 44, 48-49, 53, 56, 83, 91, 100, 108, 124, 158, 166, 170, 303.

56. Novombergskii, *Prodovol'stvennoe*, vol. 1, nos. 55, 58, 65, 101, 103, 132.

57. F. P. Sorokoletov, *Istoriia voennoi leksiki v Russkom iazyke v XVI–XVII vekakh* (Leningrad, 1970), p. 142. On cash outlay, see S. M. Troitskii, "Finansovaia politika Russkogo absoliutizma vo vtoroi polovine XVII i XVIII vv.," in AN SSSR II, *Absoliutizm v Rossii* (Moscow, 1964), p. 306; Strumilin, "K voprosu," pp. 302-8; E. D. Stashevskii, "Biudzhet i armiia, " in *Russkaia istoriia v orcherkakh i statiakh*, ed. M. V. Dovnar-Zapol'skii, 3 vols. (Kiev, 1912), vol. 3, p. 417; Pierre Goubert, *Ancien Régime French Society, 1600–1750* (New York, 1973), pp. 126-39.

58. V. P. Zagorovskii, "Donskoe kazachestvo i razmery Donskikh otpuskov v XVII veke," *Trudy Voronezhskogo universiteta*, vol. 53, vyp. 1 (1960), pp. 135, 137-38, 140-44; Novombergskii, *Prodovol'stvennoe*, vol. 1, nos. 581-83; on record keeping, see ibid., nos. 40, 48, 54, 61, 77, among others.

CHAPTER 3: ARMY REFORM AND REGIONAL CONSOLIDATION, 1663–1682

1. The simultaneous interest in both grain and cash is indicated by the existence of a Chancellery for Grain and Cash Collections between 1654 and 1682. Peter Brown, "Bureaucracy," pp. 582–609. Other chancelleries collected only cash for cash salaries, however.

2. Shelekhov, "Glavnoe," p. 3; Zaozerskii, *Tsarskaia votchina*, p. 231–33.

3. The net effect of changes cited in note 17 of chapter 2 was that the weight of one *chetverik* (i.e., 1/8 *chetvert'*) was constant throughout.

4. Unlike eighth-grain duespayers in the south, Novogorod's eighth-grain taxpayers in 1663 were peasants. Novombergskii, *Prodovol'stvennoe*, vol. 1, no. 585.

5. Modern infantrymen were supported by their former lords, and national collections continued to feed campaigning troops. Hellie, *Enserfment*, p. 196; P. Nebol'sin, "O Russkikh soldatakh i drugikh voennykh chinakh do Petra velikogo," *Sovremennik* 13 (1849): 123-54.

6. Chernov, *Vooruzhennye sily*, pp. 187-88; Anisimov, *Podatnaia*, pp. 243-44.

7. Southern grain collections are the best studied of the Military Chancellery efforts, but such studies as exist tend to see collections as intermittent phenomena. See, for example, V. M. Vazhinskii, "Sbory zaprosnogo khleba v kontse XVII veka dlia obespecheniia krimskikh i azovskikh pokhodov," *Izvestiia Voronezhskogo gospedinstituta* 153 (1975): 23-46.

8. The processes of Muscovite decision making have to be deduced; to my knowledge, governmental deliberations of this kind simply were not recorded.

9. Not all men under arms were fielded at once, but Muscovy actually mustered more than 100,000 men before 1670 for the Doroshenko campaigns. Hellie, *Enserfment*, pp. 267-73.

10. Stashevskii, *Smeta*, pp. 25–28. The Belgorod army sum is calculated from pay schedules and Hellie, *Enserfment*, pp. 227–28.

11. As above, this is deduction; the first Muscovite state budget was compiled for the year 1680.

12. K. V. Bazilevich, *Denezhnaia reforma Alekseia Mikhailovicha i vosstanie v Moskve v 1662 g.* (Moscow, Leningrad, 1936), pp. 19, 27.

13. *AMG*, vol. 3, nos. 190, 582, 644; Russia, Ministerstvo iustitsii, Moskovskii arkhiv, *Opisanie dokumentov i bumag khraniashchikhsia v Moskovskom arkhive Ministerstva iustitsii*, 21 vols. (St. Petersburg, Moscow, 1869–1921), vol. 13 (Moscow, 1903), "stolbets 989, Belgorodskogo stola"; A. G. Brueckner, *Mednye den'gi v Rossii, 1656–1663* (St. Petersburg, 1864), pp. 27–28.

14. RGADA, f. 210, Belgorodskii stb. 546, ll. 1, 5; Novombergskii, *Prodovol'stvennoe*, vol. 1, no. 77. In the Novombergskii document, the assessment was not a *chetverik*.

15. The Grain Chancellery drew no resources from the area and contributed supplies directly to campaigns, ostensibly for musketeers; it did draw farm labor for Bogoroditsa from nearby southern towns like Dedilov. Miliukov, *Gosudarstvennoe khoziaistvo*, p. 224; Zaozerskii, *Tsarskaia votchina*, pp. 21, 223–33. I have not been successful in my attempts to consult the archives of this chancellery, which were being catalogued during my visits to the former Soviet Union.

16. 20,419 *chetverti*. RGADA, f. 210, Belgorodskii stb. 546, ll. 553–82; Vazhinskii, "Sbory," p. 28. Quotation from Belgorodskii stb. 546, l. 1.

17. RGADA, f. 210, Belgorodskii stb. 546, ll. 1, 335, 391, 397, 465, 467, 469–80.

18. RGADA, f. 210, Belgorodskii stb. 545, ll. 1–4. In all likelihood, the Grain Department kept records for all provinces under the Military Chancellery's jurisdiction; it seems to have fallen into disuse after the Peace of Andrusovo. Miliukov, *Gosudarstvennoe khoziaistvo*, p. 224.

19. See notes 39–42 below.

20. Miliukov, *Gosudarstvennoe khoziaistvo*, p. 114; Bobrovskii, *Perekhod*, p. 83; Troitskii, "Finansovaia," pp. 295–96; V. O. Kliuchevskii, "Russkaia rubl' v XVI–XVII vekakh i ego otnoshchenie k rynochnom," in *Sochenenie* (Moscow, 1959), vol. 7, p. 223.

21. Grain was also probably more readily available than cash to some parts of the Muscovite population. Vazhinskii, "Melkoe," p. 142, suggests that small markets were fueled by the need for cash to pay taxes.

22. Cf. RGADA, f. 210, Belgorodskaia kn. 79, l. 372, with Denezhnaia kn. 114, l. 22; *RIB*, vol. 37, no. 9. There are a number of reasons why furs were a better substitute for cash than grain, including ease of transportation. Belgorodskaia kn. 100 lists payment in furs in lieu of cash.

23. In 1680 cash revenues totaled 1,987,000 unadjusted rubles. Using S. G. Strumilin's price of 0.5 rubles per *chetvert'*, the assessed 65,500 tons of musketeers' grain added another 303,000 rubles' value. By 1680 southern grain collections should have yielded 5,000 tons, or about 29,000 rubles' value. Strumilin, "K voprosu," p. 306; Miliukov, *Gosudarstvennoe khoziaistvo*, p. 120. On southern grain prices for the last two-thirds of the seventeenth century, see Stevens, "Food Supply," figure 2, p. 233.

24. See the account of these events recently offered by Lindsey Hughes, *Sophia, Regent of Russia* (New Haven, Conn., 1990), pp. 179–86.

25. RGADA, f. 210, Belgorodskaia kn. 78, l. 345; Belgorodskaia kn. 89, ll. 436–39; Belgorodskaia kn. 95, ll. 1–38; Vazhinskii, "Melkoe," pp. 180–84. The Sevsk region's dues paying population was calculated from the amounts of grain owing from those cities. Novombergskii, *Prodovol'stvennoe*, vol. 1, nos. 240–43. Calculations yielded from 18,000 to 22,000 households.

26. Chapter 5 discusses the provisioning of Kiev in greater detail.

27. RGADA, f. 210, Belgorodskaia kn. 79, l. 23; Belgorodskaia kn. 89, ll. 436–39; Belgorodskaia kn. 118, ll. 405, 410–11.

28. RGADA, f. 210, Belgorodskaia kn. 78, ll. 2–3.

29. RGADA, f. 210, Belgorodskii stb. 545, ll. 1–2; Novombergskii, *Prodovol'-stvennoe*, vol. 1, nos. 71, 106, 408, 412, 503; RGADA, f. 210, Belgorodskaia kn. 78, l. 48; Belgorodskii stb. 904, ll. 28–30, 121.

30. Cf. Vazhinskii, "Razvitie," p. 15, where he comments that the chief reason that eighth-grain collections were initiated was to supply grain for Don shipments.

31. RGADA, f. 210, Belgorodskaia kn. 152, ll. 338–57.

32. *DAI*, vol. 9, no. 106, pp. 248–303. These amounts exclude grain held in Belgorod, Voronezh, and Sevsk provinces because these granaries also acted as depots for the system.

33. RGADA, f. 210, Belgorodskaia kn. 152, ll. 388–456; Novombergskii, *Prodovol'stvennoe*, vol. 1, nos. 84, 169, 170, 178, 188, 190, 237, 245, 250, 256, 304, 406, 408, 411, 412, 419, 420; Veinberg and Poltoravskaia, *Materialy . . .* , vol. 1, *Voronezhskie akty*, nos. 89, 94.

34. Cf. RGADA, f. 210, Belgorodskii stb. 545, l. 1, with Belgorodskaia kn. 78, ll. 3, 5–7, 345.

35. Tatar raids on the defensive lines did great damage; there was a serious raid on Belgorod province proper in 1680. Bagalei, *Materialy*, (1890), pp. 91–101. Chapter 6 discusses garrison defense in greater detail.

36. V. M. Vazhinskii, "Khlebnaia torgovlia na iuge Moskovskogo gosudarstva vo vtoroi polovine XVII veka," *Uchenye zapiski Moskovskogo oblastnogo ped-instituta imeni N. K. Krupskoi*, vol. 127, vyp. 7 (1963), p. 22, appendices.

37. *DAI*, vol. 9, no. 106; AN SSSR, IRIa, *Pamiatniki*, vol. 1, pp. 7–20; Aleksandrov, "Streletskoe naselenie," pp. 241–48; Solov'ev, "Goroda," pp. 49–51.

38. RGADA, f. 210, Belgorodskii stb. 643, ll. 431–33; Belgorodskaia kn. 118, ll. 315–17; Belgorodskaia kn. 78, l. 245; Novombergskii, *Prodovol'stvennoe*, vol. 1, no. 176.

39. *RIB*, vol. 34, section XV, nos. 1–3; XXXVII, nos. 5, 6, 12; XLII, nos. 2–47; and others; Novombergskii, *Prodovol'stvennoe*, vol. 1, nos. 48, 89, 90, 92, 99; Zagorovskii, "Donskoe kazachestvo," pp. 144–47.

40. V. P. Zagorovskii, "Soldatskie sela i soldatskoe zemlevladenie v Voronezhskom krae v XVII veka," *Iz istorii Voronezhskogo kraia*, vyp. 4 (1972), p. 93, believes that Moscow had every intention of providing year-round support to the 1653 infantrymen.

41. Hellie, *Enserfment*, p. 228; Zagorovskii, *Belgorodskaia*, p. 156; Aleksandrov, "Streletskoe naselenie," p. 238; A. Z. Myshlaevskii, "Ofitserskii vopros v

XVII veke," *Voennyi sbornik*, 1899, no. 5: 45; *PSZ*, no. 370; RGADA, f. 210, Belgorodskaia kn. 76, ll. 72–229, 245–end; Belgorodskaia kn. 78, ll. 252–317; Belgorodskaia kn. 100, ll. 20–38.

42. RGADA, f. 210, Belgorodskaia kn. 78, l. 245; Belgorodskaia kn. 89, ll. 440–41; Vazhinskii, "Sbory," pp. 24–25; Zagorovskii, "Donskoe kazachestvo," pp. 131–47.

43. Stevens, "Food Supply," pp. 227–28; *AIIuZR*, vol. 11, nos. 76, 191.

44. "Zapisnaia kniga Moskovskogo stola, 1678–1679," *RIB*, vol. 11, p. 495.

45. RGADA, f. 210, Belgorodskaia kn. 79, ll. 271–81; Belgorodskaia kn. 78, ll. 245–317; Belgorodskaia kn. 152, ll. 388–456.

46. RGADA, f. 210, Belgorodskaia kn. 78, ll. 315–17, 345; Belgorodskii stb. 643, ll. 388–433.

47. The Belgorod army numbered 14,083 men and about 500 officers. RGADA, f. 210, Belgorodskii stb. 691, ll. 34–80, 91. I. V. Stepanov, *Krest'ianskaia voina v Rossii v 1670–1671*, 2 vols. (Leningrad, 1972), vol. 2, p. 353.

48. In 1671 musketeers' grain was collected in double its usual volume in Voronezh province, an unusual instance of that collection's local use and a precursor of the following year's reform to the tax. Supplementary collections were ordered in Kursk, Korotoiak, Zemliansk, and other cities. RGADA, f. 210, Belgorodskaia kn. 79, ll. 2–17, 24, 208–34; Belgorodskaia kn. 152, l. 458; Belgorodskii stb. 691, l. 103; Denezhnaia kn. 312, ll. 23–90; Novombergskii, *Prodovol'stvennoe*, vol. 1, no. 176; Stepanov, *Krest'ianskaia voina*, vol. 1, pp. 165–66.

49. RGADA, f. 210, Belgorodskaia kn. 81, ll. 1, 3–4; Belgorodskaia kn. 89, l. 436. The distribution of these grain dues appear to contradict Vazhinskii's statement in "Melkoe," p. 15, that the eighth-grain collections were intended primarily to provide Don shipments—at least for the period prior to the 1678–1682 reforms. After the reforms the amounts shipped down the Don certainly increased enormously, but so did contributions. As indicated earlier, some of the grain so shipped was used to feed Muscovite troops in the area.

50. *DAI*, vol 9, no. 106.

51. RGADA, f. 210, Belgorodskaia kn. 76, 78, 79, 81, 89. For example, Belgorod province listed 1,245 contributors in 1673. The closest military census identifies more than 900 middle-level servitors of the town's garrison. The remainder were 350 militarized peasants on nearby court land. There is practically no evidence of about 1,100 landholding members of the Belgorod campaign regiments. Belgorodskaia kn. 89, ll. 91, 99, 163–91, 256, 333–34; *DAI*, vol. 9, no. 106, pp. 257–303; Belgorodskaia kn. 95, ll. 1–38. See also collection orders in *PSZ*, no. 522; Novombergskii, *Prodovol'stvennoe*, vol. 1, nos. 275, 297, which refer explicitly to urban garrison payments and sizes. There were numerous irregularities; musketeers in some provinces contributed grain, and large peasant populations were exempted. Belgorodskii stb. 546 and Novombergskii, *Prodovol'stvennoe*, vol. 1, nos. 168, 180, 217, 270, 271.

52. From 1672 on, southern musketeers' grain was assessed by household; a general census in 1678 was household-based.

53. RGADA, f. 210, Belgorodskii stb. 546, ll. 9–end; Belgorodskii stb. 618, l. 478; Vazhinskii, *Zemlevladenie*, p. 209. Contributions were recorded differently in different provinces. In Belgorod province, households were listed individually and each was separately marked as paid-up or in arrears. Belgorodskaia kn. 79, ll. 20–25.

In Kozlov province, however, households were recorded as paying partially or being excused from payment on account of poverty. Brian Davies, "Dela raznykh gorodov kn. 36," ref. to ll. 448, 450.

54. Cf. *PSZ*, no. 354.

55. Vazhinskii, *Sel'skoe khoziaistvo*, p. 77, calculates that annual service expenses were 6.87 rubles for a midcentury campaign serviceman and 6.09 rubles for a town serviceman at about the same period; by the end of the century they had risen to 7.15 rubles for a campaign serviceman and to 7.72 rubles for his townservice counterpart.

56. Novombergskii, *Prodovol'stvennoe*, vol. 1, nos. 127, 219; cf. Bobrovskii, *Perekhod*, p. 15.

57. See Novombergskii, *Prodovol'stvennoe*, vol. 1, no. 585, for example.

58. Vazhinskii, "Sbory," p. 28; Novombergskii, *Prodovol'stvennoe*, vol. 1, no. 260.

59. Stevens, "Food Supply," pp. 226–29; Stevens, "Trade," pp. 184–85.

60. These stratagems are discussed further in chapter 4. See also Vazhinskii, "Usilenie," pp. 53, 56–58, 63–64. These recruitment norms and the attendant economic complications did not affect the wealthy few serving in old-style cavalry regiments (*sotni*).

61. Nor were southerners successful in getting sympathetic local servicemen appointed as investigators. A. A. Novosel'skii, "Pobegi krest'ian i kholopov i ikh sysk v Moskovskom gosudarstve vo vtoroi polovine XVII veka," *Trudy instituta istorii. Sbornik statei* (Moscow, 1926), pp. 334, 337, 342–43; A. G. Man'kov, "Voprosy krepostnogo prava na iuzhnykh i zapadnykh okrainakh Russkogo gosudarstva vo vtoroi polovine XVII veka," *EAIVE* 1960 (1962): 180–81; Keep, "Pluralism," p. 224.

62. Hellie, *Enserfment*, p. 198; see also chapter 4.

63. Novosel'skii, "Rasprostranenie," pp. 23–29; *PSZ*, nos. 516, 549, 622; Vazhinskii, *Zemlevladenie*, pp. 81–85.

64. Novosel'skii, "Rasprostranenie," p. 28–39; Novosel'skii, "Praviashchie gruppy," pp. 322–24, 329, 331; Vazhinskii, *Zemlevladenie*, pp. 82–88; RGADA, f. 210, Belgorodskaia kn. 95, ll. 122–53.

65. Novosel'skii, "Praviashchie gruppy," p. 328 It should be added that irregular military enrollments and appointments were also taking place in other parts of Russia.

66. RGADA, f. 210, Belgorodskaia kn. 95, ll. 80–98, 142–47, offers ample evidence of massive absenteeism.

67. RGADA, f. 210, Belgorodskaia kn. 79, ll. 20–25, 27–60; Belgorodskaia kn. 95, l. 67.

68. RGADA, f. 210, Belgorodskaia kn. 79, ll. 23–26; Belgorodskaia kn. 89, ll. 435–39; Belgorodskaia kn. 118, ll. 405–6.

69. RGADA, f. 210, Belgorodskaia kn. 89, ll. 46–48.

70. RGADA, f. 210, Belgorodskaia kn. 79, ll. 383–87; Belgorodskaia kn. 81, ll. 3–4, 12–24; Novombergskii, *Prodovol'stvennoe*, vol. 1, nos. 239–41.

71. RGADA, f. 210, Belgorodskaia kn. 118, ll. 117, 410; Belgorodskaia kn. 89, l. 37; Belgorodskii stb. 904, l. 180; Novombergskii, *Prodovol'stvennoe*, vol. 1, nos. 139, 140, 158, 161, 163, 164, 173, 184; Veinberg and Poltoravskaia, *Materialy . . .*, vol 1, *Voronezhskie akty*, no. 75; Solove'v, "Goroda," p. 47.

72. Novombergskii, *Prodovol'stvennoe*, vol. 1, no. 145.

73. Novombergskii, *Prodovol'stvennoe*, vol. 1, nos. 181, 270.

74. RGADA, f. 210, Belgorodskaia kn. 81, ll. 40–42; Novombergskii, *Prodovol'stvennoe*, vol. 1 nos. 15, 35 65, 70, 86, 139, 145, 148, 181, 270, 335, 399, 422, 424; Vazhinskii, *Zemlevladenie*, pp. 227–33.

75. RGADA, f. 210, Belgorodskaia kn. 78, ll. 170–72; Belgorodskaia kn. 95, ll. 13–15. Sanctions were applied against those who failed to return borrowed grain from the granaries. Belgorodskaia kn. 81, l. 6; Belgorodskii stb. 904, l. 177.

76. RGADA, f. 210, Belgorodskaia kn. 118, l. 743; Belgorodskaia kn. 81, l. 40, 202; Belgorodskaia kn. 79, l. 30; Novombergskii, *Prodovol'stvennoe*, vol. 1, no. 292.

77. Contemporaries believed that the ability to pay taxes represented ownership of undeclared labor. *Iz istorii Kurskogo kraia: Sbornik dokumentov i materialov* (Voronezh, 1965), pp. 46–47.

78. E. I. Kamentseva and N. V. Ustiugov, *Russkaia metrologiia*, 2d ed. (Moscow, 1975), p. 97.

79. Novombergskii, *Prodovol'stvennoe*, vol. 1, no. 418.

80. Cherepnin, "Klassovaia bor'ba," pp. 53–65; Birzhe, "Volnenie," pp. 150–74.

81. A. A. Novoselskii, "Otdatochnye knigi beglykh kak istochnik izucheniia narodnoi kolonizatsii na Rusi v XVII veke," *Trudy MGIAI* 2 (1946): 127–55; Novoselskii, "Vol'nye," pp. 61–77.

82. Novombergskii, *Prodovol'stvennoe*, vol. 1, nos. 75, 173, 358; vol 2, nos. 99, 241.

83. Novombergskii, *Prodovol'stvennoe*, vol. 1, nos. 74, 112, 213, 260, 374, 377; vol. 2, no. 111.

84. Birzhe, "Volnenie," pp. 150–74.

85. In 1678 the entire Belgorod region had a total of nearly 1,000 administrators within its borders; only 104 of them were exclusively involved in granary affairs, and 17 of those were in the town of Belgorod itself. There were in addition 134 clerks, who served a variety of functions, including granary ones, but their salaries were probably less than 10 rubles annually, supplemented by grain or land. A similar contingent of administrators existed in the Sevsk region. *DAI*, vol. 9, no. 106, pp. 257–303; RGADA, f. 210, Belgorodskaia kn. 152, ll. 371–82; Novombergskii, *Prodovol'stvennoe*, vol. 1, no. 178; vol. 2, nos. 288, 380. In other words, the state's cash expenditures on the system were low, but these arrangements represented considerable investment in the granary system.

86. Novombergskii, *Prodovol'stvennoe*, vol. 1, no. 64.

87. Novombergskii, *Prodovol'stvennoe*, vol. 1, no. 4.

88. Belgorod, for example, had three granary heads in 1670–1671. RGADA, f. 210, Belgorodskaia kn. 79, ll. 347–85.

89. RGADA, f. 210, Belgorodskaia kn. 79, ll. 347–50; Novombergskii, *Prodovol'stvennoe*, vol. 1, no. 234; and RGADA, f. 210, Belgorodskii stb. 546, ll. 553–82, and Belgorodskii stb. 643, ll. 388–433, describe the collection process.

90. RGADA, f. 210, Belgorodskii stb. 691, l. 103; Denezhnaia kn. 312, l. 76.

91. RGADA, f. 210, Belgorodskaia kn. 79, ll. 27, 347–50; Belgorodskaia kn. 89, l. 3; Belgorodskaia kn. 143, ll. 242–44; Belgorodskii stb. 643, ll. 399–402, 430;

Novombergskii, *Prodovol'stvennoe*, vol. 1, nos. 123, 124, 146, 147, 149, 260; vol. 2, no. 191.

92. Officer salaries were so high that payment in full could have consumed over one-half of southern grain collections prior to 1683. RGADA, f. 210, Belgorodskaia kn. 78, ll. 247–31. Cash salaries were also high. Myshlaevskii, "Ofitserskii vopros," p. 296.

93. *PSZ*, no. 276; Vazhniskii, "Usilenie," pp. 57. Thirty *altyn*, one month's food allowance, was a very high price for one *chetvert'* of rye flour by southern standards. Most contemporary European armies were issuing about two pounds of bread daily; by this standard a *chetvert'* should have lasted several months.

94. As the assessment of eighth-grain climbed toward 5,000 tons (46,000 *chetverti*) in the late 1670s, it appeared briefly that Muscovy was nearly capable of paying food allowances to the rank-and-file army and even to the officer corps, provided it abandoned all other fiscal responsibilities.

CHAPTER 4: THE INCORPORATION OF THE SOUTH: THE 1680S AND 1690S

1. The Belgorod army sent 26,731 men; the Sevsk army 5,229. Romodanovskii's forces as a whole numbered 48,866 men; 25 percent were infantry. Zagorovskii, *Iziumskaia*, p. 92.

2. Patrick Gordon engineered the destruction of Chigirin in retreat; other commanders like I. I. Rzhevskii and G. Kosagov were outsiders to the Muscovite service elite but had training and familiarity with the new formations. See Crummey, *Aristocrats*, p. 48.

3. Ironically, the Ottoman forces themselves were not trained on a European model, though they made use of European technological changes. W. H. McNeill, *The Pursuit of Power* (Chicago, 1982), p. 135; David Ralston, *Supporting the European Army* (London, 1990), p. 45–48; Carlo Cipolla, *Guns, Sails, and Empires* (New York, 1965), pp. 94–95.

4. *PSZ*, no. 744.

5. Cf. Claes Peterson, *Peter the Great's Administrative and Judicial Reforms*, trans. Michael Metcalf (Stockholm, 1979), pp. 44–48.

6. *PSZ*, no. 744; Vazhinskii, "Usilenie," p. 57.

7. *PSZ*, nos. 689, 747.

8. There is an extensive literature on the abolition of *mestnichestvo*; see, for example, A. I. Markevich, *Istoriia mestnichestva v Moskovskom gosudarstve* (Odessa, 1888); Robert O. Crummey, "Reflections on *Mestnichestvo*," FOG 27 (1980): 269–81; E. A Vasilievskaia, "Terminologiia mestnichestva i rodstva," *Trudy MGIAI* 2 (1946): 155–79; B. I. Buganov, " 'Vrazhtotvornoe' mestnichestvo," *Voprosy istorii* 1974 (November): 118–133; M. Ia. Volkhov, "Ob otmene mestnichestva v Rossii," *Istoriia SSSR* 1977 (March–April): 53–67; and Bobrovskii, *Perekhod*, p. 20.

9. RGADA, f. 210, Sevskaia kn. 18, ll. 70–85; Hellie, *Enserfment*, p. 269; Petr I. Ivanov, *Opisanie gosudarstvennogo razriadnogo arkhiva* (Moscow, 1842), appendix 10, "Rospis' ratnym liudiam," 1681.

10. V. M. Vazhinskii, "Vvedenie podushnogo oblozhenia na iuge Rossii v 90-kh godov XVII veka," *Izvestiia Voronezhskogo gospedinstituta* 127 (1973): 91.

11. Vazhinskii, "Usilenie," p. 61.

12. Chernov, *Vooruzhennye sily*, p. 156–61; Vazhinskii, "Usilenie," p. 60.

13. *PSZ*, nos. 744, 745; Zagorovskii, *Iziumskaia*, p. 114.

14. *PSZ*, nos. 516, 622; RGADA, f. 210, Belgorodskaia kn. 95, ll. 122, 154ob.; Novosel'skii, "Raspad," pp. 231–53.

15. Zagorovskii, *Iziumskaia*, p. 113.

16. Cf. registers in RGADA, f. 210, Belgorodskaia kn. 95 (1674); Belgorodskaia kn. 79 (1678); Belgorodskii stb. 1000 (1681).

17. RGADA, f. 210, Belgorodskaia kn. 161, ll. 254–63, 327–31; Belgorodskii stb. 957, ll. 19–20; Prikaznoi stb. 643, ll. 1–129.

18. RGADA, f. 210, Belgorodskii stb. 1000, ll. 108–11.

19. Vazhinskii, "Usilenie," p. 62; Zagorovskii, *Iziumskaia*, p. 39; *PSZ*, no. 982. In 1681–1682 there were 5,218 lancers and cavalrymen in five regiments based in Belgorod, Oboian, Elets, Kozlov, and Livny. RGADA, f. 210, Belgorodskaia kn. 100. The Tambov district had three cavalry regiments. A. N. Piskarev, ed., *Sobranie materialov dlia istorii zapadnogo kraia Tambovskoi gubernii i eparkhii* (Tambov, 1878), p. 99. Some cavalry regiments had members from many provinces. See RGADA, f. 210, Belgorodskaia kn. 99, for example.

20. These were territorially defined regiments from Slobodskaia Ukraina. Vazhinskii, "Vvednie," p. 91.

21. RGADA, f. 210, Belgorodskaia kn. 100, ll. 185, 191. Prior to 1678, southerners had also complained of demotions against their will. Novosel'skii, "Praviashchie gruppy," p. 328. For 1678 orders not to do so, see Belgorodskaia kn. 94, l. 395.

22. Vazhinskii, "Usilenie," pp. 61–62; Vazhinskii, *Sel'skoe khoziaistvo*, p. 48.

23. Hughes, *Sophia*, p. 106; Myshlaevskii, "Ofitserskii vopros," p. 288; *PSZ*, no. 812.

24. Epifanov, "Ocherki," p. 128; *PSZ*, no. 756 (1679); *AAE*, vol. 4, no. 280; Chernov, *Vooruzhennye Sily*, pp. 187–90.

25. The wanderers needed guarantors before they could join the infantry. Vazhinskii, "Usilenie," p. 59.

26. Vazhinskii, loc. cit.; *PSZ*, no. 847. Arsen'ev, *Dedilov*, no. 42, notes musketeers' earlier acceptance into the dragoons in 1669.

27. Vazhinskii, "Usilenie," p. 53.

28. RGADA, f. 210, Sevskaia kn. 17, ll. 17–85; Belgorodskaia kn. 152, ll. 459–96.

29. Russia, M. Iu. M. A., *Opisanie*, vol. 13, "stolbets 1228 Belgorodskogo stola."

30. RGADA, f. 210, Belgorodskaia kn. 95; Vazhinskii, "Usilenie," p. 57.

31. The Belgorod regiments attained this size just before the launching of a new campaign. RGADA, f. 210, Belgorodskaia kn. 100; Zagorovskii, *Iziumskaia*, pp. 39, 93, 113.

32. Hellie, *Enserfment*, p. 269; RGADA, f. 210, Sevskaia kn. 18, ll. 96–100.

33. RGADA, f. 210, Prikaznoi stb. 643, "Dobroe."

34. Vazhinskii, "Vvedenie," pp. 91–92.

35. *DAI*, vol. 9, no. 106; RGADA, f. 210, Moscow kn. 126. Siberia remained the exception, protected by garrison troops of mixed social origins.

36. See table 4 of appendix; Myklashevskii, *K istorii khoziaistvennogo byta*, p. 198.

37. RGADA, f. 210, Sevskaia kn. 17, ll. 203–39; Sevskaia kniga 21, ll. 68–76.

38. RGADA, f. 210, Belgorodskaia kn. 156, ll. 115–53 lists the variety of persisting ranks among dues payers in 1682.

39. Stanford Shaw, *The History of the Ottoman Empire and Modern Turkey* (Cambridge, 1976), vol. 1, pp. 213–19.

40. Even were the central government making such an attempt, it would have been unable to do so, if only from the perspective of food supply. See table 1 of appendix.

41. S. K. Bogoiavlenskii, "O pushkarskom prikaze," *Sbornik stat'ei v chest' M. K. Liubovskogo* (Moscow, 1917), p. 370.

42. Vazhinskii, *Zemlevladenia*, p. 117 n. 102; Rabinovich, "Sud'ba," pp. 448–50.

43. Hughes, *Sophia*, p. 106; Troitskii, "Finansovaia," pp. 281–319.

44. Both have been extensively analyzed by Miliukov, *Gosudarstvennoe khoziaistvo*, pp. 64–65, 71, 78–79, 554–55.

45. *PSZ*, no. 844; Myshlaevakii, "Ofitserskii," p. 45; Chernov, *Vooruzhennye sily*, pp. 187–99; Piskarev, *Sobranie materialov*, p. 99.

46. Myshlaevskii, "Ofitserskii," pp. 45–46; Chernov, "TsGADA," p. 19,.

47. Zagorovskii, *Iziumskaia*, pp. 45–46; Bagalei, *Materialy*, (1886), no. 26.

48. Vazhinskii, *Zemlevaldenie*, pp. 47–49, 54–55.

49. Vazhinskii, "Usilenie," pp. 63–66.

50. Ibid., p. 62; Brian Davies, "Service, Landholding, and Dependent Labour in Kozlov District, 1675," in *New Perspectives in Muscovite History*, ed. Lindsay A. J. Hughes (London, 1993), pp. 130, 145–46. For an example of *prokormshchik*-relatives, see L. B. Veinberg, ed., *Materialy po istorii Voronezhskoi i sosednikh gubernii*, vol. 1, *Drevnie akty XVII stoletiia* (Voroneh, 1885), no. 388.

51. See RGADA, f. 210, Sevskaia kn. 21, ll. 68–76, for example. Desertions were treated with astonishing leniency on occasion. Belgorodskii stb. 957, ll. 19–21; Belgorodskii stb. 1070, ll. 123–34.

52. RGADA, f. 210, Belgorodskaia kn. 163, l. 98; Prikaznoi stb. 1400; Chernov, *Vooruzhennye sily*, p. 188; A. K. Levykin, "Pushechnyi nariad i pushkari vo vtoroi polovine XVII veka v Rossii (po materialam iuzhno-russkikh gorodov)" (Kand. thesis, Moscow State University, 1985), p. 165; Vazhinskii, "Usilenie," pp. 60, 62. Vazhinskii cites Belgorodskii stb. 1050, that the Belgorod infantry were not paid for this active duty, though musketeers were.

53. Arsen'ev, *Dedilov*, no. 53 (1672).

54. Veinberg, *Materialy . . . sosednikh gubernii*, vol. 1, no. 395 (1697). Five hundred of the poorest men rafted logs while the rest of the assembled troops joined the army.

55. RGADA, f. 210, Belgorodskaia kn. 94, ll. 398–402; Prikaznoi stb. 1400, ll. 1–22.

56. RGADA, f. 210, Belgorodskii stb. 1314, l. 192; Novombergskii, *Prodovol'stvennoe*, vol. 1, nos. 434–37; Vazhinskii, "Melkoe," p. 184.

57. A request to list the payers of the musketeers' grain tax on the regional rolls was ignored, for example.

58. RGADA, f. 210, Belgorodskii stb. 903, ll. 59–60; Belgorodskaia kn. 100, ll. 122–22ob.; Veinberg and Poltoravskaia, *Materialy . . .* , vol. 1, *Voronezhskie akty*, no. 66; I. A. Bulygin, *Monastyrskie krest'iane Rossii* (Moscow, 1977), pp. 134–59,

209; Brown, "Bureaucracy," p. 496. For interim arrangments during the census, see *AAE*, vol. 4, no. 299. The juxtaposition of southern petty servicemen and taxpaying peasants elsewhere in Muscovy is implied, at least, by *DAI*, vol. 8, no. 36II, IV; *AAE*, vol. 4, no. 250; Golubtsov, "K istorii podatnoi," pp. 155–67.

59. Table 1 of the appendix shows a gain in ability to pay dues; the 1680 column was calculated on the basis of the new quarter-grain and its returns.

60. RGADA, f. 210, Belgorodskaia kn. 118, l. 311ob; Zagorovskii, *Izium-skaia*, pp. 87–134; Cherepnin, "Klassovaia bor'ba," pp. 53–61. Southern musketeers' grain had reduced payments that year, also. *AAE*, vol. 4, no. 250.

61. RGADA, f. 210, Belgorodskaia kn. 156, ll. 6, 703–43. Novombergskii, *Prodovol'stvennoe*, vol. 1, nos. 275, 316 are examples of the confusion of eighth-grain with quarter-grain.

62. RGADA, f 210, Belgorodskaia kn. 143 (1686) ll. 1–2; Brian Davies, "Belgorodskii stb. 1429"; Novombergskii, *Prodovol'stvennoe*, vol. 1, nos. 316, 317, 378 (1683–1684); vol. 2, no. 281 (1686), no. 322 (1692).

63. Novombergskii, *Prodovol'stvennoe*, vol. 1, no. 280, p. 244.

64. Brian Davies, "Dela raznykh gorodov 36"; Novombergskii, *Prodovol'stvennoe*, vol. 1, no. 378; vol. 2, no. 281.

65. RGADA, f. 210, Belgorodskaia kn. 143 (Kursk); Belgorodskaia kn. 159, ll. 231, 237; Belgorodskaia kn. 156, ll. 6, 115; Belgorodskaia kn. 164 ll. 1, 70; Davies, "Belgorodskii stb. 1429."

66. Brian Davies, "Dela raznykh gorodov 36."

67. Piskarev, *Sobranie materialov*, pp. 100–5; Vtorovoi and Aleksandrov-Dol'nik, *Drevnie gramoty*, no. 28; Bagalei, *Materialy* (1890), pp. 102–4; M. F. De-Pule, ed., *Materialy dlia istorii Voronezhskoi i sosednykh gubernii, sostoiashchie iz tsarskikh gramot i drugikh aktov XVII–XVIII stoletii*, kn. 1, *Orlovskie akty* (Voronezh, 1861), nos. 131, 153.

68. RGADA, f. 210, Belgorodskaia kn. 78, l. 50.

69. I have compared the number and occupations of grain contributors after 1683 with the number of service land grants, the number of peasants, and the categories and number of servicemen of twelve Belgorod region provinces. The best match was a special household census taken in 1683 with subsequent grain registers (RGADA, f. 210, Belgorodskaia kn. 159, with Belgorodskaia kn. 152, 156, "Belgorod" headings). The only unpredictable factor in that comparison was the number of peasant contributors; this is presumably explainable on the grounds that unaccountable peasants were paying musketeers' tax, as the instructions suggest. Indeed, 167 peasants were removed from the former lists for precisely that reason in 1688–1689 (Belgorodskie kn. 152, 156). Similar circumstances would eliminate most large landholders from payment of quarter-grain; however, the collection was probably not administered identically in every province.

70. Novombergskii, *Prodovol'stvennoe*, vol. 1, no. 377.

71. RGADA, f. 210, Belgorodskaia kn. 159, "Belgorod," actually lists most of them.

72. RGADA, f. 210, Belgorodskii stb. 1267, l. 444; Prikaznoi stb. 1400 petitions; Prikaznoi stb. 643, ll. 91–92; Vazhinskii, "Sbory," p. 29.

73. RGADA, f. 210, Belgorodskaia kn. 144; Cherepnin, "Klassovaia bor'ba," p. 72; Novombergskii, *Prodovol'stvennoe*, vol. 1, nos. 364, 396, 399, 413, 432, 493, 680.

74. Golubtsov, "K istorii podatnoi," p. 157.
75. Vazhinskii, "Vvedenie," p. 88–103; RGADA, f. 210, Belgorodskii stb. 1267. The basis on which the Petrine state would make the choice of who served and who paid is not entirely clear. See, for example, Anisimov, *Podatnaia,* pp. 165–67; G. Germanov, "Postepennoe rasprostranenie odnodvorcheskogo naselenie v Voronezhskoi gubernii," *Zapiski imperatorskogo Russkogo geograficheskogo obshchestva* 1857 kn. 12, pp. 209–10, 230–324; N. K. Tkacheva, "Odnodvortsy XVIII veka," *Istoriia i istoriki* 1975 (1978): 281–99; Zagorovskii, "Zemledel'cheskoe," pp. 199–207; and Rabinovich, "Sud'ba," p. 513.
76. Novombergskii, *Prodovol'stvennoe,* vol. 1, nos. 138, 367, 377, 516, 535, 585.
77. RGADA, f. 210, Sevskii stb. 9, ll. 57–112 (musketeers' grain is collected here while the serfholders were in service); Novombergskii, *Prodovol'stvennoe,* vol. 1, nos. 312, 320, 444; Veinberg and Poltoravskaia, *Materialy . . . ,* vol. 1, *Voronezhskie akty,* nos. 283, 284.
78. *AAE,* vol. 4, no. 299 (1688); Arsen'ev, *Dedilov,* no. 85.
79. RGADA, f. 210, Belgorodskaia kn. 143, "Kursk."
80. RGADA, f. 210, Belgorodskaia kn. 156, ll. 350–81, 743, 868–88; Belgorodskaia kn. 159 l. 231; Belgorodskii stb. 1314, ll. 32–55; Novombergskii, *Prodovol'stvennoe,* vol. 1, nos. 267, 279, 280, 296, 300, 308, 376, 446.
81. RGADA, f. 210, Belgorodskaia kn. 118, ll. 410–11; Novombergskii, *Prodovol'stvennoe,* vol. 1, nos. 250, 256, 262, 280, 381, 397, 499; V. M. Vazhinskii, "Sudovaia povinnost' na Donu v XVII veke," *Materialy k nauchno-teoreticheskoi konferentsii Kemerovskogo gospedinstituta, vyp.* 2 (1965), p. 56; Vazhinskii, "Sbory," p. 33. Some of the loans that were issued were used to replace spoiled grain. See, however, Piskarev, *Sobranie materialov,* pp. 96–97, for local issues.
82. RGADA, f. 210, Belgorodskaia kn. 152, ll. 459–96; Belgorodskaia kn. 156, ll. 866–82; cf. Belgorodskaia kn. 100, l. 124; Belgorodskaia kn. 118, l. 415. The muster points were Vol'nyi, Lebedian', and Khotmyzhsk.
83. Novombergskii, *Prodovol'stvennoe,* vol. 1, no. 423.
84. RGADA, f. 210, Belgorodskaia kn. 152, ll. 381–87, 410, 703–43; Novombergskii, *Prodovol'stvennoe,* vol. 1, no. 537.
85. Novombergskii, *Prodovol'stvennoe,* vol. 1, nos. 277, 337; vol 2, nos. 259, 260, 261, 263.
86. Vazhinskii, *Zemlevladenie,* p. 134.
87. RGADA, f. 210, Belgorodskaia kn. 156, ll. 383–84; 415–16; Novombergskii, *Prodovol'stvennoe,* vol. 1, nos. 284; 370, 434–37, 444, 480, 488–89, 494. Only 48 percent of the grain that was supposed to be in granaries was actually there during the audit. David Das, Bates College, tentatively identified Andrei Lyzlov, an overseer in 1694–1695, as the author of *Skifskaia istorii.* Ibid., no. 363.
88. Zagorovskii, "Donskoe kazachestvo," pp. 143–47.
89. Davies, "Belgorodskii stb. 1429," shows one collection for Russian salaries on the Don, ref. to ll. 687–88 (a special collection), and another for Don shipment to the Cossacks, ref. to ll. 40–44 in the same year (1695–1696). Novombergskii, *Prodovol'stvennoe,* vol. 1, no. 306 shows Don sales.
90. RGADA, f. 210, Belgorodskaia kn. 163, l. 98; Bagalei, *Materialy* (1890), pp. 102–4.
91. RGADA, f. 210, Belgorodskaia kn. 163 ll. 1–8, 212–32; Belgorodskii stb.

1267, ll. 165–78, 381, 384; Bagalei, *Materialy* (1890), pp. 102–4; Vazhinskii, "Sbory," p. 29; Novombergskii, *Prodovol'stvennoe*, vol. 1, nos. 77, 347, 350, 351, 442, 443, 451, 465.

92. RGADA, f. 210, Belgorodskaia kn. 163, ll. 1–3; Belgorodskii stb. 1267, l. 170; Novombergskii, *Prodovol'stvennoe*, vol. 1, no. 330.

93. RGADA, f. 210, Belgorodskii stb. 1267; Vazhinskii, "Sbory," pp. 32–33, 36–37; Novombergskii, *Prodovol'stvennoe*, vol. 1, no. 344; *AI*, vol. 4, no. 299.

94. RGADA, f. 210, Belgorodskaia kn. 174, l. 95; Veinberg and Poltoravskaia, *Materialy . . .* , vol. 1, *Voronezhskie akty*, nos. 102, 118.

95. RGADA, f. 210, Belgorodskaia kn. 163, l. 8; Novombergskii, *Prodovol'stvennoe*, vol. 1, nos. 320, 444, 491.

96. RGADA, f. 210, Belgorodskaia kn. 174, ll. 141, 164; Vazhinskii, "Sbory," pp. 36–38, 40–41.

97. RGADA, f. 210, Belgorodskaia kn. 163, ll. 183–99; Belgorodskaia kn. 164, l. 1; Novombergskii, *Prodovol'stvennoe*, vol. 1, nos. 307, 308, 310, 324, 333, 352; *Iz istorii Kuskogo kraia*, no. 75; Veinberg and Poltoravskaia, *Materialy . . .* , vol. 1, *Voronezhskie akty*, no. 100.

98. RGADA, f. 210, Belgorodskii stb. 1267, ll. 4, 5, 15; Sevskaia kn. 16, ll. 180–90, 202–14, 252–63, 393–98, 400–2.

99. See, for example, Novombergskii, *Prodovol'stvennoe*, vol. 1, no. 279.

100. Bagalei, *Materialy* (1890), pp. 102–4. There wasn't always enough. S. A. Belokurov, *Materialy dlia Russkoi istorii* (Moscow, 1888), no. 10.

101. RGADA, f. 210, Belgorodskaia kn. 174, ll. 71–95; stb. 1267, ll. 24–31, 46–47; Novombergskii, *Prodovol'stvennoe*, vol. 1, nos. 494, 510.

102. Novombergskii, *Prodovol'stvennoe*, vol. 2, nos. 270, 290, 300.

103. B. B. Kafengauz, *Ocherki vnutrennego rynka Rossii pervoi polovine XVIII veka po materialam vnutrennykh tamozhen* (Moscow, 1958), pp. 290, 293.

104. RGADA, f. 210, Belgorodskaia kn. 100, l. 41; Belgorodskaia kn. 144, l. 312; f. 137, Pskovskaia kn. 18, ll. 2–5; Novombergskii, *Prodovol'stvennoe*, vol. 1 nos. 138 (1695), 321 (1693), 361 (1696), 444 (1697), 642 (1687); Veinberg, *Materialy . . . sosednikh gubernii*, vol. 1, no. 370 (1696); Vazhinskii, "Sbory," p. 29; P. N. Petrov, "Rospis' raskhodov tsarstva Moskovskogo, 206 goda," *Zapiski otdeleniia Russkoi i slavianskoi arkheologii Russkogo arkheologicheskogo obshchestva* 4 (1887): 341. Not everyone agreed; Elets residents were offered the possibility of paying arable tenth in cash in 1699 and refused. Quarter-grain was occasionally collected in cash in the 1690s. Vazhinskii, "Melkoe," p. 177.

105. RGADA, f. 210, Belgorodskaia kn. 100, l. 41; Belgorodskii stb. 1873 (1700). Belgorodskaia kn. 100, ll. 111ob. discusses how prices were pegged to salaries. Granary contents also became less prominent features of annual accounting in inland cities. Belgorodskaia kn. 152, l. 458.

106. RGADA, f. 210, Belgorodskaia kn. 100, ll. 41–42; Belgorodskii stb. 1193 (1685).

107. Vazhinskii, "Usilenie," p. 57 and preceding note.

108. RGADA, f. 210, Belgorodskaia kn. 174, l. 25; Vazhinskii, "Sbory," p. 36.

109. Vazhinskii, "Sbory," pp. 40–41; Vazhinskii, "Vvedenie," pp. 93–97; *Iz istorii Kurskogo kraia*, no. 76; RGADA, f. 210, Belgorodskii stb. 1873, ll. 154–55.

110. See chapter 5, text and notes 55, 70.

111. Avtokratov, "Pervye komissariatskie," pp. 163–88; Vazhinskii, "Vvedenie," p. 90.

CHAPTER 5: SUPPLY TO THE CAMPAIGN FORCES

1. See, for example, Razin, *Istoriia*, vol. 3, pp. 259–61; A. K. Baiov, *Kurs istorii Russkogo voennogo isskustva*, 7 vols. (St. Petersburg, 1909–1913), vol. 3; Myshlaevskii, "Ofitserskii vopros," pp. 32–58; Bobrovskii, *Perekhod*, p. iii; N. A. Smirnov, *Rossiia i Turtsiia v XVI–XVII vekakh*, 2 vols. appear as *Uchenye zapiski MGU*, vyp. 94 (1946), vol. 1, p. 26; N. S. Golitsyn, *Russkaia voennaia istoriia*, pt. 2 of *Ot Ioanna do Petra I* (St. Petersburg, 1878), pp. 426–85; E. A. El'chaninov, "Ocherk istorii voennogo iskusstva do Petra velikogo," in *Istoriia Russkoi armii i flota*, 15 vols. (Moscow, 1911–1915), vol. 1, pp. 75–79.

2. Hughes, *Sophia*, pp. 200–14, describes Golitsyn's campaigns in some detail, mentioning in this brief discussion the importance of supply.

3. The central logs of preparation for war in 1678–1679, for example, make practically no mention of provisioning. "Zapisnaia kniga Moskovskogo stola, 1678–1679," *RIB*, vol. 10, pp. 351–525.

4. AN SSSR II, *Istoriia Kieva. Kiev perioda posdnego feodalizma i kapitalizma*, 3 vols, 4 books (Kiev, 1983), vol. 2, pp. 15–17.

5. *AIIuZR*, vol. 6, nos. 22, 35; Bobrovskii, *Perekhod*, p. 117 n. 140.

6. RGADA, f. 210, Moscow stb. 404, l. 23; *AIIuZR*, vol. 8, no. 60; vol 9, no. 25; vol. 11, nos. 184, 201; *DAI*, vol. 9, no. 47; Novombergskii, *Prodovol'stvennoe*, vol. 1, no. 438.

7. *PSZ*, no. 756; *AIIuZR*, vol. 8, no. 60; Arsen'ev, *Dedilov*, no. 53 (the musketeers were not on campaign but in garrison service).

8. RGADA, f. 210, Belgorodskii stb. 691, ll. 357–61; Belgorodskaia kn. 100, ll. 29–35; *AIIuZR*, vol. 8, no. 70.

9. RGADA, f. 210, Moscow stb. 404, ll. 24–50; *AIIuZR*, vol. 8, no. 36.

10. RGADA, f. 210, Sevskii stb. 410, ll. 191–200; Moscow stb. 404, l. 71; *AIIuZR*, vol. 11, no. 141.

11. *DAI*, vol. 9, no. 47.

12. *PSZ*, no. 756; *AIIuZR*, vol. 9, no. 131.

13. See, for example, RGADA, f. 210, Moscow stb. 404, ll. 94, 381.

14. RGADA, f. 210, Belgorodskii stb. 691, ll. 11, 358; Belgorodskii stb. 643, ll. 431–33; Belgorodskaia kn. 78, l. 48.

15. RGADA, f. 210, Belgorodskaia kn. 76, ll. 229–44; Belgorodskii stb. 904, ll. 23–56; Belgorodskii stb. 1314, ll. 32–55; Belgorodskii stb. 691, l. 205; Belgorodskii stb. 546, ll. 1, 5; Moscow stb. 404, l. 1; *AIIuZR*, vol. 11, no. 171; Novombergskii, *Prodovol'stvennoe*, vol. 1, no. 631.

16. *AIIuZR* vol. 9, no. 5; vol. 13, no. 129.

17. *AIIuZR*, vol. 9, no. 25; vol. 8, no. 36.

18. Novombergskii, *Prodovol'stvennoe*, vol. 1, no. 631.

19. *AIIuZR*, vol. 9, no. 75; vol. 8, no. 11; vol. 7, no. 8 pt. 1.

20. RGADA, f. 210, Moscow stb. 404, ll. 24, 56, 80, 86.

21. *Istoriia Kieva*, pp. 17, 22.

22. *AIIuZR* vol. 13, no. 42; vol. 8, nos. 65, 70.

23. *AIIuZR*, vol. 11, no. 100; vol 8, no. 51.

24. RGADA, f. 210, Sevskii stb. 414-I, l. 30; *AIIuZR*, vol. 13, nos. 48, 110, 114.

25. *AIIuZR*, vol. 8, no. 77.

26. *AIIuZR*, vol. 8, no. 19.

27. RGADA, f. 210, Moscow stb. 404, ll. 49–93.

28. Bagalei, *Materialy*, (1886), pp. 54–56, gives troop dispositions.

29. RGADA, f. 210, Moscow stb. 404, l. 63.

30. RGADA, f. 210, Moscow stb. 404, ll. 27, 28, 265.

31. RGADA, f. 210, Moscow stb. 404, ll. 56, 72, 80, 316.

32. RGADA, f. 210, Moscow stb. 404, ll. 23, 27, 71, 94, 270, 365, 381.

33. Arsenev, *Dedilov*, no. 23; RGADA, f. 210, Moscow stb. 404, ll. 10–13.

34. *AIIuZR*, vol. 9, no. 4; vol. 8, nos. 36, 70, 77.

35. Not until the late 1670s would the Military Chancellery solve this transportation bottleneck in supply. *AIIuZR*, vol. 9, no. 4; vol. 8, nos. 11, 19, 36, 70, 77.

36. *AIIuZR*, vol. 8, nos. 36, 60, 65.

37. *AIIuZR*, vol. 7, nos. 8, 26; vol. 8, no. 85.

38. *AIIuZR*, vol. 8, nos. 51, 96.

39. RGADA, f. 210, Belgorodskii stb. 691, l. 230.

40. *AIIuZR*, vol. 9, no. 25.

41. RGADA, f. 210, Belgorodskii stb. 691, l. 46; *AIIuZR*, vol. 11, nos. 152, 192; vol. 12, no. 77; vol. 13, no. 110.

42. This estimate is based on the official size of the garrison (see note 6 above) minus 1,000 cavalrymen.

43. RGADA, f. 210, Belgorodskii stb. 691, l. 230, but cf. ibid., ll. 49, 235; *AIIuZR*, vol. 11, no. 171.

44. *AIIuZR*, vol. 13, nos. 129, 114, 110; vol. 12, nos. 102, 27; vol. 11, nos. 1, 52, 192; vol. 8, no. 11; RGADA, f. 210, Belgorodskii stb. 691, ll. 205, 49; Moscow stb. 404 ll. 10–13, 25, 86, 228, 316; Arsen'ev, *Dedilov*, no. 23.

45. *AIIuZR*, vol. 13, no. 116.

46. See Parker, *Military Revolution*, pp. 42–43.

47. *AIIuZR*, vol. 8, no. 77.

48. *AIIuZR*, vol. 11, nos. 113, 145; vol. 13, no. 114.

49. *PSZ*, no. 1204; S. M. Solov'ev, *Istoriia Rossii s drevneishchikh vremen*, 29 vols. in 15 books (Moscow, 1959–1966), vol. 16, p. 391.

50. *PSZ*, no. 1204 discusses costs for 60,000 men and their officers; 75,000 men in new formation regiments participated in the campaign. Hellie, *Enserfment*, p. 272.

51. Hellie, loc. cit.

52. L. J. D. Collins, "The Military Organization and Tactics of the Crimean Tatars during the Sixteenth and Seventeenth Centuries," in *War, Technology, and Society in the Middle East*, ed. V. J. Parry and M. E. Yapp (London, 1975), pp. 273–74; Zagorovskii, "Donskoe kazachestvo," pp. 131–47.

53. Vazhinskii, "Sbory," pp. 24–25.

54. See RGADA, f. 210, Belgorodskii stb. 1000, l. 7, ll. 5–6, on the usual availability of provisions, and ll. 34–143 for calculations city-by-city of the number of arms still needed.

55. This sum includes one carter for each of the 20,000 carts that Patrick Gordon counted and 5,000 others as replacements, trumpeters, and the like. Perjès

estimates that seventeenth-century armies had baggage trains that numbered half again as many men as the fighting force. On European provisioning rates, see Parker, *Military Revolution*, p. 75.

56. Perjès, "Provisioning," pp. 5–11, 14–17.

57. Perjès, "Provisioning," pp. 4, 15.

58. Perjès, "Provisioning," p. 11.

59. Bobrovskii, *Perekhod*, pp. 81–83, describes the process.

60. Novombergskii, *Prodovol'stvennoe*, vol. 1, nos. 278, 378, 436; RGADA, f. 210, Belgorodskaia knigi 132, 133 (city-by-city inventories); Zagorovskii, *Izium-skaia*, pp. 146–47; Novombergskii, *Prodovol'stvennoe*, vol. 1, no. 383.

61. Novombergskii, *Prodovol'sdtvennoe*, vol. 1, no. 302, p. 270. Repairs were undertaken and paid for locally. Mtsensk was told to send its grain directly to Belgorod; because the province collected so little, it would be wasteful to rebuild its granary. Ibid., no. 279.

62. RGADA, f. 210, Belgorodskii stb. 1267, ll. 14–23; Vazhinskii "Sbory," pp. 29–30.

63. RGADA, f. 210, Belgorodskaia kn. 143. The two collections overlapped by about 25 percent, but fell short by about 200 *chetverti* (22 tons).

64. See RGADA, f. 210, Belgorodskaia kn. 144, ll. 289, 312; kn. 156, ll. 381–84; Vazhinskii, "Sbory," p. 32.

65. Novombergskii, *Prodovol'stvennoe*, vol. 1, no. 279.

66. Novombergskii, *Prodovol'stvennoe*, vol. 1, no. 281.

67. RGADA, f. 210, Sevskii stb. 11, ll. 5, 17, 26, 107; Sevskii stb. 414-I, l. 184; Sevskii stb. 4, l. 2ob; Sevskii stb. 5, l. 51.

68. A number of landholders paid the wrong city. RGADA, f. 210, Sevskii stb. 5, ll. 51, 119; Sevskii stb. 11, l. 103. In towns where a major landholder refused to pay or was slow in doing so, the commander complained of general lethargy. And despite a general inclination to unite all taxes to be used for the campaign, musketeers' grain was still sent to Moscow, including that of campaign commanders. Sevskii stb. 11, ll. 17–26; Novombergskii, *Prodovol'stvennoe*, vol. 1, no. 312. Other landholders refused to relinquish their receipts, and still others were believed to hold false receipts. Scribes were moved in midtask from post to post. Ominously, the early reports of receipts were low. Sevskii stb. 4, ll. 2–23; Sevskii stb. 11, ll. 3–4, 104; Novombergskii, *Prodovol'stvennoe*, vol. 1, no. 278.

69. Vazhinskii, "Sbory," p. 30. Some shortfalls were recorded. Voronezh was still suffering from three consecutive bad harvests, as was Palatov. Novombergskii, *Prodovol'stvennoe*, vol. 1, no. 281; vol. 2 no. 280. Some grain was spoiled and was resold to local inhabitants. Novombergskii, *Prodovol'stvennoe*, vol. 1, nos. 379, 381.

70. On-demand grain taxpayers were peasant households belonging either to ecclesiastical establishments that often paid musketeers' grain or to servicemen who did not serve in 1687 (or who were otherwise occupied). RGADA, f. 210, Belgorodskii stb. 1267, l. 444; Sevskii stb. 9, l. 253. There were few peasants in the Belgorod region and fewer still fitting this description. The province of Belgorod, with a quarter-grain assessment of 2,136 households, only contributed to the levy from 371 households. Belgorodskii stb. 1267, ll. 14–19; Belgorodskaia kn. 159; Novombergskii, *Prodovol'stvennoe*, vol. 1, no. 378. In some areas, such as Ryl'sk province, grain contributors were often widows and minors on tenanted estates. By

southern standards, the demand was less than extravagant; not least of all, the harvest was good. Bobrovskii, *Perekhod*, p. 85 n. 98.

71. RGADA, f. 210, Sevskaia kn. 16, l. 214.

72. RGADA, f. 210, Belgorodskaia kn. 144, l. 289; Sevskaia kn. 16, l. 214.

73. Levykin, "Pushechnyi nariad," pp. 125–27.

74. RGADA, f. 210, Belgorodskii stb. 1070, l. 130 (Golitsyn asked for two more guns). N. G. Ustrialov, *Istoriia tsarstvovaniia Petra velikogo*, 5 vols. (St. Petersburg, 1858–1863), vol. 1, *Gospodstvo tsarevny Sofii*, pp. 302–3.

75. RGADA, f. 210, Sevskaia kn. 16, l. 368; Veinberg, *Materialy . . . sosednikh gubernii*, vol. 1, nos. 375, 387.

76. RGADA, f. 210, Sevskaia kn. 18, by regiment.

77. On origins of skilled craftsmen and materials, see RGADA, f. 210, Belgorodskaia kn. 144, ll. 2–176.

78. N. I. Novombergskii, ed., *Vrachebnoe stroenie v doPetrovskoi Rusi* (St. Petersberg, 1903), nos. 33, 34, 37, 38; Novombergskii, *Materialy po istorii meditsiny*, 2 vols. (St. Peterburg, 1907), vol. 2, pp. xvii, xxii, xxiv, nos. 198, 199.

79. RGADA, f. 210, Sevskaia kn. 17, ll. 240–42; Veinberg, *Materialy . . . sosednikh gubernii*, vol. 1, nos. 363, 364, 365.

80. Likhvin and Kaluga sent men to Briansk, while Vorotynsk, Kozelsk, Peremyshl', Serpeisk, and Mosal'sk supported Smolensk's effort. RGADA, f. 210, Sevskii stb. 414-I, ll. 2–5, 48, 420–21, 483, 608, 787. Sevsk cities contributed one boat per 60–80 households. Belgorodskii stb. 1040, l. 182; Sevskii stb. 414-I, ll. 137, 610–29.

81. Ibid., ll. 24–25.

82. RGADA, f. 210, Sevskii stb. 414-I, ll. 48, 547–49, 578–80, 738, 750, 753. Various devices were used to avoid direct participation. One alternative was to pay for a complete boat. In Ustiug province peasants paid about one ruble per household for this purpose. Belokurov, *Materialy*, no. 15. A number of landholders chose instead to purchase boards. Likhvin agreed to send more grain instead of workers. About 120 skilled men appeared from twenty-four cities. RGADA, f. 210, Sevskii stb. 414-I, ll. 578–80, 629, 750, 805–11.

83. RGADA, f. 210, Sevskii stb. 414-I, l. 629. Meanwhile, forty-five scribes had been assembled to oversee and direct not only the boat-building but also the arrival, storage, and then loading of grain. Sevskii stb. 414-I, ll. 573–79, 629, 730–32. Kaluga complained that it lost its only scribe, but this was not an unusual occurrence. N. F. Demidova, *Sluzhilaia burokratiia v Rossii XVII veka i ee rol' v formirovanii absoliutizma* (Moscow, 1987), p. 186. Sumy apparently lost its clerk altogether in the process. Ibid., p. 48.

84. RGADA, f. 210, Sevskii stb. 414-I, ll. 19–20, 30, 33, 450–54, 765.

85. Novombergskii, *Prodovol'stvennoe*, vol. 1, no. 276; RGADA, f. 210, Sevskii stb. 414-I, ll. 450–54.

86. RGADA, f. 210, Belgorodskii stb. 1267. A total of 22,043 households provided 4,411 carts to accompany the army from its muster points, one from every five households. The militarized Komaritskii district paid at more than double that rate, one from every two households, or 2,232 carts.

87. Even this was not entirely adequate; the authorities initiated a local census near Putivl' for the express purpose of identifying new households to contribute fodder. RGADA, f. 210, Sevskii stb. 33, ll. 76, 84.

88. RGADA, f. 210, Sevskii stb. 32, l. 218; Sevskii stb. 33, ll. 1–5, 14–26, 66, 84, 96, 127, 143, 207, 216; Novombergskii, *Prodovol'stvennoe*, vol. 1, no. 284.

89. RGADA, f. 210, Belgorodskaia kn. 98, l. 101; Patrick Gordon, *Tagebuch des Generals Patrick Gordon*, ed. M. A. Obolenskii and M. C. Posselt, 3 vols. (Moscow, 1849–1852), vol. 2, p. 172; Perjès, "Provisioning," p. 16.

90. RGADA, f. 210, Belgorodskaia kn. 144, l. 5.

91. A. A. Tan'kov, *Istoricheskaia letopis' Kurskogo dvorianstva*, vol. 1 (Moscow, 1913), p. 464; De-Pule, *Orlovskie akty*, no. 162, p. 175; *DAI*, vol. 12, no. 36.

92. RGADA, f. 210, Sevskaia kn. 17, ll. 204ob.–5, 228ob.–35.

93. RGADA, f. 210, Sevskaia kn. 17, ll. 98–99, 107; Bobrovskii, *Perekhod*, p. 10.

94. Gordon, *Tagebuch*, p. 172; Perjès, "Provisioning," pp. 18–19.

95. Solov'ev, *Istoriia*, vol. 16, pp. 391–95; Perjès, "Provisioning," p. 39. Perjès, p. 11, believes an 11,000-cart baggage train would not be manageable.

96. This calculation allows no stops for anything besides gathering. The Russian army seems to have avoided delays related to baking and the like by carrying much of its food as biscuit and hardtack. Hughes, *Sophia*, p. 200, calculates the army's movement by dividing the miles covered by the number of days traveled; the text here divides mileage by the number of days on the move, that is, total days minus foraging days.

97. See Gordon, *Tagebuch*, pp. 171–74, for an account of the early days of the campaign.

98. See, for example, Alan Fisher, *The Crimean Tatars* (Palo Alto, Calif., 1978), p. 50.

CHAPTER 6: THE RUSSIAN DEFENSIVE FORCES

1. Parker, *Military Revolution*, p. 39.

2. For example, see Vazhinskii, *Sel'skoe khoziaistvo*, pp. 6–7; Anisimov, *Podatnaia*, pp. 166–80, offers an account of the process of legal recategorization in eighteenth-century Russia.

3. McNeill, *Steppe Frontier*, chapter 4.

4. Hellie, *Enserfment*, pp. 175–79; Zagorovskii, *Belgorodskaia*, p. 25.

5. Zagorovskii, *Iziumskaia*, pp. 214–22, 226; Zagorovskii, *Belgorodskaia*, p. 288. Zagorovskii offers no estimate of the cost of constructing either the Izium or the Belgorod Defensive Line.

6. Zagorovskii, *Belgorodskaia*, pp. 197, 215 (illustrations), 240–43. Cf. Zagorovskii, *Iziumskaia*, pp. 190, 210, 212 (illustrations).

7. Stevens, "Food Supply," table 4, p. 69; Zagorovskii, *Belgorodskaia*, pp. 179–81; Zagorovskii, *Iziumskaia*, p. 79.

8. See, for example, C. B. O'Brien, *Muscovy and the Ukraine* (Berkeley, 1963), p. 114.

9. A. A. Novosel'skii, *Bor'ba Moskovskogo gosudarstva s Tatarami v pervoi polovine XVII veka* (Moscow, 1948), conclusion; Vodarskii, *Naselenie*, p. 173.

10. Cf. Nikitin, *Sluzhilye liudi*, chap. 1.

11. See, for example, *PSZ*, nos. 7399, 9672, cited in Thomas Esper, "The Odnodvortsy and the Russian Nobility," *Slavonic and East European Review* 45 (1967): 127.

12. Myshlaevskii, *K istorii khoziaistvennogo byta*, pp. 14–15, argues that the fortresses fell into disrepair and that some of the military institutions common to southern cities in the seventeenth century disappeared as the frontier moved south. Aleksandrov, "Streletskoe voisko," p. 48, argues that there was no demilitarization of the central Belgorod region in the 1650s with respect to the musketeer forces. On p. 13 he demonstrates that the number of musketeers in southern towns remained quite stable from 1632 to 1678, except for a brief increase in the 1650s.

13. See, for example, *DAI*, vol. 9, no. 106, p. 231, where a garrison of 1,161 males is described for Tula. Of these, 177 have military functions (*vorotniki, stanichniki, zasechnye storozha, pushkarei*, and musketeers). The remainder are townsmen, postal service personnel, blacksmiths, locksmiths, and brick makers, and the children, relatives, and in-laws of those listed. None are actually described as garrison servicemen.

14. Vazhinskii, "Usilenie," pp. 56, 58, 60; RGADA, f. 210, Belgorodskaia kn. 100, ll. 4–10.

15. RGADA, f. 210, Belgorodskaia kn. 95 (1676) identifies the numbers of both campaign and garrison servicemen originating from each province it surveys.

16. Hellie, "Warfare," p. 92.

17. Vazhinskii, "Usilenie," p. 56, lists the dates of major recruitments. The implementation of other reforms in the south is recorded in RGADA, f. 210, Belgorodskie kn. 95 (1675–1676) and 100. For the content of the reforms, see chapter 4.

18. Davies, "Service," p. 136. Servicemen described their supporting laborers as cripples or half-wits or testified they personally had been retired to town service because of poverty and solitude, p. 145.

19. Davies, "Service," 138. More than 10 percent of Dobryi's garrison were solitary. Novombergskii, *Prodovol'stvennoe*, vol. 2, no. 203.

20. Vazhinskii, "Usilenie," p. 65.

21. *AIuB*, vol. 3, no. 300, describes cavalrymen serving in a garrison because of poverty and solitude.

22. The percentage of distressed garrison service households was 65.2 percent—compared to 40.7 percent for regimental service—although the economic differences between regimental servicemen and garrison servicemen, on the whole, were not pronounced. Davies, "Service," pp. 140–41, 144; Novombergskii, *Prodovol'stvennoe*, vol. 1, no. 630. I know of no study that would supply similar information for contract or recruited servicemen.

23. RGADA, f. 210, Belgorodskaia kn. 78, "Kursk"; Belgorodskaia kn. 143, "Kursk." Likewise, there appeared to be little consistency in garrison service personnel for a district of Belgorod province. Cf. Belgorodskaia kn. 79, ll. 29–62; Belgorodskaia kn. 152, ll. 115–53; Davies, "Service," pp. 149–51.

24. Chernov, *Vooruzhennye Sily*, p. 133; Novosel'skii, "Dvorstovye," p. 65–80; RGADA, f. 210, Belgorodskaia kn. 143, "Kursk." Moskovskii stb. 404, ll. 133, 180, shows the Komaritskii dragoons undertaking first campaign and then garrison service again.

25. Zagorovskii, *Iziumskaia*, p. 38.

26. Demotion into the garrison services was invoked as a penalty for failure to report for campaign service; infantrymen appear more frequently on the garrison rolls after 1679. Kalynchev, *Pravovye voprosy*, p. 77; *PSZ*, no. 1218 (1686).

27. See, for example, Novombergskii, *Prodovol'stvennoe*, vol. 1, no. 236.

28. L. B. Veinberg, ed., *Materialy po istorii goroda Ostrogozhska* (Voronezh, 1886), no. 165, records an instance, however, when an effort to reinforce a garrison with contract regimental servitors was overruled by the regimental commander.

29. See Bagalei, *Materialy* (1886), pp. 54–74, 205–10, for example.

30. *DAI*, vol. 9, no. 106; RGADA, f. 210, Sevskaia kn. 16, ll. 508–68.

31. On the whole, these garrisons were poorly armed, and it was not uncommon to find garrisons where more than half the hereditary servicemen lacked firearms, unless these were issued from the state armory. Because it was expected that recruited servicemen would be armed from the armory, they were often better provided for in this regard. RGADA, f. 210, Belgorodskaia kn. 77, "Bolkhov," "Cherniavsk"; Belgorodskaia kn. 82, "Novosil."

32. Many dragoons had entered the army as militarized peasants, then been used in the campaign regiments under the manpower pressures of the 1670s, and finally returned to local defense and garrison service in the 1680s, when active campaign service exhausted their resources.

33. See Beliaev, "Dlia sravnitel'noi statistiki," pp. 39–40, on the growing size of the regimental versus the garrison service in Khar'kov. Zagorovskii, *Iziumskaia*, pp. 72–73. The proportion of hereditary servicemen who were retired rose a bit in both military regions, from 5 to 7 percent.

34. Dmitrii I. Bagalei, *K istorii zaselenie i khoziaistvennogo byta Voronezhskogo i Kurskogo kraia* (St. Petersburg, 1896), pp. 105–6, describes Belgorod's long distance patrols between 1623 and 1636. These patrols' warnings of Tatar approach called up the regular army.

35. Quotation from RGADA, f. 210, Balgorodskii stb. 691, l. 277; the responsible tasks of guarding and patrolling traditionally had been allotted to hereditary servicemen. Miklashevskii, *K istorii khoziaistvennogo byta*, p. 15.

36. Zagorovskii, *Belgorodskaia*, pp. 24–32.

37. RGADA, f. 210, Belgorodskii stb. 691, l. 277; Belgorodskaia kn. 79 (Valuiki); cf. Belgorodskii stb. 545, ll. 61–62 (Valuiki, 1664–1665).

38. Garrisons usually served in halves, that is, with one complete relief rotation. Golitsyn, *Voennaia istoriia*, p. 437.

39. *DAI*, vol. 9, no. 106 p. 282; other examples of town duties are listed throughout document no. 106, a military estimate.

40. RGADA, f. 210, Belgorodskaia kn. 95 (*razbor* and *smeta*, 1677), "Korotoiak."

41. *AI*, vol. 4, no. 148 (Bolkhov, 1660).

42. RGADA, f. 210, Belgorodskaia kn. 79, p. 30; Zagorovskii, *Belgorodskaia*, p. 251. Hereditary servicemen also acted as police. Golitsyn, *Voennaia istoria*, p. 436.

43. A group of Voronezh Cossacks, for example, list their garrison responsibilities in 1672 in Vtorovoi and Aleksandrov-Dol'nik, *Drevnie gramoty*, no. 313, pp. 649–50. In the territories of the four Ukrainian regiments, most garrison servicemen were listed as *cherkassy* (Ukrainian). Zagorovskii, *Iziumskaia*, pp. 58–59.

44. Tan'kov, *Kurskogo dvorianstva*, p. 400.

45. *DAI*, vol. 9 , no. 106, pp. 249–50.

46. For guard duties at Pskov fortress in 1661, see *AI*, vol. 4, no. 161.

47. Arsen'ev, *Dedilov*, nos. 20, 22 (1969).

48. Davies, "Prikaznoi stb. 385." In 1679 the Komaristkii dragoons served as baggage train orderlies for the infantry regiments. *RIB*, vol. 10, p. 396; Chernov, *Vooruzhenye sily*, pp. 165–67; *AAE*, vol. 4, no. 206 (1675).

49. See Stevens, "Food Supply," table 4, p. 69; Golitsyn, *Voennaia istoria*, p. 437.

50. Zagorovskii, *Belgorodskaia*, p. 251.

51. Zagorovskii, *Iziumskaia*, pp. 58–59, 61; Stepanov, *Krest'ianskaia voina*, vol. 2, pt. 2, pp. 56–88; Piskarev, *Sobranie materialov*, p. 50.

52. For example, see Brian Davies, "Prikaznoi stb. 859," ref. to l. 150.

53. *PSZ*, nos. 8, 207–I; Solov'ev, "Goroda," p. 49; Davies, "Prikaznoi stb. 859," ref. to l. 50.

54. See, for example, Vtorovoi and Aleksandrov-Dol'nik, *Drevnie gramoty*, no. 168.

55. RGADA, f. 210, Belgorodskii stb. 971, 986.

56. RGADA, f. 210, Belgorodskii stb. 986, l. 62; Novombergskii, *Prodovol'stvennoe*, vol. 1, no. 244; Zagorovskii, *Belgorodskaia*, pp. 121, 288.

57. Novombergskii, *Prodovol'stvennoe*, vol. 1, no. 244. Arable tenth calculations were taken from Iablonov's fields before the Izium Defensive Line was completed; men and women both worked at harvest time. Miklashevskii, *K istorii khoziaistvennogo byta*, appendix.

58. *AIuZR*, vol. 11, no. 152; Arsen'ev, *Dedilov*, no. 23; RGADA, f. 210, Belgorodskii stb. 691, l. 13; Sevskii stb. 13, l. 72.

59. Towns along the Don disproportionately contributed to the annual boat-building from their garrisons because this was, for them, a local project. On isolated occasions, one boat was built by as few as twenty garrison households, but forty to seventy-five households were more usual prior to 1678. RGADA, f. 210, Belgorodskii stb. 691; Novombergskii, *Prodovol'stvennoe*, vol. 1, nos. 166, 341; Piskarev, *Sobranie materialov*, pp. 100–5; Veinberg and Poltoravskaia, *Materialy . . .* , vol. 1, *Voronezhskie akty*, no. 76–77; Vtorovoi and Aleksandrov-Dol'nik, *Drevnie gramoty*, nos. 153, 168. The same group of towns would provide escorts, at the rate of one serviceman from four to six garrison households in the early 1670s. Voronezhskaia kn. 1, l. 69ob; Novombergskii, *Prodovol'stvennoe*, vol. 1, no. 177.

60. See *AIuZR*, vol. 9, no. 5, for example.

61. Vtorovoi and Aleksandrov-Dol'nik, *Drevnie gramoty*, no. 75; Arsen'ev, *Dedilov*, no. 51.

62. Vtorovoi and Aleksandrov-Dol'nik, *Drevnie gramoty*, no. 75; Novombergskii, *Prodovol'stvennoe*, vol. 1, no. 341; Arsen'ev, *Dedilov*, no. 48; Voronezhskaia kn. 1, l. 69ob.

63. Boat-building continued to be a significant demand. De-Pule, *Orlovskie akty*, no. 131; Novombergskii, *Prodovol'stvennoe*, vol. 1, no. 382; Veinberg, *Materialy . . . Ostrogozhska*, no. 100; RGADA, f. 210, Prikaznoi stb. 1400. The boats required military escort; one man from eighty households was sent in 1686. In Valuiki, as at other points on the frontier, when supplies were not forthcoming, its servicemen made up the quantities. Veinberg, *Materialy . . . , sosednikh gubernii*, vol. 1, no. 366 (1697).

64. RGADA, f. 210, Belgorodskaia kn. 98, ll. 84–88; Belgorodskaia kn. 144, l. 406; De-Pule, *Orlovskie akty*, nos. 167, 170, 173.

65. Chernov, *Vooruzhenye sily*, p. 188; Sevskii stb. 410, ll. 4–7, lists soldiers

from Trubchevsk and Karachev in the Sevsk region who deserted the Kievan garrison.

66. De-Pule, *Orlovskie akty*, p. 435, cited by Myklashevskii, *K istorii khoziaistvennogo byta*, p. 14.

67. See, for example, RGADA, f. 210, Belgorodskii stb. 1267, l. 444; Prikaznoi stb. 1400 (1693); Tan'kov, *Kurskogo dvorianstva*, pp. 38, 464; RGADA, f. 210, Sevskaia kn. 18, l. 216; Davies, "Dela raznykh gorodov 36." In some individual towns the growth of the campaign army imposed an immediate hardship on garrisons by reducing their numbers.

68. It was openly remarked that the Belgorod line would need no upkeep in the areas where it was protected by the Izium defenses. Tan'kov, *Kurskogo dvorianstvo*, p. 462.

69. No less than thirteen additional garrisons were converted into interior towns by 1680 alone.

70. Compare granary holdings in RGADA, f. 210, Belgorodskie kn. 57, 77, 79, 82, 87, 89, 94, 95, 100, 118, 132, 133, 144, 151, 152, 159, 163, 164; Belgorodskie stb. 545, 690, 691, 904, 957, 1000, 1070, 1314; Moskovskie kn. 103, 126; Moskovskii stb. 404; Sevskie kn. 14, 17, 18, 33; Sevskii stb. 414-I; Davies, "Dela raznykh gorodov 36"; Belgorodskie stb. 921, 1429, 1557; *PSZ*, no. 522; Vodarskii, "Naselenie," pp. 104–7, 198–212, 225–32; *DAI*, vol. 9, no. 106; Vazhinskii, *Zemlevladenia*, pp. 104, 122–23; Piskarev, *Sobranie materialov* pp. 78–81, 109, 192.

71. The entries in RGADA, f. 210, Belgorodskie kn. 132–33, were absent or illegible.

72. In 1686 artillery is calculated for towns that appear in all three registers, 1678, 1682, and 1686.

73. Levykin, "Pushechnyi nariad," pp. 125–27.

74. Table 5 totals do not include either nonfunctioning artillery or shot that did not fit any of the town's artillery.

75. Collins, "Military Organization," esp. pp. 270–71.

76. Davies, "Prikaznoi stb. 643"; for Kozlov town garrison's relative poverty before the reforms, see Davies, "Service," pp. 129–53.

77. Vazhinskii, "Sbory," p. 30. Anisimov, *Podatnaia*, p. 166, argues that this change from military serviceman to taxpayer was not fully accomplished until the Petrine period.

78. See Anisimov, *Podatnaia*, pp. 165–88, esp. p. 166, for a judicious example.

79. RGADA, f. 210, Sevskii stb. 414-I, ll. 2, 24–25, 449–54; Novombergskii, *Prodovol'stvennoe*, vol. 1, no. 631; Sevskii stb. 33, l. 104; Belgorodskaia kn. 163, l. 3ob.

CHAPTER 7: THE COLLAPSE OF SOUTHERN STATUS: THE *ODNODVORTSY*

1. Quoted in Novosel'skii, "Pobegi," p. 352; and cited in Gregory Freeze, "The *Soslovie* (Estate) Paradigm and Russian Social History," *American Historical Review* 1986 (February): 14 n. 14.

2. See chapter 2 for more detailed description.

3. The enrollment of fugitive serfs in southern service garrisons, some of them as hereditary servicemen, is only one example of such movement between

larger categories (taxpaying to service). It is, however, a telling one because it had the tacit approval of the state, which then limited the owners' ability to reclaim their former peasants.

4. V. O. Kliuchevskii, *Istoriia soslovii v Rossii* (Moscow, 1913), esp. lectures 1, 2, 20, applies the word *soslovie* or "estate" to the seventeenth century, comparing that period's characterizations to western European estates of a much earlier period.

5. Freeze, "The *Soslovie* Paradigm," pp. 15–16, 23, 28–29, 31, discusses alternative terms and their success in describing the social realities of the eighteenth and nineteenth centuries.

6. V. A. Aleksandrov, "Streletskoe voisko na iuge Russkogo gosudarstva v XVII veke" (Kand. thesis, Moscow State University, 1947), p. 250. Also note, in chapter 4 above, the shift of musketeers into new formation regiments and the subsequent division and disbanding of remaining musketeers regiments.

7. Anisimov, *Podatnaia*, p. 180.

8. Esper, "*Odnodvortsy*," p. 129, discusses the smallholders as an intermediate social category but largely with reference to subsequent centuries.

9. For example, see Germanov, "Rasprostranenie," pp. 183–326; Ia. Solov'ev, "Ob odnodvortsakh," *Otechestvennye zapiski* 69 (1850): esp. p. 88; N. D. Chechulin, "Neskol'ko slov o starykh sluzhb v XVIII veke," in *Sbornik statei v chest' Matveia K. Liubovskogo*, ed. D. I. Bagalei (Moscow, 1917), pp. 32–39; Judith Pallot and Denis Shaw, *Landscape and Settlement in Romanov Russia* (Oxford, 1990), pp. 33, 36, 46; P. I. Ivanov, "Siabry-pomeshchiki," *ZhMNP* 1903 (December): 406–22.

10. *AMG*, vol. 2, nos. 62, 112, 382, 387, for the 1630s and 1640s, and also cited in Esper, "*Odnodvortsy*"; Solov'ev, "Ob odnodvortsakh," p. 90.

11. Nikitin, *Sluzhilye liudi*, p. 254.

12. Solov'ev, "Ob odnodvortsakh," pp. 91–92. Anisimov, *Podatnaia*, pp. 178–79, 166, identifies the shift away from an emphasis on service as key.

13. The Kozlov province example comes from Rabinovich, "Sud'ba," p. 513, but the same diversity is noted by Solov'ev, "Ob odnodvortsakh," p. 81. Davies, "Dela raznykh gorodov 36," ref. to ll. 987, 990–91, identifies 2,967 hereditary garrison servicemen among the 25,000 servicemen in Kozlov province.

14. Vazhinskii, *Zemlevladenie*, p. 122–23.

15. Cf. Bobrovskii, *Perekhod*, p. 61; Polkovnik Gudim-Levkovich, "Ocherk istoricheskogo razvitia vooruzhennykh sil Rossii do 1708," *Voennyi sbornik* 107 (1876): 22; Hellie, *Enserfment*, pp. 229–30.

16. This rather uncontrolled access to initiation, in conjunction with other conditions, clearly promoted exceptional social mobility. Solov'ev, "Ob odnodvortsakh," p. 87. Nevertheless, in the 1646 census some careful distinctions were recorded: hereditary servicemen who happened to be members of the steppe patrol (*stanichniki deti boiarskie*) and Cossack leaders who could own service land (*pomestnye atamany*). Tan'kov, *Kurskogo dvorianstvo*, appendix, pp. 38–50, reproduces entries for Belgorod province.

17. Miklashevskii, *K istorii khoziaistvennogo byta*, p. 26.

18. RGADA, f. 210, Belgorodskii stb. 772, ll. 142–48; Novosel'skii, "Raspad," pp. 231–53; Aleksandrov, "Streletskoe," p. 250; Nikolai P. Pavlov-Sil'vanskii, *Gosudarevye sluzhilye liudi: Proizkhozhdenie russkogo dvorianstva* (St. Petersburg, 1898), p. 243. V. I. Nedosekin, "Chetvertnoe zemlepol'zovanie odnodvertsev

iuga Rossii v XVIII veke," *Trudy Voronezhskogo universiteta* 53 (1960): 107, indicates misleadingly that eighteenth-century smallholders were recruited servicemen. A hint of the complexities involved is Nedosekin's categorization of hereditary service dragoons as recruited servicemen.

19. Pavlov-Silvanskii, *Gosudarevye sluzhilye liudi*, pp. 236–38; Zagorovskii, "Soldatskie sela," pp. 94–95.

20. Zagorovskii, "Soldatskie sela," pp. 94–95. An analogous situation to that of the soldiers, but from an earlier period, would be that of the *pomestnyi ataman*. Tan'kov, *Kurskogo dvorianstva*, p. 42.

21. Davies, "Service," p. 139.

22. Zagorovskii, "Soldatskie sela," p. 95; Solov'ev, "Ob odnodvortsakh," p. 88, offer other examples.

23. Birzhe, "Volnenie," no. 1; RGADA, f. 210, Belgorodskaia kn. 89, ll. 179–91; Belgorodskaia kn. 118, l. 289. The request for initiation was also, obviously, itself an indication of the confusion of status and service categories.

24. Novosel'skii, "Raspad"; PSZ, no. 1103; Anisimov, *Podatnaia*, pp. 174–75, discusses the continuation of these policies in the Petrine period.

25. See examples cited in Vazhinskii, *Zemlevladenie*, pp. 121, 145, 178, 179.

26. RGADA, f. 210, Belgorodskii stb. 618, l. 498.

27. Aleksandrov, "Streletskoe naselenie," p. 250; Vazhinskii, *Zemlevladenie*, pp. 144–45. There were attempts to limit shifts of recruited servicemen to full-fledged hereditary service. Pavlov-Silvanskii, *Gosudarevye sluzhilye liudi*, pp. 223–24. This part of the eighteenth-century social recategorization process has been less fully studied than that affecting the smallholders.

28. The term *pomeshchik* was not retired from official use until the Petrine censuses, however. Anisimov, *Podatnaia*, p. 168.

29. *PSZ*, no. 1003.

30. Vazhinskii, *Zemlevladenie*, pp. 107–8.

31. Vazhinskii, *Zemlevladenie*, pp. 94, 104, 116–17, 122–25.

32. Land shortage seems a less plausible explanation. Germanov, "Rasprostranenie," pp. 218–19, asserts the presence of empty lands in the Don River provinces. Also, land parcels granted late in the century tended to be issued at full size. Stevens, "Food Supply," pp. 41–42.

33. Kursk, Belgorod, Usman', and Khar'kov were also among the areas where Moscow-ranked servicemen were prohibited from acquiring service land; Usman' and Khar'kov were founded in the 1640s. Vazhinskii, *Zemlevladenie*, pp. 122–25; Zagorovskii, *Belgorodskaia*, pp. 24–25.

34. RGADA, f. 210, Sevskaia kn. 18, ll. 70–96: "1686–1687 Muster of Starodubtsy"; Davies, "Service," esp. pp. 139–41. For similar results in other provinces, see Vazhinskii, *Zmelevladenie*, p. 11; Zagorovskii, "Soldatskie sela," p. 95.

35. Vazhinskii, *Zemlevladenie*, pp. 122–25; his, *Sel'skoe khoziaistvo*, pp. 23–25. Zagorovskii, "Zemledel'cheskoe," p. 202, adds that the recruited men's lands weren't much larger than the peasantry's.

36. See chapters 2–4 above; Vazhinskii, *Sel'skoe khoziaistvo*, pp. 33–50.

37. We lack specific information on southern peasant economies. In a brief examination of their dues-paying records, it appeared that servicemen who were ex-peasants were at least as reliable contributors as others, both serf and free. Stevens, "Food Supply," chapter 6, esp. p. 259. At the end of the seventeenth century,

northern monastic peasants paid 4–5 rubles annually in state taxes, while southern servitors contributed 7–8 rubles' worth (the latter is a more comprehensive calculation, including labor and service). Vazhinskii, *Sel'skoe khoziaistvo*, pp. 77–80.

38. Novombergskii, *Prodovol'stvennoe*, vol. 1, nos. 299, 233; Solov'ev, "Goroda," pp. 54–55; Vazhinskii, *Zemlevladenie*, p. 24.

39. Vazhinskii, "Usilenie," pp. 52, 63–66.

40. See, for example, RGADA, f. 210, Sevskaia kn. 18.

41. *PSZ*, nos. 982, 991.

42. Vazhinskii, *Zemlevladenie*, p. 25.

43. *PSZ*, nos. 1113, 1148.

44. See, for example, Anisimov, *Podatnaia*, p. 165.

45. Vazhinskii, *Sel'skoe khoziaistvo*, p. 52; Cherepnin, "Klassovaia bor'ba," p. 55.

46. Cherepnin, "Klassovaia bor'ba," pp. 53–61; *Iz istoriia Kurskogo kraia*, pp. 46–47; Miliukov, *Gosudarstvennoe khoziaistvo*, pp. 5–9; Vazhinskii, *Sel'skoe khoziaistvo*, p. 52; Pavlov-Silvanskii, *Gosudarvye sluzhilye liudi*, p. 251.

47. Cf. Bobrovskii, *Perekhod*, p. 62; Bobrovskii, *Istoriia leib-gvardii Preobrazhenskogo polka* (St. Petersburg, 1900), vol. 1, p. 15.

48. Siberian contributions were somewhat similar. Nikitin, *Sluzhilye liudi*, pp. 32–33.

49. By V. M. Vazhinskii's calculation, in *Sel'skoe khoziaistvo*, p. 77, garrison servicemen contributed about four rubles more in taxes, dues, and labor than campaign servicemen.

50. The single exception would have been large estateholders, whose peasants might have contributed but who would personally have had no relationship to the fortress garrison and would therefore have been exempt from payment of military dues.

51. Arsen'ev, *Dedilov*, no. 73.

52. Veinberg and Poltoravskaia, *Materialy* . . . , vol. 1, *Voronezhskie akty*, no. 76; Novombergskii, *Prodovol'stvennoe*, vol. 1, no. 341; V. P. Zagorovskii, "Sudostroenie pod Voronezhem v XVII veke," *Trudy Voronezhskogo kraevedcheskogo muzeia* 1 (1960): 51–73. See also Zagorovskii, *Iziumskaia*, pp. 99, 107; Vazhinskii, *Sel'skoe khoziaistvo*, p. 56.

53. Vazhinskii, *Sel'skoe khoziaistvo*, p. 56.

54. Novosel'skii, "Dvortsovaia"; Novombergskii, *Prodovol'stvennoe*, vol. 1, no. 123.

55. Novombergskii, *Prodovol'stvennoe*, vol. 1, nos. 166, 171, 341; Piskarev, *Sobranie materialy*, pp. 100–5; Veinberg and Poltoravskaia, *Materialy* . . . , vol. 1, *Voronezhskie akty*, nos. 28, 76, 77; RGADA, f. 210, Sevskii stb. 414-I, ll. 2, 48, 430–54, 579–80.

56. One tax that continued to differentiate by status and wealth was the postal tax, which was assessed on acreage of land under cultivation until 1678.

57. Solov'ev, "Goroda," pp. 54–56.

58. But cf. Kliuchevskii, *Istoriia soslovii*, lecture 5.

59. RGADA, f. 210, Sevskii stb. 414-I, ll. 2–3, 420–21, 483, 608, 787; Belgorodskii stb. 1040, l. 182; Veinberg and Poltoravskaia, *Materialy* . . . , vol. 1, *Voronezhskie akty*, no. 28. Occasionally, designating a service or status group as contributors seems intended to vary the pool of contributors. RGADA, f. 210, Belgorodskii stb.

1267; Belgorodskaia kn. 163, l. 3ob.; Veinberg and Poltoravskaia, *Materialy* . . . , vol. 1, *Voronezhskie akty*, no. 425; Miklashevskii, *K istorii khoziaistvennogo byta*, pp. 198–99; Bagalei, *Materialy* (1890), pp. 102–4.

60. See RGADA, f. 210, Belgorodskaia kn. 143, for example.

61. Novombergskii, *Prodovol'stvennoe*, vol. 1, no. 377.

62. Novombergskii, *Prodovol'stvennoe*, vol. 1, no. 630; RGADA, f. 210, Moskovskaia kn. 404, l. 160; Belgorodskaia kn. 144; Novosel'skii, "Dvortsovie," pp. 65–80; Belgorodskii stb. 904, ll. 180–82. Cf. RGADA, f. 210, Denezhnaia kn. 312, ll. 10–11; Arsen'ev, *Dedilov*, no. 53.

63. S. B. Veselovskii, "Materialy po istorii obshchego opisaniia vsekh zemel' Russogo gosudarstva v knotse XVII veka," *Istoricheskii arkhiv* 7 (1951): 300–15; Vazhinskii, *Zemlevladenia*, p. 169.

64. For example, Peter I's government tried to protect hereditary servicemen from the shock of serving in the same regiments as their social inferiors but did not apply this ruling in the south. V. N. Avtokratov, "Voennyi prikaz," in AN SSSR II, *Poltava* (Moscow, 1959), p. 237.

65. Vazhinskii, "Vvedenie," pp. 91–92.

66. Anisimov, *Podatnaia*, p. 167.

67. Anisimov, *Podatnaia*, p. 168–71; Esper, "Odnodvortsy," p. 127.

GLOSSARY

The historian of pre-Petrine Russia writing in English confronts the unfortunate necessity of intelligibly translating the myriad social and military service categories so important to Muscovite life. Some of these terms, such as *pomest'e* (land held in service tenure or service land), have in the recent past been translated by and large consistently in the English-language literature. Where such standard terms exist, I have of course used them. Elsewhere, I have endeavored to be merely consistent and, where possible, to chose relatively euphonious English equivalents.

altyn   0.03 rubles (1 ruble = 33 *altyn*, 2 *den'gi* = 200 *den'gi*).

ataman   Title of Cossack military commanders.

batraki   Hired laborers.

Belgorodskaia zasechanaia cherta   Belgorod Defensive Line, defensive abatis line built through town of Belgorod, 1630s–1650s.

Belgorodskii polk   Belgorod Army Group, supported and recruited from cities of Belgorod Military-Administrative Region. Similar army group existed in Sevsk.

Belgorodskii razriad   Belgorod Military-Administrative Region. Similar regions existed in Sevsk, Tambov, and elsewhere.

bobyl(i)   Cotter(s).

Boiarskaia duma   Boyar Council.

Bol'shaia kazna   Great Treasury.

chetverik   Dry measure equal to one-eighth *chetvert'*. It was equivalent to 27 pounds of rye from 1650 to 1678; 36 pounds of rye thereafter.

chetverikovyi khleb   "Eighth-grain": in-kind grain dues levied from 1663 to 1683 in southern regions; named after dry measure *chetverik* (one-eighth *chetvert'*).

chetvert'   (1) Land measure; 1 *chetvert'* = 0.5 *desiatina* = 1.35 acres (640 acres = 1 sq. mi.). (2) Dry measure for official deposits in state granaries, equivalent to 216 pounds of rye from 1650s until 1670s; 288 pounds rye thereafter. *Razdatochnaia chetvert'* (issuing *chetvert'*) was used for payments from granary; it was 0.75 of *priemnaia chetvert'* (deposit *chetvert'*), used to measure payments into granary.

chin dumnyi   Rank commensurate with participation in Boyar Council.

chin gorodovoi, po gorodovomu spisku   Rank of provincial hereditary servicemen; members of middle service class.

chin moskovskii   Rank commensurate with service assignment to capital.

datochnye liudi   Army recruits of taxpaying background.

den'ga   0.005 ruble (1 ruble = 200 *den'gi*).

desiatina   Land measure, equivalent to ca. 2.7 acres. Cf. *chetvert'*.

desiatinnaia pashnia, pashnia   "Arable tenth": court land cultivated in south by servitors for emergency grain supply.

desiatinnyi khleb   "Tenth-grain": in-kind grain dues that replaced arable tenth in southern provinces. See *desiatinnaia pashnia, pashnia*.

dvoinoe vino   "Double wine": double-distilled grain liquor, alcohol, vodka.

dvoriane, deti boiarskie   Ranks of middle service class; provincial servicemen, in descending order of prestige. Sing., *dvorianin, syn boiarskii.*

golova   Head; commander of musketeer unit.

gorodovaia sluzhba   Town or garrison service. Cf. *polkovaia sluzhba.*

gorodovoi, dvorovoi, vybornoi   Echelons of provincial service in ascending order.

gosudarevye zhitnitsy   Tsar's granaries.

guberniia   Provincial administrative unit of Peter I, introduced in 1708.

guliashchie liudi   Wandering people; those whose location and occupation were not fixed by census takers.

iama, iamskaia gon'ba   Postal system, similar to state-run pony express.

iamshchik   Servitor in postal system; member of lower service class.

Inozemskii prikaz   Foreigners' Chancellery.

iz cheti, s gorodom   Indications that cash entitlements for hereditary servicemen came, respectively, from center or local sources.

Khlebnyi prikaz   Grain Chancellery, 1663–1683; collected grain from escheated and mortgaged land for campaign troops.

Khlebnyi stol   Grain Department of Military Chancellery; supervised collection of southern grain dues.

kopeishchiki   Lancers.

kormovye den'gi   Food allowance in cash.

kvas   Popular Muscovite near beer.

mestnichestvo   Precendence-ranking system used at Muscovite court, abolished in 1682.

na pashne   "On the land": left to farm family fields for relatives in garrison or regimental service.

nadel   Land parcel in collective holding, typically belonging to member of lower service class.

novo-okladnyi khleb   "Newly assessed grain"; another name given to quarter-grain. See *poluosminyi khleb.*

novyi stroi   New formation; modern regiments of seventeenth-century Muscovite army.

odnodvorets (pl., *odnodvortsy*)   Smallholder; petty serviceman with small land grant and little dependent labor (see chapter 7).

oklad   Entitlement, typically in cash and land, assigned to hereditary serviceman at initiation.

okladshchik   Official who assigned entitlements at initiations.

osadnyi khleb   "Siege-grain": among earliest regular southern grain collections.

otpusk   Shipment, delivery. Don shipments (*Donskie otpuski*) and Kievan shipments (*Kievskie otpuski*) were sent by south to support Don Cossacks and Russian troops.

otsypnoi khleb   "Tenth-grain": in-kind grain dues that replaced arable tenth in southern provinces. See *desiatinnaia pashnia, pashnia.*

pod'iachii   Clerk.

polkovaia sluzhba   Campaign, field, or regimental service. Cf. *gorodovaia sluzhba.*

polkovnik   Colonel; commander of modern regiment.

polovinchik   Individual with whom landholder halved his duties, service, and land. Cf. *prokormshchik.*

poluosminyi khleb   "Quarter-grain": in-kind grain dues collected in south after 1683. Named after its one-quarter *chetvert'* assessment. See *chetvert'.*

polupolkovnik   Lieutenant colonel.

pomeshchik   Service landholder. See *pomest'e.*

pomest'e (pl., *pomest'ia*)   Land received contingent on lifelong military service; service land typically belonging to an hereditary serviceman.

pud   36.11 pounds; 16.38 kilograms.

posadskie liudi   Townspeople.

Posol'skii prikaz   Chancellery of Foreign Affairs.

posopnyi khleb   "Tenth-grain": in-kind grain dues that replaced arable tenth in southern provinces. See *desiatinnaia pashnia, pashnia.*

prikaz   Chancellery; musketeer regiment.

Prikaz dragunskogo stroia   Dragoons' Chancellery.

prokormshchik   "Feeder": assigned individual (often not family member) who farmed to support others away in service. Also called *pod"emshchik, podmoshchnik.*

pushkar'   Artilleryman dealing with heavy and mounted guns; member of lower service class.

razbor   Military review for all categories of servicemen.

razborshchik   Military reviewer.

Razriad, razriad   Military Chancellery; or military-administrative region such as those at Belgorod, Sevsk, Tambov.

reitary   New formation light cavalrymen. See *novyi stroi.*

rugi   Contributions (to clergy).

sbornyi khleb   Southern regional grain dues of 1690s, similar to eighth-grain. See *chetverikovyi khleb.*

s"ezzhaia izba   Local administration.

sluzhilye liudi   Military servicemen.

sluzhilye liudi po gorodovomu spisku   Provincial hereditary servicemen. See *chin gorodovoi, po gorodovomu spisku.*

sluzhilye liudi po otechestvu   Hereditary servicemen, born to service ranks; members of middle and upper service class.

sluzhilye liudi po priboru   Recruited servicemen; men recruited or contracted to military service; members of lower service class.

smeta   Military estimates, listing available men, supplies, fortifications.

soldaty   Infantrymen, soldiers.

sotnia (pl., *sotni*)   Old-style heavy cavalry unit of one hundred men.

stanichniki   Steppe patrolmen; special frontier branch of early southern military service.

stol'nik   Russian court rank.

streletskii khleb   "Musketeers' grain": national grain collections paid by taxable population for support of musketeers.

Streletskii prikaz   Musketeers' Chancellery.

strel'tsy (sing., *strelets*)   Musketeers.

sukhari   Hardtack.

syn boiarskii   Sing. of *deti boiarskie.* See *dvoriane.*

tiaglye liudi   Taxable population.

tretchiki   Individuals with whom landholder divided his lands, service, and duties into thirds. Cf. *prokormshchik, polovinchik.*

tseloval'nik   Sworn deputy.

Ulozhenie   Law Code of 1649.

verstan'e, verstan'ia   Military initiation for hereditary servicemen.

vino   "Wine": distilled alcohol.

voevoda   Military commander; military town governor.

volost'   Territory or district, often with resident peasant community; often referred to territories in south held by dragoons, former peasants.

vorotniki   Guards of fortress gates; recruited servicemen.

votchina   Hereditary land and estates.

vybornyi   "Select."

vybornyi soldat   Member of elite infantry regiment.

vyt   Taxable unit often encompassing 12–20 *chetverti* of land.

zaprosnyi khleb   "On-demand grain" collections; extraordinary levies used to supply particular military campaigns, especially toward end of seventeenth century.

zasechanaia cherta   Defensive abatis line.

zatinshchik   Artilleryman dealing with light weapons; member of lower service class.

zemlia soderzhit voiska   "The land/nation supports the army."

zhalovan'e   Support payment, not necessarily regular or annual.

zhitennyi golova   Head of state granary.

BIBLIOGRAPHY

ABBREVIATIONS USED

AAE   *Akty sobrannye, v bibliotekakh i arkhivakh Rossiiskoi imperii Arkheograficheskoiu ekspeditseiu imperatorskoi Akademii nauk.* 4 vols. 1836. Reprint. Ann Arbor: University Microfilms, 1962.

AI   *Akty istoricheskie, sobrannye i izdannye Arkheograficheskoiu komisseiu.* 4 vols. St. Petersburg, 1841–1842.

AIIuZR   *Akty, otnosiashchiesia k istorii iuzhnoi i zapadnoi Rossii, sobrannye i izdannye Arkheograficheskoiu komissieu.* 15 vols. St. Petersburg, 1846–1892.

AIuB   *Akty otnosiashchiesia do iuridicheskogo byta drevnei Rossii, izdannye Arkheograficheskoii komisseiu.* 3 volumes. St. Petersburg, 1857–1884.

AMG   *Akty Moskovskogo gosurdarstva. Razriadnyi prikaz. Moskovskii stol, 1571–1664.* 3 vols. Vols. 1 and 2 edited by N. A. Popov. Vol. 3 edited by D. Ia. Samokvasov. St. Petersburg, 1890, 1894, 1901.

AN SSSR II   Akademiia nauk SSSR. Institut istorii.

ChOIDR   *Chteniia v Imperatorskom obshchestve istorii i drevnostei rossiiskikh pri Moskovskom universitete.*

DAI   *Dopolneniia k aktam istoricheskim.* 12 vols. St. Petersburg, 1846–1875.

EAIVE   *Ezhegodnik po agrarnoi istorii vostochnoi Evropy.*

FOG   *Forschungen zur Osteuropaischen Geschichte.*

JGOE   *Jahrbücher für Geschichte Osteuropas.*

IZ   *Istoricheskie zapiski.*

PSZ   *Polnoe sobranie zakonov Rossiiskoi imperii.* First Series. 45 vols. St. Petersburg, 1830.

RIB   *Russkaia istoricheskaia biblioteka, sobrannye i izdannye Arkheograficheskoiu komissieu.* Vols. 1–39. St. Petersburg, 1872–1927.

Trudy MGIAI   *Trudy moskovkogo gosudarstvennogo istoriko-arkhivnogo instituta. ZhMNP*   *Zhurnal ministerstva narodnogo prosveshcheniia.*

ARCHIVAL MATERIALS CONSULTED

Moscow. Rossiiskii gosudarstvennyi arkhiv drevnikh aktov (RGADA). Fond 210 (Razriad). Belgorodskii stol: knigi 57, 72, 76, 77, 78, 79, 81, 82, 87, 89, 94, 95, 98, 99, 100, 115, 118, 132, 133, 143, 144, 152, 156, 159, 161, 163, 164, 174; stolbtsy: 436, 463, 545, 546, 618, 643, 691, 772, 903, 904, 922, 957, 971, 986, 1000, 1036, 1070, 1193, 1267, 1314, 1873.

RGADA. F. 210. Denezhnyi stol: knigi 114 (opis' 6zh.), 118, 132, 312, 313.

RGADA. F. 210. Moskovskii stol: knigi 103, 126; stolbtsy 403, 404.

RGADA. F. 210. Prikaznyi stol: knigi 9, 77; stolbets 1400.

RGADA. F. 210. Razriadnyi stol: kniga 2.

RGADA. F. 210. Sevskii stol: knigi 14, 15, 16, 17, 18, 21, 23; stolbtsy 4, 5, 9, 11, 13, 32, 33, 313, 410, 414.

RGADA. Smotrennye knigi 35, 52, 53.

RGADA. F. 137 (Boiarskie i gorodovye knigi). Boiarskie knigi 12, 14; Gorodovye knigi; op. 2 Maiatsk ed. khr. 216; Mtensk kniga 1; op. Novgorod. ed. khr. 137; Pskov knigi 16, 18; Torsk ozera ed. khr. 1; Voronezh kniga 1; op. 2 ed. khr. 129; op. 2 ed. khr. 220.

Davies, Brian, "Manuscript notes: Belgorodskie stolbtsy 921, 1429, 1557; Dela raz-nykh gorodov 36; Prikaznoi stol, stolbtsy 385, 643, 859." Used largely for statistical information.

SELECTED PRIMARY MATERIALS

AN SSSR Institut Russkogo iazyka. *Pamiatniki iuzhno-velikorusskogo narechiia.* 2 vols. Vol. 1: *Otkaznye knigi.* Vol. 2: *Tamozhennye knigi.* Moscow, 1977, 1982.

Arkhiv iugo-zapadnoi Rossii, izdannyi vremennoi komisseiu dlia razbora drev-nikh aktov (Kiev), vysochiashei Arkheograficheskoi komissii. 1918. Reprint, Wurtzburg, 1976.

Arkhiv iugo-zapadnoi Rossii, izdannyi Vremennoi komisseiu dlia razbora drev-nikh aktov, uchrezhdenii pri Kievskom voennom, Podol'skom i Volynskom general-gubernatorakh. 37 vols. Kiev, 1859–1914.

Arsen'ev, Iuri Vasil'evich, ed. *Dedilov i ego uezd v voennom otnoshenii po neiz-dannym aktam XVII veka.* Kiev, 1913.

Bagalei, D. I., ed. *Materialy dlia istorii kolonizatsii i byta Khar'kovskoi i otchasti Kurskoi i Voronezhskoi gubernii.* Khar'kov, 1890. Often cited as vol. 2 of following.

———. *Materialy dlia istorii kolonizatsii i byta stepnoi okrainy Moskovskogo go-sudarstva v XVI–XVII stoletiiakh.* Khar'kov, 1886. Often cited as companion volume to above.

Beauplan, Guillaume le Vasseur de. *A Description of Ukraine Containing Several Provinces of the Kingdom of Poland.* New York, 1959.

———. *Description de l'Ukraine depuis les confins de la Moscovie jusqu'à la lim-ite de la Transylvanie.* Paris, 1861.

Beliaev, I. S., ed. "Dlia sravnitel'noi statistiki drevnei Rusi: Smetnye rospisi gorodo-voi sluzhby 7194 (1686)." *ChOIDR,* god 3: 39–40.

———. *Rospisnoi spisok goroda Moskvy, 1638 goda.* Vol. 1 of *Trudy moskovskogo otdela Imperatorskogo russkogo voenno-istoricheskogo obshchestva.* Mos-cow, 1911.

Belokurov, S. A., ed. *Materialy dlia Russkoi istorii.* Moscow, 1888.

———. *ChOIDR* 1902, no. 1, pt. 4: 10–11.

Birzhe, A., ed. "Volnenie krest'ian Belgorodskikh metropolichikh dereven' v 1682 godu." *Krasnyi arkhiv* 79 (1939): 150–74.

De-Pule, M. F., ed. *Materialy dlia istorii Voronezhskoi i sosednykh gubernii sostoi-ashchie iz tsarskikh gramot i drugikh aktov XVII–XVIII stoletii.* Vol. 1, *Or-lovskie akty.* Voronezh, 1861.

Dovnar-Zapol'skii, M. V., ed. *Materialy dlia biudzheta Razriadnogo prikaza.* Mos-cow, 1900.

Efremenko, S. N., ed. "Dvizhenie tsen na krest'ianskoi dukhi i na khleb s 1689, po arkhivnym dokumentam." *Izvestiia Kurskogo obshchestva kraevedeniia* 1928, no. 3 (9): 815–32.

Gordon, Patrick. *Tagebuch des Generals Patrick Gordon, wahrend seiner Kriegsdienste unter den Schweden und Polen vom Jahre 1655 bis 1661 und sienes Aufenhaltes in Russland vom Jahre 1661 bis 1699.* Edited by M. A. Obolenskii and M. C. Posselt. 3 vols. Moscow, 1849–1852.

Gurliand, I. I., ed. *Rospis' kakie goroda v kakom prikaze vedomy. Materialy dlia istorii prikazov XVII veka.* Iaroslavl', 1901.

Iz istorii Kuskogo kraia: Sbornik dokumentov i materialov. Voronezh, 1965.

Khoziaistvo krupnogo feodala-krepostnika. 2 vols. Moscow and Leningrad, 1933, 1936.

Kotoshikhin, Grigorii Karpovich. *O Rossii v tsarstvovanie Alekseia Mikhailovicha.* Translated and annotated by Benjamin P. Uroff. Ph.D. diss., Columbia University, 1970.

———. *O Rossii v tsarstvovanie Alekseia Mikhailovicha: Sovremennoe sochinenie.* Edited and with commentary by A. E. Pennington. Oxford, 1980.

Krest'ianskaia voina pod predvoditel'stvom Stepana Razina: Sbornik dokumentov. 4 vols. Moscow, 1954–1967.

Novombergskii, N. I., ed. *Materialy po istorii meditsiny.* 2 vols. St. Petersburg, 1907.

———. *Ocherki vnutrennego upravleniia moskovskoi Rusi XVII stoletiia: Prodovol'stvennoe stroenie: Materialy.* 2 vols. Vol. 1, Tomsk, 1914. Vol. 2, Moscow, 1915.

———. *Vrachebnoe stroenie v doPetrovskoi Rusi.* St. Petersburg, 1903.

Piskarev, A. N., ed. *Sobranie materialov dlia istorii zapadnogo kraia Tambovskoi gubernii i eparkhii.* Tambov, 1878.

Russia. Ministerstvo iustitsii. Moskovskii arkhiv. *Opisanie dokumentov i bumag khraniashchikhsia v Moskovskom arkhive ministerstva iustitsii.* 21 vols. St. Petersburg, Moscow, 1869–1921.

Simbirskii sbornik. Vol. 1, Istoricheskaia chast'. Simbirsk, 1870.

"Smety Voronezha, 1666, 1669, 1683, 1700." *Voronezhskii iubileinyi sbornik* 1886, no. 3: 203–11; no. 5: 212–40; no. 7: 253–61, no. 10: 260–65.

United States. Department of Agriculture. *Agricultural Statistics for 1980.* Washington, D.C., 1980.

Vasil'ev, A., ed. "Dokument o vosstanii 1650 goda vo Pskove." *Istoricheskii Arkhiv* 1 (1936): 67–72.

Veinberg, L. B., ed. *Materialy po istorii goroda Ostrogozhska.* Voronezh, 1886.

———. *Materialy po istorii Voronezhskoi i sosednikh gubernii.* Vol. 1, *Drevnie akty XVII stoletiia.* Voroneh, 1885.

Veinberg, L. B., and Poltoravskaia, A., eds. *Materialy dlia istorii Voronezhskoi i sosednykh gubernii.* 2 vols. Vol. 1, *Voronezhskie akty.* Vol. 2, *Pistsovye knigi Voronezha.* Voronezh, 1887, 1891.

Veselovskii, S. B. "Smety voennykh sil Moskovskogo gosudarstva, 1662–1663 g." *ChOIDR* 1911, no. 3.

———, ed. *Akty pistsovogo dela.* 3 vols. Vol. 1, *1614–1627.* Vol. 2, *1627–1649.* Vol. 3, *1644–1661.* Moscow, 1913, 1917, 1977.

Vtorovyi, N., and Aleksandrov-Dol'nik, K., eds. *Drevnye gramoty i drugie pismennye pamiatniki, kasaiushiesia Voronezhskoi gubernii i chastiu Azova: Voronezhskie akty.* 2d ed. Voronezh, 1851–1853.

Zaitsev, F., ed. "Tsarskie gramoty na Korochu voevodam i chelobitnye Korochu tsariam." *ChOIDR* 1859, no. 2: i–ii, 1–54, 1–254.

Zertsalov, A. N., ed. "Okladnaia raskhodnaia rospis' denezhnogo i khlebnogo zhalovan'ia za 1681 (K istorii gosudarstvennykh rospisei XVII veka)." *ChOIDR* 1893, no. 4, sect. 1: i–iv, 1–70.

SECONDARY WORKS CITED

Adams, Simon. "Tactics or Politics? The Military Revolution and Hapsburg Hegemony, 1525–1648." In *Tools of War: Instruments, Ideas, and Institutions of Warfare, 1445–1871*, ed. John A. Lynn, pp. 44–59. Urbana, Ill., 1990.

AN SSSR. Arkheograficheskaia komissiia. *Novoe o proshlom nashei strane: Pamiati akademika M. N. Tikhomirovu.* Moscow, 1967.

AN SSSR. Geograficheskoe obshchestvo SSSR. Moskovskii filial. *Materialy: Voprosy istoricheskoi geografii i istorii geografii.* Moscow, 1973.

AN SSSR II. *Absoliutizm v Rossii.* Moscow, 1964.

———. *Goroda feodal'noi Rossii.* Ed. N. V. Ustiugov and V. I. Shunkov. Moscow, Leningrad, 1966.

———. *Istoriia Kieva: Kiev perioda posdnego feodalizma i kapitalizma.* 3 vols. 4 books. Kiev, 1983.

———. *Poltava. K 250-letiia Poltavskogo srazheniia: Sbornik statei.* Moscow, 1959.

———. *Russkoe gosudarstvo v XVII veke: Novye iavleniia v sotsial'no-ekonomicheskoi, politicheskoi, i kul'turnoi zhizni.* Moscow, 1961.

———. *Trudy instituta istorii: Sbornik statei.* Moscow, 1926.

———. *Vossoedenenie Ukrainy s Rossii, 1654–1954 gg.: Sbornik statei.* Moscow, 1954.

AN SSSR II. Sibirskoe otdelenie. *Istochnikovedenie i istoriografiia gorodov Sibiri v kontse XVI–pervoi polovine XIX vv.* Ed. O. N. Vil'kov. Novosibirsk, 1987.

Alef, Gustave. "Muscovite Military Reforms in the Second Half of the Fifteenth Century." In *Rulers and Nobles in Fifteenth-Century, Muscovy*, his, pp. 73–108. London, 1983.

Aleksandrov, V. A. "K voprosu o proiskhozhdenii sosloviia gosudarstvennykh krest'ian." *Voprosy istorii* 1950, no. 10: 86–95.

———. "Streletskoe naselenie iuzhnykh gorodov Rossii v XVII veke." In AN SSSR, Arkheograficheskaia komissiia, *Novoe o proshlom nashei strane*, pp. 235–50. Moscow, 1967.

———. "Streletskoe voisko na iuge Russkogo gosudarstva v XVII veke." Kand. thesis, Moscow State University, 1947.

Alekseev, V. P. *Budzhet razriada v 1650–1652 gg.: Novyi dokument k istorii zemskogo sobora, 1648–1649.* Moscow, 1900. (And in *Drevnosti: Trudy arkheograficheskoi komissiei Moskovskogo arkheologicheskogo obshchestva.* 1900.)

Anisimov, E. V. *Podatnaia reforma Petra I: Vvedenie podushnoi podati v Rossii, 1719–1728 gg.* Leningrad, 1982.

Avtokratov, V. N. "Pervye komissariatskie organy Russkoi reguliarnoi armii, 1700–1710 gg." *IZ* 68 (1961): 163–88.

———. "Voennyi prikaz. K istorii komplektovaniia i formirovaniia voisk v Rossii v nachale XVIII veka." In AN SSSR II, *Poltava: K 250–letiia Poltavskogo srazheniia: Sbornik statei*, pp. 228–45. Moscow, 1959.

Babushkina, G. K. "Mezhdunarodnoe znachenie krymskikh pokhodov 1687 i 1689 gg." *IZ* 33 (1950): 158–72.

Bagalei, D. I. *K istorii zaselenie i khoziaistvennogo byta Voronezhskogo i Kurskogo kraia*. St. Petersburg, 1896.

——. "K istorii zaseleniia stepnoi okrainy Moskovskogo gosudarstva." *ZhMNP* 245 (May 1886): 87–105; (June 1886): 250–87.

——, ed. *Sbornik statei v chest' M. K. Liubovskogo*. 1917. Reprint, Dusseldorf, 1970.

Baiov, A. K. *Kurs istorii Russkogo voennogo iskusstva*. 7 vols. St. Petersburg, 1909–1913.

Bakulin, V. S. "Orel kak khlebnyi rynok vo vtoroi polovine XVII veka." In AN SSSR II, *Goroda feodal'noi Rossii*, ed. N. V. Ustiugov and V. I. Shunkov, pp. 256–63. Moscow, Leningrad, 1966.

——. "Torgovye oboroty i sotsial'nyi sostav torgovtsev na Belevskom rynke v 60-kh–70-kh godakh XVII veka." *Trudy MGIAI* 21 (1965): 289–313.

Bater, James H., and French, R. A., eds. *Studies in Russian Historical Geography*. 2 vols. London, 1983.

Bazilevich, K. V. *Denezhnaia reforma Alekseia Mikhailovicha i vosstanie v Moskve v 1662 g.* Moscow, Leningrad, 1936.

——. "Elementy merkantilizma v ekonomicheskoi politiki pravitel'stva Alekseia Mikhailovicha." *Uchenye zapiski MGU* 41 (1940): 3–34.

Beliaev, I. D. *O Russkom voiske v tsarstvovanie Mikhaila Feodorovicha i posle ego, do preobrazovanii, sdelannykh Petrom velikim: Istoricheskoe issledovanie*. Moscow, 1846.

Beliaev, I. D. *O dokhodakh Moskovskogo gosudarstva*. Moscow, 1885.

——. *ChOIDR* 1902, no, 1: 10–11.

Bercé, Yves-Marie. "Guerre et état." *XVII siècle* 148 (July–September 1985): 257–66.

Bertin, Jacques; Hémardinquer, Jean-Jacques; Keul, Michael; and Randles, W. G. L. *Atlas des cultures vivrières*. Paris, 1971.

Bobrovskii, Petr Osipovich. "K kharakteristike voennogo iskusstva i distsipliny v voiskakh XVII i nachala XVIII stoletii." *Voennyi sbornik* 9–10 (1891): 5–27, 177–96.

——. *Perekhod Rossii k reguliarnoi armii*. St. Petersburg, 1885.

——, comp. *Istoriia leib-gvardii preobrazhenskogo polka*. Vol. 1. St. Petersburg, 1900.

Bogoiavlenskii, S. K. "O pushkarskom prikaze." In *Sbornik statei v chest' M. K. Liubovskogo*, ed. D. I. Bagalei, pp. 361–85. 1917. Reprint, Dusseldorf, 1970.

Brandenburg, N. E. "Ocherki sostoianiia voennogo dela na Rusi v polovine XVII veka." *Voennyi sbornik* 66 (1869): 153–80; 69 (1869): 5–28.

Braudel, Fernand. *The Structures of Everyday Life*. 2 vols. Translated by Sian Reynolds. New York, 1981.

Brewer, John. *The Sinews of Power: War, Money, and the English State, 1688–1783*. New York, 1989.

Brown, Peter B. "Early Modern Russian Bureaucracy: The Evolution of the Chancellery System from Ivan III to Peter the Great, 1478–1717." Ph.D. diss., University of Chicago, 1978.

———. "The Pre-1700 Origins of Peter the Great's Provincial Administrative (*Guberniia*) Reform: The Significance of the Frontier." Paper delivered at the Conference on the Role of the Frontier in Rus'/Russian History. Chicago, 29–31 May 1992.

Brueckner, A. G. *Mednye den'gi v Rossii, 1656–1663*. St. Petersburg, 1864.

Buganov, V. I. " 'Vrazhdotvornoe' mestnichestvo." *Voprosy istorii* 1974 (November): 118–33.

Bulygin, I. A., *Monastyrskie krest'iane Rossii v pervoi chetverti XVIII veka*. Moscow, 1977.

Bushkovitch, Paul Alexander. *The Merchants of Muscovy, 1580–1650*. Cambridge, 1980.

Chagniot, Jean. "Guerre et societé au XVII siècle." *XVII siècle* 1985 (July–September): 249–56.

Chayanov, Aleksandr Vasilievich. *Problemy urozhaia*. Moscow, 1927.

Chechulin, N. D. "Neskol'ko slov o starykh sluzhb v XVII veke." In *Sbornik stat'ei v chest' Matveia K. Liubovskogo*, ed. D. I. Bagalei, pp. 32–39. 1917. Reprint, Dusseldorf, 1970.

Cherepnin, L. V. "Klassovaia bor'ba na iuge Moskovskogo gosudarstva v 1682 godu." *IZ* 4 (1938): 41–75.

Chernov, A. V. "TsGADA kak istochnik po voennoi istorii Russkogo gosudarstva do XVIII veka." *Trudy MGIAI* 4 (1948): 115–60.

———. *Vooruzhennye sily Russkogo gosudarstva v XV–XVII vv.: S obrazovaniia tsentralisovannogo gosudarstva do reform pri Petre I*. Moscow, 1954.

Chistiakova, E. V. "Volneniia sluzhilykh liudei v iuzhnykh gorodakh Rossii v seredine XVII veka." In AN SSSR II, *Russkoe gosudarstvo v XVII veke*, pp. 254–72. Moscow, 1961.

Cipolla, Carlo. *Guns, Sails, and Empires*. New York, 1965.

Collins, L. J. D. "The Military Organization and Tactics of the Crimean Tatars during the 16th and 17th Centuries." In *War, Technology, and Society in the Middle East*, ed. V. J. Perry and M. E. Yapp, pp. 257–76. London, 1975.

Corvisier, André. *Armies and Societies in Europe, 1494–1789*. Translated by A. T. Siddall. Bloomington, Ind., 1979.

———. "Guerre et mentalités au XVII siècle." *XVII siècle* 1985 (July–September): 219–32.

Crummey, Robert O. *Aristocrats and Servitors: The Boyar Elite in Russia, 1613–1689*. Princeton, 1983.

———. "Reflections on *mestnichestvo*." *FOG* 27 (1980): 269–81.

Davies, Brian L. "From Village into Garrison." *Russian Review* 51 (October 1992): 481–501.

———. "Service, Landholding, and Dependent Labour in Kozlov District, 1675." In *New Perspectives in Muscovite History*, ed. L. Hughes, pp. 129–55. London, 1993.

———. "*Voevody* and the *Verstan'e* Process." Paper delivered at Midwest Slavic Conference, 1982.

Davis, John Cushman. *The Decline of the Venetian Nobility as a Ruling Class*. Baltimore, 1962.

Demidova, N. F. *Sluzhilaia biurokratiia v Rossii XVII veka i ee rol' v formirovanii absoliutizma*. Moscow, 1987.

Dix-septieme siècle 1985 (July–September): "Présence de la guerre au XVIIe siècle."

Dovnar-Zapol'skii, M. V., ed. *Russkaia istoriia v ocherkakh i statiakh.* 3 vols. Kiev, 1912.

Downing, Brian M. *The Military Revolution and Political Change: The Origins of Democracy and Autocracy in Early Modern Europe.* Princeton, 1992.

Eaton, H. L. "Decline and Recovery of Russian Cities from 1500 to 1700." *Canadian-American Slavic Studies* 11–12 (Summer 1977): 220–52.

———. "Early Russian Censuses and the Population of Muscovy, 1550–1650." Ph.D. diss., University of Illinois, 1971.

Efremenko, S. N. "Cherty zhizni Kurskogo kraia po arkhivnym materialam 17-ogo veka." *Izvestiia Kurskogo gubernskogo obshchestva kraevedeniia* 1–2 (January–April 1927): 31–37.

El'chaninov, A. G. "Ocherk istorii voennogo isskustva do Petra Velikogo." In *Istoriia Russkoi armii i flota, 1802–1902.* 15 vols. Vol. 1, pp. 9–79. Moscow, 1902–1915.

Epifanov, P. P. "Ocherki iz istorii armii i voennogo dela v Rossii vo vtoroi polovine XVII veka–pervoi polovine XVIII veka." Dok. diss., Moscow State University, 1969.

Esper, Thomas. "The *Odnodvortsy* and the Russian Nobility." *Slavonic and East European Review* 45 (1967): 124–35.

Finkel, Caroline. *The Administration of Warfare: The Ottoman Military Campaigns in Hungary, 1593–1606.* Beihefte zur Weiner Zeitschrift für die Kunde des Morgenlandes. Vol. 14. Vienna, 1988.

Fisher, Alan. *The Crimean Tatars.* Palo Alto, Calif., 1978.

———. "Muscovite-Ottoman Relations in the Sixteenth and Seventeenth Centuries." *Humaniora Islamica* 1 (1973): 207–17.

Freeze, Gregory. "The *Soslovie* (Estate) Paradigm and Russian Social History." *American Historical Review* 91 (February 1986): 11–36.

Germanov, G. "Postepennoe rasprostranenie odnodvorcheskogo naselenie v Voronezhskoi gubernii." *Zapiski Imperatorskogo Russkogo geograficheskogo obshchestva* 12 (1857): 183–326.

Gibson, James H. *Feeding the Russian Fur Trade: The Provisionment of the Okhotsk Seaboard and the Kamchatka Peninsula, 1639–1856.* Madison, Wis., 1969.

Gokbilgin, O., and Desaive, D. "Le khanat de Crimée et les campagnes militaries de l'Empire Ottoman, fin du XVII–debut du XVII siècle, 1687–1736." *Cahiers du monde russe et sovietique* 11 (January–March 1970): 110–17.

Golitsyn, Nikolai Sergeevich. *Russkaia voennaia istoriia.* Pt. 2, *Ot Ioanna do Petra I.* St. Petersburg, 1878.

Golubtsov, I. A. "K istorii podatnoi reformy 1679–1681 gg." *Istoricheskii Arkhiv* 1959, no. 5: 155–67.

Gordon, Linda. *Cossack Rebellions: Social Turmoil in the Sixteenth-Century Ukraine.* Albany, N.Y., 1983.

Gorskaia, N. A. "Obrabotka zerna i zernoproduktov v tsentral'noi chasti Russkogo gosudarstva vo vtoroi polovine XVI–nachale XVII vv." *Materialy po istorii sel'skogo khoziaistva i krest'ianstva SSSR* 6 (1965): 36–65.

Goubert, Pierre. *Ancien Régime French Society, 1600–1750.* New York, 1973.

Gromov, G. G. "Zhilishche." In *Ocherki Russkoi kul'tury XVII veka*, vol. 1, ed. A. V. Artisikhovskii, pp. 194–201. Moscow, 1979.

Gudim-Levkovich, Polkovnik. "Ocherk istoricheskogo razvitiia vooruzhennykh sil Rossii do 1708." *Voennyi sbornik* 107 (1876), no. 1: 5–40, no. 2: 213–32; vol. 108 (1876), no. 3: 5–32; no. 4: 237–83.

Guéry, Alain. "Les finances de la monarchie française sous l'Ancien Régime." *Annales: ESC* 33 (March–April 1978): 216–39.

Hellie, Richard. *Enserfment and Military Change in Muscovy*. Chicago, 1971.

———. *Introduction to Muscovite Society*. Chicago, 1968.

———. "Ulozhenie Commentary: Preamble and Chapters 1–2." *Russian History* 15 (Summer–Fall–Winter 1988): 181–224.

———. "Warfare, Changing Military Technology, and the Evolution of Muscovite Society." In *Tools of War: Instruments, Ideas, and Institutions of Warfare, 1445–1871*, ed. John A. Lynn, pp. 74–99. Urbana, Ill., 1990.

Hoszowski, Stanislas. "L'Europe centrale et la révolution des prix." *Annales: ESC* 33 (March–April 1978): 215–45.

Hughes, Lindsay A. J. *Sophia: Regent of Russia*. New Haven, 1990.

———, ed. *New Perspectives in Muscovite History: Selected Papers from the Fourth World Congress for Soviet and East European Studies*. London, 1993.

Iakovlev, A. I. *Zasechnaia cherta Moskovskogo gosudarstva v XVII veke: Ocherk iz istorii oborony iuzhoi okrainy Moskovskogo gosudarstva*. Moscow, 1916.

Iatsunskii, V. K. "K voprosu o sobranii i publikatsii materialov po istorii urozhaev i tsen v Rossii." *Problemy istochnikovedeniia* 1955, no. 4: 350–59.

Indova, E. I. "Zemledel'cheskaia praktika v tsentral'noi Rossii XVIII veka." *Materialy po istorii sel'skogo khoziaistva i krest'ianstva SSSR* 7 (1969): 32–44.

Ivanov, Petr I. "Siabry-pomeshchiki (neskol'ko novykh materialov po istorii zemlevladeniia)." *ZhMNP* 1903 (December): 406–22.

———, ed. *Opisanie gosudarstvennogo razriadnogo arkhiva s prisovokupleniem so mnogikh khraniashchikhsia v onom liubopytnykh dokumentov*. Moscow, 1842.

Kabuzan, V. M. "Izmeneniia v chistlennosti i razmeshchenii Ukrainskogo naseleniia na territorii Rossiiskoi imperii v XVII–XIX vekakh." In AN SSSR, Geograficheskoe obshchestvo SSSR, Moskovskii filial, *Materialy: Voprosy istoricheskoi geografii i istorii geografii*, pp. 21–22. Moscow, 1973.

Kafengauz, B. B. *Ocherki vnutrennego rynka Rossii v pervoi polovine XVIII veka po materialam vnutrennykh tamozhen*. Moscow, 1958.

Kahan, Arcadius. "Natural Calamities and Their Effect upon Food Supply in Russia." *JGOE* 16 (September 1968): 353–77.

Kalachov, N., ed. *Arkhiv istoricheskikh i prakticheskikh svedenii otnosiashchikhsia do Rossii*. Vol. 3. St. Petersburg, 1862.

Kalynchev, Feodor Ivanovich. *Pravovye voprosy voennoi organizatsii Russkogo gosudarstva vtoroi poloviny XVII veka*. Moscow, 1954.

Kamentseva, E. I., and Ustiugov, N. V. *Russkaia metrologiia*. 2d ed. Moscow, 1975.

Kaplan, Steven. *Bread, Politics, and Political Economy in the Reign of Louis XV*. 2 vols. The Hague, 1976.

Kauffman-Rochard, Jacqueline. *Les origines d'une bourgeoisie Russe, XVI–XVII siècles: Marchands de Moscovie*. Paris, 1969.

Keenan, Edward L. "Muscovite Political Folkways." *Russian Review* 45 (1986): 115–81.
Keep, John L. H. "The Muscovite Elite and the Approach to Pluralism." *Slavonic and East European Review* 48 (1970): 201–31.
———. *Soldiers of the Tsar: Army and Society in Russia, 1462–1874.* Oxford, 1985.
Kirby, David. *Northern Europe in the Early Modern Period: The Baltic World, 1492–1772.* London, New York, 1990.
Kleimola, Ann. "Holding on in the Stamped-over District: The Survival of a Provincial Elite." Paper delivered at the Conference on the Role of the Frontier in Rus'/Russian History. Chicago, 29–30 May 1992.
Kliuchevskii, Vasilii O. *Istoriia soslovii v Rossii.* Moscow, 1913.
———. "Russkaia rubl' v XVI–XVII vekakh i ego otnoshchenie k rynochnom." In *Sochenenie,* his, pp. 170–236. Moscow, 1959.
Klochkov, M. V. *Naselenie Rossii pri Petre velikom po perepisiam togo vremeni.* St. Petersburg, 1911.
Koretskii, V. I. "Krest'ianskaia kolonizatsiia i osobennosti protsessa zakreposheniia na iuge Rossii v kontse XVII veka." *EAIVE* 1964 (1966): 90–103.
Kotel'nikov, V. L. "Ob izmenenii geograficheskoi sredy sel'sko-khoziaistvennoi deiatel'nosti cheloveka." *Izvestiia vsesoiuznogo geograficheskogo obshchestva* 82 (1950): 138–51.
Lappo-Danilevskii, A. S. "O velichine dvorovykh i ogorodnykh mest drevnerusskogo goroda po nekotorym dannym pervoi polovine XVII veka." *Zapiski Russkogo archeologicheskogo obshchestva* n.s., 3, vyp. 3–4 (1888): 307–16.
Lavrionov, I. M. "Rabotniki Voronezhskikh verfei (k istorii Voronezhskogo korablestroeniia, 1696–1711 gg.)." In *Voronezhskii krai na iuzhnykh rubezhakh Rossii (XVII–XVIII vv.),* pp. 77–89. Voronezh, 1981.
LeDonne, John. *Absolutism and the Ruling Class: The Formation of the Russian Political Order, 1700–1825.* Oxford, 1991.
Lemercier-Quelquejay, Chantal. "Les relations entre la Porte Ottamane et les cosaques Zaporogues au milieu du XVII siècle." *Cahiers du monde russe et sovietique* 11 (July–September 1970): 454–61.
Levykin, A. K. "Pushechnyi nariad i pushkari vo vtoroi polovine XVII v. v Rossii (po materialm iuzhno-russkikh gorodov)." Kand. thesis, Moscow State University, 1985.
Lynn, John A., ed. *Tools of War: Instruments, Ideas, and Institutions of Warfare, 1445–1871.* Urbana, Ill., 1990.
McNeill, William H. *Europe's Steppe Frontier, 1500–1800.* Chicago, 1964.
———. *The Pursuit of Power.* Chicago, 1982.
Magoesi, P. R. *Ukraine: A Historical Atlas.* Toronto, 1985.
Man'kov, A. G. "Dvizheniie i geografiia khlebnykh tsen v Russkom gosudarstve XVI veka." *IZ* 28 (1949): 132–63.
———. "Voprosy krepostnogo prava na iuzhnykh i zapadnykh okrainakh Russkogo gosudarstva vo vtoroi polovine XVII veka." *EAIVE* 1960 (1962): 179–88.
Margolin, S. L. "K voprosu ob organizatsii i sotsial'nom sostave streletskogo voiska v XVII veke." *Uchenye zapiski Moskovskogo oblastnogo pedinstituta.* Vol. 27, *Trudy kafedry istorii SSSR,* vyp 1. (1953), pp. 63–96.
Markevich, A. I. *Istoriia mestinchestva v Moskovskom gosudarstve.* Odessa, 1888.
Martin, Janet. "Frontier Policies of the Muscovite State." Paper delivered at the

Conference on the Role of the Frontier in Rus'/Russian History. Chicago, 29–31 May 1992.

———. "The Novokreshcheny of Novgorod." Paper delivered at the 21st National Conference of the American Association for the Advancement of Slavic Studies. 4 November 1989.

Maslovskii, D. F. "Pomestnye voiska Russkoi armii v XVII stoletii." *Voennyi sbornik* 195 (1890) no. 9: 5–36.

Meuvret, Jean. "Le commerce des grains et des farines à l'époque de Louis XIV." *Revue d'histoire moderne et contemporaine* 3 (1956): 169–203.

Meyer, Jean. " 'De la guerre' au XVII siècle." *XVII siècle* 1985 (July–September): 267–90.

Miklashevskii, I. N. *K istorii khoziastvennogo byta Moskovskogo gosudarstva.* Pt. 1, *Zaselenie i sel'skoe khoziaistvo iuzhnoi okrainy XVII veka.* Moscow, 1894.

Miliukov, Pavel Nikolaevich. *Spornye voprosy finansovoi istorii Moskovskogo gosudarstva.* St. Petersburg, 1892.

———. *Gosudarstvennoe khoziaistvo Rossii v pervoi chetverti XVIII stoletiia i reforma Petra velikogo.* 2d ed. St. Petersburg, 1905.

Mironov, Boris N. "O metodike obrabotki istochnikov po istorii tsen." *Arkheograficheskii ezhegodnik* 1968 (1970): 154–65.

———. "Dvizhenie tsen rzhi v Rossii v XVIII veke" *EAIVE* 1965 (1970): 156–63.

Mueller, Hans Eberhard. *Bureaucracy, Education, and Monopoly.* Berkeley, 1984.

Myshlaevskii, A. Z. "Ofitserskii vopros v XVII veke." *Voennyi sbornik* 1899, no. 5: 32–58; no. 6: 285–310.

Navrot, M. I., "Okladnaia kniga Sibirii, 1697." *Problemy istochnikovedeniia* 1956, no. 5: 184–209.

Nebol'sin, Pavel, "O russkikh soldatakh i drugikh voennykh chinakh do Petra velikogo." *Sovremennik* 13 (1849): 123–54.

Nedosekin, V. I. "Chetvertnoe zemlepol'zovanie odnodvertsev iuga Rossii v XVIII veke." *Trudy Voronezhskogo universiteta* 53 (1960): 104–21.

Nikitin, A. V. "Belgorodskaia krepost' v XVI–XVII vekakh." *Sovietskaia arkheologiia* 1962, no. 3: 260–78.

———. *Sluzhilye liudi v zapadnoi Sibirii.* Novosibirsk, 1988.

Novosel'skii, Aleksei Andreevich. *Bor'ba Moskovskogo gosudarstva s Tatarami v pervoi polovine XVII veka.* Moscow, 1948.

———. "Dvortsovye krest'iane Komaritskoi volosti vo vtoroi polovine XVII veka." In AN SSSR II, *Voprosy istorii sel'skogo khoziaistva, krest'ianstva, i revoliutsionnogo dvizheniia v Rossii,* pp. 65–80. Moscow, 1961.

———. "Otdatochnye knigi beglykh, kak istochnik izucheniia narodnoi kolonizatsii na Rusi v XVII veke." *Trudy MGIAI* 2 (1946): 127–55.

———. "Pobegi krest'ian i kholopov i ikh sysk v Moskovskom gosudarstve vo vtoroi polovine XVII veka." In AN SSSR II, *Trudy instituta istorii. Sbornik statei,* pp. 327–54. Moscow, 1926.

———. "Praviashchie gruppy v sluzhilom gorode XVII veka." *Uchenye zapiski RANION* 5 (1928): 315–35.

———. "Raspad zemlevladeniia sluzhilogo goroda v XVII veke (po desiatniam)." In AN SSSR II, *Russkoe gosudarstvo v XVII veke,* pp. 231–53. Moscow, 1961.

———. "Rasprostranenie krepostnicheskogo zemlevladeniia v iuzhnykh uezdakh Moskovskogo gosudarstva v XVII veke." *IZ* 4 (1938): 21–40.

———. "Vol'nye i perekhozhye liudi iuzhnykh uezdov Russkogo gosudarstva v XVII veke." *Materialy po istorii sel'skogo khoziaistva i krest'ianstva SSSR* 5 (1962): 61–77.

O'Brien, Charles Bickford. *Muscovy and the Ukraine.* Berkeley, 1963.

Ocherki Russkoi kul'tury XVII veka. 2 vols. Vol. 1, *Material'noe iskusstvo*, ed. A. V. Artisikhovskii. Moscow, 1979.

Optukhin, L. "O khlebnoi chetverti v drevnei Rossii." In *Arkhiv istoricheskikh i prakticheskikh svedenii otnosiashchiesiia do Rossii*, vol. 3, ed. N. Kalachov, pp. 15–26. St. Petersburg, 1862.

Pallot, Judith, and Shaw, Dennis. *Landscape and Settlement in Romanov Russia.* Oxford, 1990.

Parker, Geoffrey. *The Army of Flanders and the Spanish Road, 1567–1659: The Logistics of Spanish Victory and Defeat in the Low Countries' Wars.* Cambridge, 1977.

———. *The Military Revolution: Military Innovation and the Rise of the West, 1500–1800.* Cambridge, 1988.

Pavlov-Sil'vanskii, Nikolai P. *Gosudarevye sluzhilye liudi: Proizkhozhdenie Russkogo dvorianstva.* St. Petersburg, 1898.

Perjès, G. "Army Provisioning, Logistics, and Strategy in the Second Half of the Seventeenth Century." *Acta Historica Academiae Scientarum Hungaricae* 16 (1970): 1–51.

Perry, V. J. and Yapp, M. E., eds. *War, Technology, and Society in the Middle East.* London, Oxford, 1975.

Peterson, Claes, *Peter the Great's Administrative and Judicial Reforms.* Translated by Michael Metcalf. Stockholm, 1979.

Petrov, P. N. "Rospis' raskhodov tsarstva Moskovskogo, 206 goda (1698)." *Zapiski otdeleniia Russkoi i slavianskoi arkheologii Russkogo arkheologischeskogo obshchestva* 4 (1887): 330–51.

Pintner, Walter, and Rowney, Don, eds. *Russian Officialdom: The Bureaucratization of Russian Society from the 17th–20th Centuries.* Chapel Hill, N.C., 1980.

Plavsic, Borivoj. "Seventeenth-Century Chancelleries and Their Staffs." In *Russian Officialdom: The Bureaucratization of Russian Society from the 17th–20th Centuries*, pp. 19–45. Chapel Hill, N.C., 1980.

Pozdniakov, L. N. "Belgorod s uezdom XVII veka." *Izvestiia Kurskogo gubernskogo obshchestva kraevedeniia* 1927 (September–October): 68–77.

Preobrazhenskii, A. A. "Bor'ba Verkhoturskikh krest'ian protiv kazennykh zakupok khleba v seredine XVII veka." In *Voprosy sotsialno-ekonomicheskoi istorii i istochnikovdeniia perioda feodalizma v Rossii*, pp. 61–67. Moscow, 1961.

Rabinovich, Moishe Davidovich. "Odnodvortsy v pervoi polovine XVIII veka." *EAIVE* 1971 (1974): 137–45.

———. "Strel'tsy v pervoi chetverti XVIII veka." *IZ* 58 (1956): 273–305.

———. "Sud'ba sluzhilykh liudei starykh sluzhb i odnodvortsev v periode oformlenii regulianoi Russkoi armii v nachale XVIII veka." Kand. thesis, Moscow State University, 1953.

Ralston, David. *Supporting the European Army*. Chicago, 1990.

Razin, Evgenii Andreevich. *Istoriia voennogo iskusstva*. 3 vols. Moscow, 1955–1961.

Roberts, Michael. *The Military Revolution*. Belfast, 1956.

Shaw, Dennis J. B. "Urbanism and Economic Development in a Pre-Industrial Context: The Case of Southern Russia." *Journal of Historical Geography* 3 (1977): 107–22.

Shaw, Stanford. *History of the Ottoman Empire and Modern Turkey*. 2 vols. Cambridge, 1976.

Shchmelev, G. N. *Neskol'ko zamechanii ob odnodvortsakh: Razbor issledovaniia N. A. Blagoveshchenskogo*. Khar'kov, 1901.

Shelekhov, F. P. "Glavnoe intendantskoe upravlenie. Istoricheskii ocherk." In *Stoletii voennogo ministerstva, 1802–1902*, vol. 5, pt. 1, pp. 1–18. St. Petersburg, 1903.

Shvetsova, E. A. "Sotsial'no-ekonomicheskie otnosheniia v Tambovskom uezde v 70-kh godakh XVII veka, po pistsovym, obrochnym knigam, i knigi perepisi v gumnakh khleba." *EAIVE* 1962 (1964): 212–20.

Skobelkin, O. V. "Mery feodal'nogo gosudarstva po borbe s pobegami Voronezhskikh sluzhilykh liudei na Don v poslednei treti XVII veka." In *Obshchestvennoe dvizhenie v Voronezhskom krae v XVII–nachale XX vv.*, pp. 116–26. Voronezh, 1986.

Slicher van Bath, B. H. "Yields of Different Crops in Relation to the Seed, c. 870–1820." *Acta historiae Neerlandica* 2 (1967): 26–106.

Sliusarskii, A. G. *Sotsial'no-ekonomicheskoe razvitie Slobozhanshchiny v XVII–XVIII vekakh*. Khar'kov, 1964.

Smirnov, N. A. *Rossiia i Turtsiia v XVI–XVII vekakh*. 2 vols. appear as *Uchenye zapiski MGU*, vyp. 94 (1946).

Smith, Dianne L. "Muscovite Logistics, 1462–1598." *SEER* 71 (January 1993): 35–65.

Smith, R. E. F. *Peasant Farming in Muscovy*. Cambridge, 1977.

Smith, R. E. F., and Christian, David. *Bread and Salt: A Social and Economic History of Food and Drink in Russia*. Cambridge, 1984.

Sofronenko, K. *Malorossiiskii prikaz Russkogo gosudarstva vtoroi poloviny XVII i nachala XVIII vv*. Moscow, 1960.

Solov'ev, Ia. "Ob odnodvortsev." *Otechestvennye zapiski* 69 (1850), otd. 2: 81–100.

Solov'ev, N. I. *Istoricheskie ocherki ustroistva i dovol'stviia Russkikh reguliarnykh voisk v pervoi polovine XVIII stoletia*. St. Petersburg, 1900.

Solov'ev, Sergei M. *Istoriia Rossii s drevneishchikh vremen*. 29 vols. in 15. Moscow, 1959–1966.

Solov'ev, V. M. "Goroda Belgorodskoi cherty nakanune krest'ianskoi voiny, 1670–1671 gg." *Problemy istorii SSSR* 10 (1979): 42–59.

Sorokoletov, Fedor Pavlovich. *Istoriia voennoi leksiki v Russkom iazyke v XVI–XVII vekakh*. Leningrad, 1970.

Speranskii, A. N. "K voprosu o sushnosti i kharaktere Psovskogo vostaniia, 1650 g." *Istorik-marksist* 57 (1936): 124–38.

Stashevskii, E. D. "Biudzhet i armiia." In *Russkaia istoriia v ocherkakh i statiakh*. 3 vols., ed. M. V. Dovnar-Zapol'skii. Vol. 3, pp. 411–17. Kiev, 1912.

———. *Smeta voennykh sil Moskovskogo gosudarstva v 1663 g.* Kiev, 1910.

Stebelsky, I. "Agriculture and Soil Erosion in the European Forest Steppe." In *Studies in Russian Historical Geography*, ed. J. H. Bater and R. A. French, pp. 45–64. London, 1983.

Stepanov, I. V. *Krest'ianskaia voina v Rossii v 1670–1671 gg.* 2 vols. Leningrad, 1972.

Stevens, Carol B. "Belgorod: Notes on Literacy and Language in the Seventeenth-Century." *Russian History* 7 (1980): 113–24.

———. "Trade and Muscovite Economic Policy toward the Ukraine." In *Ukrainian Economic History: Interpretive Essays*, ed. I. S. Koropeckyj, pp. 172–85. Cambridge, Mass., 1991.

———. "Status and Solvency: The Impact of Military Reform, 1678–1682." In *New Perspectives in Muscovite History: Selected Papers from the Fourth World Congress for Soviet and East European Studies*, ed. Lindsey Hughes, pp. 156–73. London, 1993.

———. "The Politics of Food Supply: Grain and the State in Southern Russia." Ph.D. diss., University of Michigan, 1985.

Strumilin, S. G. *Ocherki ekonomicheskoi istorii Rossii i SSSR.* Moscow, 1960.

Tan'kov, A. A. *Istoricheskaia letopis' Kurskogo dvorianstva.* Moscow, 1913.

Teodorczyck, J. "L'armeé polonaise dans la première moitié du XVIIe siècle." In *Histoire militaire de la Pologne: Problèmes choisis*, ed. W. Bieganskii, pp. 95–113. Warsaw, 1970.

Ternovskii, D. A. "K istorii Nizhegol'skogo uezda v 17-om i 18-om vekakh." *Izvestiia Kievskogo gubernskogo obshchestva kraevedeniia* 1927 (September–October): 57–68.

Tikhomirov, Mikhail Nikolaevich. *Pskovkoe vosstanie 1650 goda.* Moscow and Leningrad, 1935.

———. "Pskovskii miatezh." In his *Klassovaia bor'ba v Rossii XVII veka*, pp. 352–96. Moscow, 1969.

Tikhonov, Iu. A. *Pomeshchich'e krest'iane v Rossii: Feodal'naia renta v Rossii v XVII–nachale XVIII vv.* Moscow, 1974.

Tilly, Charles. *As Sociology Meets History.* New York, 1981.

———. "Food Supply and Public Order in Modern Europe." In *The Formation of National States in Western Europe*, ed. Charles Tilly, pp. 380–455. Princeton, 1975.

Tilly, Louise. "The Food Riot as a Form of Political Conflict in France." *Journal of Interdisciplinary History* 2 (1971): 23–57.

Tkacheva, N. K. "Odnodvortsy XVIII veka v otechestvennoi istoriografii." *Istoriia i Istoriki* 1975 (1978): 281–99.

———. "Iz istorii odnodvortsev v XVIII veke." *EAIVE* 1968 (1972): 133–40.

Tkhorzhevskii, S. I. "Gosudarstvennoe zemlevladenie na iuzhnoi okraine Moskovskogo gosudarstva v XVII veke." *Arkhiv istorii truda v Rossii* 8 (1923): 64–78.

Torke, Hans Joachim. "Gab es in Moskauer Reich des 17 Jahrhunderts eine Burokratie?" *FOG* 38 (1986): 276–98.

Troitskii, S. M. "Finansovaia politika Russkogo absoliutizma vo vtoroi polovine XVII i XVIII vv." In AN SSSR II, *Absoliutizm v Rossii*, pp. 281–319. Moscow, 1964.

Tverskoi, L. *Russkoe gradostroitel'stvo do kontsa XVII veka: Planirovka i zastroika Russkikh gorodov.* Leningrad, 1953.

Urlanis, B. Ts. *Voiny i narodo-naselenie Evropy: Liudskie poteri vooruzhennykh sil Evropeiskikh stran v voinakh XVII–XX vv. (Istoriko-statisticheskoe issledovanie)*. Moscow, 1960.

Ustrialov, N. G., graf. *Istoriia tsarstvovaniia Petra velikogo*. 5 vols. St. Petersburg, 1858–1863.

Vasil'evskaia, E. A. "Terminologiia mestnichestva i rodstva." *Trudy MGIAI* 2 (1946): 155–79 .

Vazhinskii, V. M. "Ia. E. Vodarskii, *Naselenie Rossii v kontse XVII–nachale XVIII vv. (Chislenost', soslovno-klassovoi sostav, razmeshchnie)*: retsenziia." *Istoriia SSSR* 1980, no. 1: 216–19.

———. "Khlebnaia torgovlia na iuge Moskovskogo gosudarstva vo vtoroi polovine XVII veka." *Uchenye zapiski Moskovskogo oblastnogo pedinstituta imeni N. K. Krupskoi* 127, vyp. 7 (1963) *Istoriia SSSR*: 3–30.

———. "Melkoe sluzhiloe zemlevladenie odnodvortsev v XVII veke po materialam iuzhnykh uezdov Rossii." Dok. diss., Moscow State University, 1975.

———. "Razvitie rynochnykh sviazei v iuzhnykh Russkikh uezdakh vo vtoroi polovine XVII veka." *Uchenye zapiski Kemerovskogo pedinstituta* 5 (1963): 102–41.

———. "Razvitie rynochnykh sviazei v iuzhnykh uezdakh Rossii." Kand. thesis, Moscow State University, 1963.

———. "Sbory zaprosnogo khleba v kontse XVII veka dlia obespecheniia krimskikh i azovskikh pokhodov." *Izvestiia Voronezhskogo gospedinstituta* 153 (1975): 23–46.

———. *Sel'skoe khoziaistvo v chernozemnom tsentre Rossii v XVII veke*. Voronezh, 1983.

———. "Sudovaia povinnost' na Donu v XVII veke." *Materialy k nauchno-teoreticheskoi konferentsii Kemerovskogo gospedinstituta* 2 (1965): 54–61.

———. "Torgovye sviazi iuzhnykh gorodov v tret'oi chetverti XVII veka." In AN SSSR II, *Goroda feodal'noi Rossii*, ed. N. V. Ustiugov and V. I. Shunkov, pp. 298–307. Moscow, Leningrad, 1966.

———. "Usilenie soldatskoi povinnosti v Rossii v XVII veka po materialam iuzhnykh uezdakh." *Iz istoriia tsentral'no-chernozemnogo kraia. Izvestiia Voronezhskogo pedinstituta* 157 (1976): 52–68.

———. "Vvedenie podushnogo oblozheniia na iuge Rossii v 90-kh godov XVII veka." *Izvestiia Voronezhskogo gospedinstituta* 127 (1973): 88–103.

———. *Zemlevladenie i skladyvanie obshchiny odnodvortsev v XVII veke po materialam iuzhnykh uezdakh*. Voronezh, 1974.

Vazhinskii, V. M., and Vodarskii, Ia. E. "K voprosu o razmeshchenie sluzhilykh liudei i ikh krepostnykh na iuge Rossii (v Sevskom polku) v kontse XVII veka." *Voprosy istoricheskoi geografi i istorii geografii*, pp. 12–15. Moscow, 1973.

———. "Razmeshchenie sel'skogo naselenie na iuge Rossii v kontse XVII veka." In *Materialy Moskovskogo filiala geograficheskogo obshchestva SSSR: Istoriia geograficheskikh znanii i istoricheskaia geografiia*, vyp. 5, *Etnografiia*, pp. 58–61. Moscow, 1971.

Vdovina, L. N. "Pishcha i utrav." In *Ocherki Russkoi kul'tury XVII veka*. 2 vols. Vol. 1, pp. 219–33. Moscow, 1979.

Veselovskii, Stepan Borisovich. *Soshnoe pis'mo: Issledovanie po istorii kadastra i pososhnogo oblozheniia Moskovskogo gosudarstva*. 2 vols. Moscow, 1915–1916.

———. "Zametki po istorii budzheta XVII veka." In *Sbornik statei v chest' Matveia Kuzmicha Liubovskogo*, ed. I. Bagalei, pp. 181–89. 1917. Reprint, Dusseldorf, 1970.

———. "Materialy po istorii obshchego opisaniia vsekh zemel' Russkogo gosudarstva v kontse XVII veka." *Istoricheskii arkhiv* 7 (1951): 300–96.

Vodarskii, Ia. E. "Krest'iane i sel'skie bobyli v Rossii v kontse XVII veka." *EAIVE* 1968 (1972): 55–61.

———. "Naselenie Rossii v kontse XVII–nachale XVIII veka (problemy, metodika issledovaniia, resul'taty)." In AN SSSR, Nauchnyi Soviet po istoricheskoi geografii i kartografii, *Problemy istoricheskoi demografii SSSR: Sbornik statei*, pp. 50–60. Tallinn, 1977.

———. *Naselenie Rossii v kontse XVII–nachale XVIII vv.* Moscow, 1977.

———. "Opis' vladeniia Khlebnogo prikaza kak istochnik sotsial'no-ekonomicheskoi istorii i istoricheskoi geografii Rossii vo vtoroi polovine XVII veka." *Arkheograficheskoi ezhegodnik* 1970 (1971): 138–44.

———. "Podvornyi perepisi XVII v. kak istoricheskii istochnik." In AN SSSR, Geograficheskoe obshchestvo SSSR, Moskovskii filial, *Materialy: Voprosy istoricheskoi geografii i istorii geografii*, pp. 26–27. Moscow, 1973.

———. "Sluzhiloe dvorianstvo v Rossii v kontse XVII–nachale XVIII vv." *Voprosy voennoi istorii* 1969: 233–38.

Volkhov, M. Ia. "Ob otmene mestnichestva v Rossii." *Istoriia SSSR* 1977 (March–April): 53–67.

———. *Ocherki istorii promyslov Rossii, vtoraia polovina XVII–pervaia polovina XVIII vv.: Vinokurinnoe proizvodstvo*. Moscow, 1979.

Will, Pierre-Etienne. *Bureaucratie et famine en Chine au XVII siècle*. Paris, 1980.

Worobec, Christine. "Contemporary Historians on the Muscovite Peasantry" *Canadian Slavonic Papers* 23 (September 1981): 315–27.

Zagorovskii, Vladimir Pavlovich. *Belgorodskaia cherta*. Voronezh, 1969.

———. "Donskoe kazachestvo i razmery Donskikh otpuskov v XVII veke." *Trudy Voronezhskogo universiteta* 53 (1960): 131–47.

———. "Formirovanie i zaselenie Dankovskogo uezda v XVII veke" *Iz istorii Voronezhskogo kraia* 5 (1975): 52–66.

———. *Iziumskaia cherta*. Voronezh, 1980.

———. "Nekotorye osobennosti kolonizatsionnogo protsessa iuzhnoi okrainy Rossii v XVII veke i ego periodizatsii." *Iz istorii Voronezhskogo kraia* 3 (1969): 83–93.

———. "Soldatskie sela i soldatskoe zemlevladenie v Voronezhskom krae v XVII veke." *Iz istorii Voronezhskogo kraia* 4 (1972): 90–97.

———. "Sudostroenie pod Voronezhem v XVII veke." *Trudy Voronezhskogo kraevedcheskogo muzeia* 1 (1960): 51–73.

———. "Zemledel'cheskoe naselenie v pridonskikh uezdakh na Belgorodskoi cherte i vozniknovenie pervykh sel 'za chertoi.' " *EAIVE* 1964 (1966): 199–207.

Zagoskin, N. P. *Ocherki organizatsii i proiskhozhdeniia sluzhilogo sosloviia v do-Petrovskoi Rusi*. Kazan', 1875.

Zanicheva, L. G. "Krest'ianskie pobegi vo vtoroi polovine XVII veka." *EAIVE* 1964 (1966): 231–39.

Zaozerskii, A. I. *Tsarskaia votchina XVII veka. Iz istorii khoziaistvennoi i prikaznoi politike tsaria Alekseia Mikhailovicha.* Moscow, 1937.

Zimin, A. A. "Khoziaistvennyi god v sele Pavlovskom, seredina XVII veka." *Materialy po istorii sel'skogo khoziaistva i krest'ianstva SSSR* 6 (1965): 64–83.

Zverev, P. "Kurskie starozaimochniki i odnodvortsy." *Iuridicheskii vestnik* 28 (1888): kn. 2–3.

INDEX